Gerald Griffin

The Poetical and Dramatic Works

Gerald Griffin

The Poetical and Dramatic Works

ISBN/EAN: 9783337304331

Printed in Europe, USA, Canada, Australia, Japan

Cover: Foto ©Thomas Meinert / pixelio.de

More available books at **www.hansebooks.com**

The Poetical and Dramatic Works of Gerald Griffin.

CONTENTS.

	PAGE
The Fate of Cathleen	1
The Bridal of Malahide	17
Shanid Castle	23
Orange and Green	47
The Traveller and the Moon	53
Anna Blake	55

LYRICAL POEMS.

My Spirit is Gay	62
The Tie is Broke, my Irish Girl	63
When Love in a Young Heart	65
Sleep, that like the Couched Dove	65
The Sally-coop, where once I Strayed	67
The Mie-na-mallah now is Past	67
The Wanderer's Return	69
Old Times! Old Times!	70
A Place in thy Memory, Dearest	72
My Mary of the Curling Hair	73
Gilli-ma-chree	75
For I am Desolate	78
The Bridal Wake	79
Once I had a True Love	80

CONTENTS.

	PAGE
Hark! Hark! the soft Bugle	82
Farewell!	83
The Mother's Lament	86
To a Lady	87
Let Others Breathe in Glowing Words	89
You Never Bade me Hope, 'tis True	89
A Soldier, a Soldier, to-night is our Guest	90
Duet (from the Duke of Monmouth)	91
Though lonely here by Avon's Tide	93
Monmouth's Address	95
Like the Oak by the Fountain	96
Falta Volla! Falta Volla!	97
Cead Millia Falta! Elim!	98
The Isle of Saints	99
No! Not for the Glories of Days that are Flown	104
Come to Glengariff! Come!	105
The Phantom City	106
While the Stars of Heaven are Shining	106
War! War! Horrid War!	108
War Song of O'Driscol	108
Fare thee well! my Native Dell	109
Aileen Aroon	112
Gone! Gone! for ever Gone!	114
Ancient Lullaby	115
Know ye not that Lovely River?	116
I Love my Love in the Morning	117
Merrily Whistles the Wind on the Shore	118
When Filled with Thoughts of Life's Young Day	120
Hark, Erin! the Blast is Blown	121
The Merriest Bird on Bush or Tree	122
'Tis, it is the Shannon's Stream	124
I am Alone! I am Alone!	125

SONNETS.

	PAGE
To Friends in America	127
To his Native Glens	128
To a Friend	129
The Future	130
A Fragment	131
To his Sister	131
Benevolence	133
Friendship	133
Fame	134
Mitchelstown Caverns	134
Written in Adare, in 1820	135

MISCELLANEOUS POEMS.

On Remembering an Inadvertent Jest on Lord Byron's Poetry	135
Lines to a Departed Friend	136
Sweet Taunton Dene	141
Adieu to London	142
My Spirit is of Pensive Mould	144
Lines on a Lady's Seal Box	146
A Portrait	148
Lines addressed to a Young Lady, on reading a Poem of hers, addressed to Death	151
Inscription on a Cup formed of a Cocoa-nut	152
Impromptu (on seeing an Iris formed by the Spray of the Ocean, at Miltown-Malbay)	153
The Wake without a Corpse	153
To a Young Friend on his Birth-day	154
To a Friend	158

CONTENTS.

	PAGE
On Pulling some Campanulas in a Lady's Garden	159
They Speak of Scotland's Heroes Old	161
O Brazil, the Isle of the Blest	162
To a Seagull, seen off the Cliffs of Moher, in the County of Clare	164
Past Times	165
The Wreck of the Comet	167
The Sister of Charity	169
Nano Nagle	171
To Memory	174
To * * * *	175
The Nightwalker	178
The Danish Invasion	189
The Joy of Honour	190
Would you Choose a Friend	193
When some Unblest and Lightless Eye	194
The Song of the Old Mendicant	196
Mary-le-bone Lyrics	197
Mr. Graham to Miss Dawson in the Clouds	197
To Claude Seurat, on Leaving London	200
When Dulness, Friend of Peers and Kings	203
Matt Hyland	206

Gissipus, a Play in Five Acts — 293

The Fate of Cathleen.

A WICKLOW STORY.

I.

In Luggelaw's deep-wooded vale
  The summer eve was dying;
On lake, and cliff, and rock, and dale
  A lulling calm was lying;
And virgin saints and holy men
  The vesper song were singing,
And sweetly down the rocky glen
  The vesper bell was ringing.

II.

Soft gloom fell from the mountain's breast,
  Upon the lake declining;
And half in gentle shade was drest,
  And half like silver shining—
And by that shore young Kevin stands,
  His heart with anguish laden;
And timid there, with wreathed hands,
  A fair and gentle maiden.

III.

And "Oh," she said, "I've left for thee
  My own beloved bowers,
The walks I trod in infancy,
  My father's ancient towers;
I've left for thee my natal hall,
  Where late I lived in splendour,
And home, and friends, and fame, and all
  I sighed not to surrender."

B

IV.

Away!" he muttered low; "in youth
    A vow to heaven I've spoken,
And I will keep my boyish truth
    To age and death unbroken.
Oh, woulds't thou bribe my heart to sin
    Against that high endeavour,
And cast those tempting eyes between
    That heaven and me for ever?"

V.

The maid looked up in still surprise,
    Her cheeks with tear-drops streaming;
A guileless light was in her eyes,
    Like childhood's sorrow gleaming.
Oh, had I here a heaven to give,
    Thou should'st be blest this hour;
Then how should *I* thine hope bereave
    Of that eternal dower?

VI.

Ah, no—Cathleen will ask no more,
    For home and friends forsaken,
Than here, upon his peaceful shore,
    To see the morn awaken:
Beneath thy holy roof to dwell,
    A lorn and timid stranger;
And watch thee, in thy lonely cell,
    In sickness and in danger.

VII.

To rouse thee when the cowled train
    Their matin beads are telling;
To hear young Kevin's fervent strain
    Amid the anthem swelling;

To smile whene'er thy smiles I see,
  To sigh when thou art sighing,
To live while life is left to thee,
  And die when thou art dying."

VIII.

"My prayers," he said, "were little worth
  While thou wert kneeling near me;
My hymns were dull as songs of earth,
  If thou wert by to hear me.
Oh, you are young and guiltless still,
  To sin and shame a stranger,
And what to thee seems pure from ill
  To me looks dark with danger.

IX.

"There is a heaven in yon blue sphere,
  Where joy abounds for ever,
There may we fondly meet; but here,
  In this cold exile, never.
There may we look with loving eyes,
  While happy souls are singing,
While angel smiles light all the skies,
  And the bells of heaven are ringing.

X.

"But here—but here—ah, fair Cathleen,
  Through all this wild creation,
In all that's bright there lurketh sin,
  In all that's fair, temptation.
It tracks the steps of young Delight,
  When souls are gay and tender;
It walketh in the dark midnight,
  And in the noonday splendour.

XI.

"It murmurs in the rising wind
    That stirs the morning flowers,
On Friendship's lap it lies reclined,
    And sighs in Love's own bowers;
It shines o'er all the summer skies,
    When dews the wild buds cherish;
And, worst of all, in woman's eyes—
    Ah, hide them! or I perish."

XII.

The maiden calmly, sadly smiled,
    She plucked an opening flower,
She gazed along the mountain wild,
    And on the evening bower.
"I've looked," she said, "from east to west,
    But sin has never found me;
I cannot feel it in my breast,
    Nor see it all around me.

XIII.

"The light that fills those summer skies,
    The laugh that flows the freest,
I've marked with loving ears and eyes,
    Nor saw the ill thou seest.
I always thought that morning air
    Blew on my bosom purely;
The worst *I* find in all that's fair
    Is that it fades too surely.

XIV.

"If it be sin to love thy name,
    And tire of loving never,
Why am I spared the inward shame
    That follows sin for ever?

For I can l'ft my hands and eyes
    To that bright heaven above me;
And gaze upon the cloudless skies,
    And say, aloud—I love thee!

XV.

" I had a brother in my home
    I loved—I love him truly—
With him it was my wont to roam
    When morn was breaking newly;
With him I've cheered the weary time
    With cruit* soft, or story;
He never spake of secret crime,
    Of sin, or tainted glory.

XVI.

" But thou"—" But I," young Kevin said,
    " Will love thee like that brother;
And wilt thou be content, sweet maid,
    To find in me another?
And seek ye but a brother's grace,
    A brother's calm caresses"—
The maiden hid her burning face
    Within her golden tresses.

XVII.

" Farewell!" she sighed, " I plead in vain,
    My dream of love is ended;
Thy thoughts of me with thoughts of pain
    Shall never more be blended.
But now the even is falling late,
    The way is long and lonely—
Oh, let me rest within thy gate
    Till morning rises only!"

* A small harp.

XVIII.

Young Kevin paused—the dew fell chill,
  The clouds rolled black and swelling
Ah, no—he could not deem it ill
  To lodge her in his dwelling;
For churls, like Nabal, deeply sin,
  And lasting pains inherit,
And those who take the stranger in
  Have patriarchal merit.

XIX.

But oft he thought, 'mid holy strains,
  Upon that lovely woman;
For, oh, the blood within his veins
  Was warm, and young, and human.
He told his nightly beads in vain—
  Sleep never came so slowly—
And all that night young Kevin's brain
  Was filled with dreams unholy.

XX.

The young man rose at dawning hour,
  To chaunt his first devotion,
And, tiptoe, then to Cathleen's bower
  He stole, in still'd emotion.
Breathless above the maiden's form
  He hung—and saw her sleeping;
Her brow was damp—her cheek was warm,
  And wore the stains of weeping.

XXI.

Beside her couched an aged hound
  (Her Kevin's sole attendant),
One hand his sable neck around,
  Like light in gloom resplendent.

The dog sprung up, that hand fell down,
  As Kevin's sigh came deeper;
He crouched him at his master's frown,
  And never woke the sleeper.

XXII.

And scenes of calm, domestic bliss
  On Kevin's soul came thronging;
Endearments soft, and smiling peace,
  And love, the young heart's longing.
Why did he swear in youth to live
  For saintly duties only?
And leave those joys that love can give,
  To lead a life so lonely?

XXIII.

Oh!—were he now a bridegroom gay
  Lord in his natal tower,
And were this morn his bridal day,
  And this his marriage bower:—
Where were the wondrous ill, he said,
  To him, to earth, to heaven?
Just then the dreamer turned her head,
  And murmured deep, "My Kevin!"

XXIV.

He started, trembled, burned, his limbs
  Shook with the sudden passion;
His eye in sudden moisture swims,
  And stirs in maniac fashion;
A whirlwind in his brooding soul
  Arose, and tossed it madly;
Then swift away the storm clouds roll,
  And leave him drooping sadly.

XXV.

Again, that fond, impassion'd moan
    Upon her warm lip lingers;
He stoops, and twines within his own
    Those white and taper fingers.
He bends—ah, hark! the convent toll!
    Another knell! another!
They peal a requiem to the soul
    Of a departed brother!

XXVI.

Up, and away! With freezing blood
    He rushes from the bower,
And seeks the beechen solitude,
    Beside the convent tower.
There hooded maids and cowled men
    The dirge of death were singing,
And sullen down the rocky glen
    The knell of death was ringing.

XXVII.

He raised to heaven his hands and eyes,
    Lone, in the silent morning,
And said, through humble tears and sighs—
    "I bless thee for the warning!
Oft dost thou thus with sounds of awe
    My slumbering soul awaken:
If I forsake thy love and law,
    Oh, let me be forsaken!

XXVIII.

"Thou hast a golden crown for those
    Who leave earth's raptures hollow,
And firmly still, through wiles and woes,
    The light of virtue follow.

Oh, be this weak heart still thy care,
  Be still my soul's defender,
And grant that crown for me may wear
  No soil upon its splendour.

XXIX.

" If tears, and prayers, and vigils lean,
  A sin like mine may cover,
I'll weep while summer woods are green,
  And watch till time is over.
But mighty armour must I weave
  Against that tempting woman;
For, oh, she haunts me morn and eve,
  And I am weak and human."

XXX.

A counsel woke within his heart,
  While yet the youth was kneeling,
It whispered to his soul—" Depart,
  And shun the war of feeling.
Courage on battle fields is shown
  By fighting firm and dying;
But in the strife with Love alone
  The glory lies in flying."

XXXI.

Swift as the sudden wind that sings
  Across the storm-roused ocean;
Swift as the silent prayer that springs
  Up, warm, from young Devotion:
Swift as the brook, the light, the air,
  As death, time, thought, or glory,
Young Kevin flies that valley fair,
  That lake, and mountain hoary.

XXXII.

And far away, and far away,
  O'er heath and hill he speeds him,
While virtue cheers the desert gray,
  And light immortal leads him;
And far away, and far, and far
  From his accustomed fountain,
Till quench'd in light the morning star,
  And day was on the mountain.

XXXIII.

In Luggelaw's deep-wooded vale
  The summer dawn was breaking,
On lake, and cliff, and wood, and dale
  Light, life, and joy were waking;
The skylark in the car of morn
  His shrilly fife was sounding,
With speckled side, and mossy horn,
  The deer were up and bounding.

XXXIV.

Young Nature now all bustlingly
  Stirs from her nightly slumber,
And puts those misty curtains by
  Her mighty couch that cumber;
And dews hang fresh on leaf and thorn,
  And o'er each eastern highland
Those golden clouds at eve and morn
  That grace our own green island.

XXXV.

Light laughed the vale, gay smiled the sun,
  Earth's welcome glad returning,
Like Valour come when wars are done
  To Beauty in her mourning.

The night calm flies, the rustling breeze,
    Sports on the glancing water,
And gently waves the tangled trees
    Above the chieftain's daughter.

XXXVI.

Like one in pain, athwart her brow,
    One hand her hair draws tightly,
Now falls that glance in tears, and now
    It glimmers quick and brightly:
For she has missed her votive love
    Within his lonely bower,
Nor is he in the beechen grove,
    Nor in the convent tower.

XXXVII.

"I fear," she sighed, and bowed her head,
    "I fear he told me truly,
That sin is in the sunshine bred,
    And roses springing newly;
For dreary looks this bower to me,
    Even while those roses wreathe it;
And even that sunshine beaming free
    Hides something dark beneath it.

XXXVIII.

"That dew"— she paused! What foot has been
    Upon its early brightness?
And left a track of deepening green
    Across its silver whiteness?
She traced it by the ravell'd brake,
    And by the silent fountain,
And o'er that lawn, and by that lake,
    And up that hoary mountain.

XXXIX.

But there the thirsty morning sun
   Had dewless left the heather;
Her eye, o'er all the desert dun
   No single trace can gather.
Yet on she went, for in her breast
   Deep passion fierce was burning—
Passion, that brooks not pause nor rest,
   And sickens at returning.

XL.

And far away—and far away—
   O'er heath and hill she speeds her,
While Hope lights up that desert gray,
   And love untiring leads her.
And far away—and far—and far
   From lake and convent tower,
Till div'd in gloom day's golden car,
   And night was on the bower.

XLI.

Now thridding lone the rugged Scalp,
   With wounded feet and weary:
Now toiling o'er each mimic Alp
   Of Wicklow's desert dreary.
Oh, lonely Bray, thy basin'd tide
   She passed at sunset mellow,
And Ouler's lake, where far and wide
   Its haunted flame shone yellow.

XLII.

Night fell—day rose—night fell again,
   And the dim day-dawn found her
On Glendalough's deep bosomed plain,
   With lake and cliff around her

There, tired with travel long and vain,
    She sinks beside that water;
For toil, and woe, and wasting pain
    Have worn the Chieftain's daughter.

XLIII.

Tall, darkening o'er her high, Lugduff
    Gathered his lordly forehead,
And sheath'd his breast in granite rough,
    Rent crag and splinter horrid.
His helm of rock beat back the breeze,
    Without a leaf to wreathe it,
The vassal waves rolled in to kiss
    His mailed foot beneath it.

XLIV.

Sudden, with joyous yelp and bound,
    A dog comes swiftly by her;
She knows—she knows that aged hound,
    And he she loves is nigh her!
The warden flies—she follows swift—
    The dangerous footway keeping,
Till, deep within the jagged clift,
    She found her Kevin sleeping.

XLV.

With hair tossed out and hands clench'd tight,
    The rugged granite hugging,
Like those who with the Hag of Night
    For voice and breath are tugging
For, oh, he had a horrid dream,
    And every nerve has felt it;
And ruin was the gloomy theme,
    And Cathleen's hand had dealt it.

XLVI.

He dreamed that at the golden gate
  Of heaven, flung wide and gleaming,
He heard soft music as he sate,
  And saw bright pinions beaming;
Millions of sainted shapes he saw,
  In light and fragrance ranging,
And calm delight, and holy awe,
  In speaking looks exchanging.

XLVII.

He strove to join that angel band;
  But, in the porch before him,
With mocking eye and warning hand.
  Cathleen stood glooming o'er him,
She thrust him from the sainted crowd,
  The gates rang clanging after,
And on his ear came, long and loud
  A peal of fearful laughter.

XLVIII.

Again it opes, again he tries
  To join that glorious vision;
Again, with lifted hands and eyes,
  Deep fixed in keen derision,
That minion of the burning deep
  Stands wrapt in gloom before him—
Up springs he from his broken sleep,
  And sees her trembling o'er him!

XLIX.

Vengeance!" he yelled, and backward toss'd
  His arms, and muttered wildly:
The frighted maid her forehead crossed,
  And dropped before him mildly.

Oh, slay me not—Oh, Kevin, spare
  The life thy Lord has given!"
He paused, and fixed his barren stare
  Upon the brightening heaven.

L.

Cathleen," he sighed, "that timely word
  Has left my hands unbloody;
But see, the early morning bird
  Sings in the sunshine ruddy;
Before that matin strain be o'er
  Fly far, and hate and fear me;
For Death is on this gloomy shore,
  And madness haunting near me."

LI.

With clenched teeth, and painful smile
  (Love's last despairing token),
She flung her arms around him, while
  Her heart beat thick and broken.
She clasp'd him as she would have grown
  Into his breast for ever:
Then fixed her gaze upon his own,
  And sternly whispered—"Never!"

LII.

Again, again! those madding dreams
  Upon his soul awaken,
The fiend athwart his eye-ball swims—
  Those golden gates are shaken!
Again he hears that ringing mock
  The vision'd stillness breaking,
And hurls the maiden from the rock
  Into the black lake, shrieking.

LIII.

Down gazed he, frenzied, on the tide—
  Cathleen! How comes he lonely?
Why has she left her Kevin's side
  That lived for Kevin only?
What mean those circles in the lake
  When not a wind is breathing?
What bubbles on the surface break?
  What horrid foam is wreathing?

LIV.

Oh, never more—oh, never more,
  By lake or convent tower,
Shall poor Cathleen come, timid, o'er
  To haunt his evening bower;
Oh, never more shall that young eye
  Beam on his prayer and break it,
And never shall that fond heart's sigh
  Thrill to his own and wake it.

LV.

The fiend that mocks at human woes
  Frowned at that maniac minute,
For well the baffled demon knows
  The hand of heaven was in it.
Oh, tempted at that saintly height,
  If they to earth sunk lowly,
She ne'er had been an angel bright,
  Nor he a victor holy!

LVI.

Ay, they are in their bowers of rest,
  With light immortal round them;
Yet pensive heaves the pitying breast
  To think how soon it found them.

The lark ne'er wakes the ruddy morn
　　Above that gloomy water,
Where sudden died, and passion lorn,
　　Cathleen, the Chieftain's daughter.

The Bridal of Malahide.

AN IRISH LEGEND.

I.

The joy-bells are ringing
　　In gay Malahide,
The fresh wind is singing
　　Along the sea-side;
The maids are assembling
　　With garlands of flowers,
And the harpstrings are trembling
　　In all the glad bowers.

II.

Swell, swell the gay measure!
　　Roll trumpet and drum!
'Mid greetings of pleasure
　　In splendour they come!
The chancel is ready,
　　The portal stands wide
For the lord and the lady,
　　The bridegroom and bride.

III.

What years, ere the latter,
 Of earthly delight
The future shall scatter
 O'er them in its flight!
What blissful caresses
 Shall Fortune bestow,
Ere those dark-flowing tresses
 Fall white as the snow!

IV.

Before the high altar
 Young Maud stands array'd
With accents that falter
 Her promise is made—
From father and mother
 For ever to part,
For him and no other
 To treasure her heart.

V.

The words are repeated,
 The bridal is done,
The rite is completed—
 The two, they are one
The vow, it is spoken
 All pure from the heart,
That must not be broken
 Till life shall depart.

VI.

Hark! 'mid the gay clangour
 That compass'd their ear,
Loud accents, in anger,
 Come mingling afar!

The foe's on the border,
His weapons resound
Where the lines in disorder
Unguarded are found.

VII.

As wakes the good shepherd,
The watchful and bold,
When the ounce or the leopard
Is seen in the fold;
So rises already
The chief in his mail,
While the new-married lady
Looks fainting and pale.

VIII

"Son, husband, and brother,
Arise to the strife,
For sister and mother,
For children and wife!
O'er hill and o'er hollow,
O'er mountain and plain,
Up, true men, and follow!—
Let dastards remain!"

IX.

Farrah! to the battle!
They form into line—
The shields, how they rattle
The spears how they shine
Soon, soon shall the foeman
His treachery rue—
On, burgher and yeoman,
To die, or to do!

X.

The eve is declining
 In lone Malahide,
The maidens are twining
 Gay wreaths for the bride:
She marks them unheeding—
 Her heart is afar,
Where the clansmen are bleeding
 For her in the war.

XI.

Hark! loud from the mountain,
 'Tis Victory's cry!
O'er woodland and fountain
 It rings to the sky!
The foe has retreated!
 He flies to the shore;
The spoiler's defeated—
 The combat is o'er!

XII.

With foreheads unruffled
 The conquerors come—
But why have they muffled
 The lance and the drum?
What form do they carry
 Aloft on his shield?
And where does he tarry
 The lord of the field?

XIII.

Ye saw him at morning,
 How gallant and gay
In bridal adorning,
 The star of the day:

Now weep for the lover—
   His triumph is sped,
His hope it is over!
   The chieftain is dead!

XIV.

But, oh, for the maiden
   Who mourns for that chief,
With heart overladen
   And rending with grief!
She sinks on the meadow—
   In one morning-tide,
A wife and a widow,
   A maid and a bride!

XV.

Ye maidens attending,
   Forbear to condole!
Your comfort is rending
   The depths of her soul.
True—true, 'twas a story
   For ages of pride;
He died in his glory—
   But, oh, he *has* died!

XVI.

The war cloak she raises
   All mournfully now,
And steadfastly gazes
   Upon the cold brow.
That glance may for ever
   Unalter'd remain,
But the bridegroom will never
   Return it again.

XVII.

The dead-bells are tolling
    In sad Malahide,
The death-wail is rolling
    Along the sea-side;
The crowds, heavy hearted,
    Withdraw from the green,
For the sun has departed
    That brighten'd the scene!

XVIII.

Ev'n yet in that valley,
    Though years have roll'd by,
When through the wild sally
    The sea breezes sigh,
The peasant, with sorrow,
    Beholds in the shade,
The tomb where the morrow
    Saw Hussy convey'd.

XIX.

How scant was the warning,
    How briefly reveal'd,
Before on that morning
    Death's chalice was fill'd!
The hero who drank it
    There moulders in gloom,
And the form of Maud Plunket
    Weeps over his tomb.

XX.

The stranger who wanders
    Along the lone vale,
Still sighs while he ponders
    On that heavy tale:

"Thus passes each pleasure
That earth can supply—
Thus joy has its measure—
We live but to die!"

Shanid Castle.

I.

On Shannon side the day is closing fair,
 The kern sits musing by his shieling* low,
And marks, beyond the lonely hills of Clare,
 Blue, rimm'd with gold, the clouds of sunset glow.
 Hush in that sun the wide spread waters flow,
Returning warm the day's departing smile;
 Along the sunny highland pacing slow,
The keyriaght† lingers with his herd the while,
And bells are tolling faint from far Saint Sinon's isle.‡

---

* Hut.

† The *Keyriaght* in ancient Ireland was a kind of wandering shepherd, or herdsman. It would appear, from their being prohibited by the Kilkenny General Assembly of Confederate Catholics, that the number of persons who pursued this roving, pastoral life, must have been at one time considerable.

‡ Few landscapes, on a calm and sunny evening, present a scene of sweet and solemn beauty exceeding that of the little island of Scattery, or Iniscatha, near the mouth of the Shannon, with its lofty round tower, and the ruins of its numerous churches, said to have been founded by St. Sinon or Senanus, one of the brightest ornaments of the ancient Irish church. The peasantry still point out the tomb of the saint, about the centre of the islet, and, as may be judged, the place is not without its share of legendary anecdote.

II.

Oh, loved shore! with softest memories twined.
　　Sweet fall the summer on thy margin fair!
And peace come whispering, like a morning wind
　　Dear thoughts of love to every bosom there!
　　The horrid wreck and driving storm forbear
Thy smiling strand—nor oft the accents swell
　　Along thy hills of grief or heart-wrung care;
But heav'n look down upon each lowly dell,
And bless thee for the joys I yet remember well!

III.

Upon that spot where Corgrig's* lofty tower
　　A lengthen'd shadow casts along the green,
The lord of Shanid summons all his power;
　　And knight and galloglas and kern are seen,
　　Marking the targe with arrow barbed keen,
And javelin light, and musket ringing loud.
　　Wide flies each shot, and still, throughout the scene,
Low smother'd laughter shakes the merry crowd,
And on the chieftain's brow dark looms the angry cloud.

IV.

Apart from these, upon a rising hill,
　　Where yellow furze and hazel scent the breeze,
An aged woman sat in posture still,
　　With tragic forehead bending to her knees.

---

* The Castle of Corgrig, one of the many fortresses along the Shannon side, dependant on the Earls of Desmond, was taken by the troops of the Lord President Carew, in the reign of Elizabeth, after a siege of two days. The fragments of the wall, still visible, show it to have been once a place of considerable strength.

She joins not in the laughter when she sees
By some new hand the harmless musket plied;
  Or when some eye unskill'd the arrow frees,
Or whirling sling its burthen scatters wide;
'Alas! the times are changed in Desmond now!" she sigh'd.

V.

" It was not thus in Desmond's happier day,
  When young Fitz-Gerald held these princely bow'rs.
Alas, that I should live to weep and say
A low-born vassal rules my chieftain's tow'rs.
Oh, come again, ye well-remember'd hours,
When he, loved relic of a kingly line,
Review'd on yonder plain his glittering pow'rs,
And many a loving glance was bent on thine;
O knight without reproach! O stainless Geraldine!"*

---

* Master Staniburst, one of the quaintest and most loquacious authorities in Holingshed, favours us with the following account of the remarkable family of the Geraldines or Fitz-Geralds, in his "Description of Ireland."

"This house was of the nobilitie of Florence, came from thence into Normandie, and so with the ancient Earle Strongbow, his kinsman, whose arms he giveth, into Wales, neare of bloud to Rice ap Griffin, prince of Wales, by Nesta, the mother of Maurice Fitz-Gerald and Robert Fitz-Stephans, with the said Earle Maurice Fitz-Gerald removed into Ireland in the yeare 1169. The corrupt orthographie that diverse use in writing this name, doth incorporate it to houses thereto linked in no kinred, and consequentlie blemisheth worthie exploits atchieved as well in England and Ireland, as in forren countries and dominions. Some write Gerold, sundry Gerald, diverse verie corruptlie Gerrat, others Gerald. But the true orthographie is Girald, as maie appear both by Giraldus Cambrensis, and the Italian authors that make mention of the familie. As for Gerrot, it differeth flat from Girald: yet there be some in Ireland that name, and write themselves Gerrots, notwithstanding they be Giraldins, whereof diverse gentlemen are in Meeth. But there is a sept of the Gerrots in Ireland, and they seeme, forsooth, by threatening kindnesse and kindred of the true Giraldins, to fatch their petit degrees from their

VI.

And is not he our lord who stands below?"
  A fair-hair'd stripling ask'd, with accent mil
"Son of my heart," the matron answer'd, "No!
  Shame on the churl! a wretched harper's child.
Oh! never joy on alter'd Desmond smiled,
  Since he by treason did these towers obtain;
And though they bend before that breast defiled,
  A spectral loyalty what heart can chain?
Their love is yet with Desmond far beyond the main."

VII.

"How lost the Geraldine his tow'rs and lands?"
  "Long time the leaguer closed his castle walls;
At length, with proffer'd peace, a knightly band
  At morning sought him in his lordly halls.
'Desmond, the queen her menaced wrath recalls,
  Receive her grace and yield.' With lofty brow,
'Within these tow'rs the Desmond stands or falls.
  A boy,' he said, 'may trust a woman's vow;
But I am old in war—my lip is bearded now.'

ancestors, but they are so neere of bloud one to the other, that two bushels of beanes would scantlie count their degrees. Another reason why diverse strange houses have been shuffled in among this familie, was, for that sundrie gentlemen at the christening of their children would have them named Giralds, and yet their surnames were of other houses; and if, after it happened that Girald had i sue Thomas, John, Robert, or such like, they would then beare the name of Girald, as Thomas Fitz-Girald, and thus, taking the name of their ancestors for their surname, within two or three descents they s oore themselves among the kindred of the Giraldins. This is a general fault in Ireland and Wales, and a great confusion and extinguishment of houses.'

The Fitz-Geralds were amongst the earlier settlers in Ireland John Fitz-Girald was created Earl of Kildare in 1315 Maurice Fitz-Thomas (a Giraldine), Earl of Desmond in 1809.

VIII.

"They part. Again, from each surrounding height,
    Thunder'd the loud artillery on the tow'r;
And all that day, and all that fearful night,
    Thick fell as hail the muskets' deadly show'r.
Where now the sunbeams light each peaceful flower
Spring daisy sweet, and opening marigold,
    Thou might'st have seen the horrid war-cloud lour,
Till settling dark, in sulph'rous volume roll'd,
It capp'd in sablest gloom the Desmond's lofty hold.

IX.

"Thou know'st where high in Shanagolden vale,
    The hill of Shanid views the plains around;
A solitary cone it meets the gale,
    Like warrior helm'd with threat'ning turret crown'd.
Steep tapering upward from the rushy ground,
A stately peak it stands:—a footway, known
    To few save Desmond, tow'rd the summit wound,
'Mid tangled sally, crag, and mossy stone,
By Desmond form'd for need, by Desmond used alone.

X.

"It chanced that night, when summer's crescent dim
    On tow'r and steep a silver paleness cast,
I mark'd a figure in the tintless beam
    Along that secret path descending fast;
It gains the outer ward—the bridge is past,
And now that form is lost in vapours dun,
    And now the warder blew his latest blast,
And all were muster'd in the court but one,
The same who rules it now—the harper's traitor son.

XI.

" Yet never came suspicion on my mind;
  Calm fell as wont on every wearied breast
Within th' embattled fortress safe reclined,
  Night's holy pause of sweet oblivious rest,
  War lost awhile his soul-devouring zest.
Hush'd was the hoarse artillery's angry roar;
  The haughty leaguer shared the influence blest.
There clamour 'woke the peopled tents no more,
But stillness sank serene on camp, and tow'r, and shore.

XII.

" ' Shanid-a-bo!* there's treason in the hold!'
  At midnight rose the cry within our halls.
' Shanid-a-bo! the Geraldine is sold!
  The English banner scoffs our armed walls!'
  Too late—too late the startled warder calls—
A host resistless fill'd the captured tow'r;
  Life after life in fruitless contest falls.
The Geraldine surrendered land and pow'r—
All lost but life and fame in that accursed hour.

XIII.

" I heard the din upon my darkling bed,
  And to my lady flew in speechless fear;
While swell'd within the hold the tumult dread
  Of clattering brand, and targe, and crackling spear.
  Ne'er may again such sounds assail mine ear!
The crash of broken blade, the shout, the moan,
  Menace and pray'r unheard, came mingling near;
And rallying call and conquest thundering on,
And the blasphemer's oath with warrior's parting groan."

Shanid-a-bo! the war-cry of the Earls of Desmond.

XIV

"We *had* a lady then?" the stripling said.
　A moment paused the matron in her tale,
And, resting on the hand her aged head,
　Burst from her inmost soul the sudden wail.
That question did her very heart assail,
For Desmond's countess had to her been kind,
　When queen-like once she ruled that lovely vale;
And all her goodness rush'd upon her mind
Ere her sweet soul had left this weary world behind.

XV.

Poor soul! affection was her little world,
　And natural love the kingdom where she reign'd;
But there had death with ruthless hand unfurl'd
　His ensign black, with many a heart's blood stain'd,
　Of all she loved this youth alone remain'd.
Forbear to ask, why spared such keen distress,
　Bad hearts rejoiced while hers was inly pain'd.
Let sweet religion meet each dubious guess,
God still severely tries the hearts he means to bless.

XVI.

"We had a lady then," the matron said—
　"Go ask the widow shivering at the gate,
Or orphan weeping in his lowly shed,
　How Desmond's countess filled her high estate.
　Not hers the soul with selfish pride elate,
Her tender heart with other's grief was riv'n;
　There grace divine and secret virtue sate.
Her heart was shared between her lord and heav'n,
And surely to her God the larger part was given.

XVII.

"God help our slothful souls!" the speaker sigh'd,
   And clasped her hands, and shook the aged head;
"She was to us a lesson and a guide,
   For holiest light in all her works was shed,
   With counsel sweet she cheered the sufferer's bed;
With gentlest hand she dried the mourner's tear,
   For all her pow'r relieved—her bounty fed,
Duly each morn arose her pray'r sincere,
And, for her Saviour's sake, her very foes were dear

XVIII.

"But she shall bless our earthly eyes no more;
   Sweet is her sleep in yonder abbey gray,
Where 'mid the summer dews descending hoar,
   The lonely redbreast sings his evening lay.
   There still our kerne their secret off'rings pay,
At solemn feast retired or vigil lone;
   For there with that same moon's declining ray,
The wretched Desmond rear'd her funeral stone,
And poured above her grave a widow'd husband's moan."

XIX.

She ceased—and bending low her aged head,
   With paly brow upon her hand reclined;
While memory woke each thought of rapture fled,
   With rocking motion soothed her anguish'd mind.
   Say Muse (for thou canst all the chain unwind
Of link'd events by History's finger wove),
   How sped the Desmond in that tumult blind,
Hemm'd in by adverse spears, a bristling grove,
Where point with point enlaced in fell discussion strove.

XX.

Pale on the midnight floor the Countess stands,
    When hark! the Desmond bursts the chamber door
Like warning sprite with wide extended hands,
    And scared gaze, and armour stained with gore.
"Betrayed! the tow'r is lost, and all is o'er!
Fair dreams of independence ruling free;
    Thou hear'st the victor Saxon's gathering roar,
Country and home and lands are lost to me,
And nothing now remains," he said, "but life and thee."

XXI.

Short time for speech. One vigorous arm he wound
    Around the trembling lady's lovely frame.
Lightly he raised her from the stony ground,
    High flash'd his reeking blade like meteor flame.
Resistless on the struggling press he came,
Back from his path the weakling commons reel,
    Some held their swords aloof in generous shame,
Who dared to thwart him rued his ruffian zeal,
For stern was the rebuke of that avenging steel.

XXII.

Right on the hero drove—oh, wondrous sight!
    Oh, fearful beauty of the warrior's ire!
Death haunts his downward track and wild affright,
    Shriek, yell, and groan confess'd his presence dire.
    Inch after inch the 'wilder'd foe retire;
Yet, cool amid the dying and the dead,
    With stilly rage he wrought and govern'd fire,
Unmoved as who the peaceful rinky tread,
More like an angel sent to wreak heaven's vengeance
    dread.

XXIII.

Son of the Geraldine,* renown'd in song!
  To that bold-mettled race, resolved and high,
Alone such giant might of arm belong,
  And purpose undismay'd of nerve and eye.
Fly! loved son of sires beloved—fly!
Thy foes are gath'ring close in flank and rear;
  Thick press'd the living fence-work circling nigh,
With rattling brand and targe and level spear,
Hip, knee, and shoulder join'd, and gnashed teeth austere.

---

* Many amusing anecdotes are related in Holingshed, illustrative of the character of this distinguished family.

"Kildare was open and plaine, hardlie able to rule himself when he were moved to anger, not so sharpe as short, being easily displeased and sooner appeased. Being in a rage with certaine of his servants for faults they committed, one of his horssemen offere Mester Boise (a gentleman that retained to him) an Irish hobbie, on conditione that he would plucke an haire from the earle his beard. Boice, taking the proffer at rebound, stept to the earle (with whose good nature he was thoroughly acquainted), parching in the heat of his choler, and said: 'So it is, and if it like your good lordship, one of your horssemen promised me a choice horsse if I snip one hair from your beard.' 'Well,' quoth the Earl, 'I agree thereto; but if thou pluck anie more than one, I promise thee to bring my fist from thine eare.'

"The branch of this good nature hath been derived from him to an earle of his posteritie, who, being in a chafe, for the wrong saucing of a partridge, arose suddenly from the table, meaning to have reasoned the matter with his cooke. Having entered the kitchen, drowning in oblivion his challenge, he began to commend the building of the roome, wherein he was at no time before, and so leaving the cooke uncontrolled, he returned to his guests merrilie. . . .

"In his warres, he (the former Kildare) used for policie a retchlesse kind of diligence or a headie carelessnesse, to the end his souldiers should not faint in their attempts, were the enemie of never so great power. Being generall in the field of Knocktow, one of the earle his captains presented him a band of kerns even as they were ready to joine battele, and withal demanded of the earle in what service he would have them imploied? Quoth he, 'Let them stand by and give se the gaze.' Such was his courage that, notwithstanding his enemies were two to one, yet would he set so good a face on the matter, as his souldiers should not once suspect that he either needed or lought for anie further helpe."

XXIV.

Onward the hero drove—crash targe and helm;
  Crash shield and mail beneath his action fell;
Each blow a subject gained to death's black realm;
  Each hollow-sounding stroke a hero's knell;
  Each glimmer of the blade a soul's farewell.
Right on his gory pathway still he hew'd;
  Ah, ruthless War, thy woes what tongue shall tell!
Three paces from the rampart yet he stood,
And those three paces cost a lake of Christian blood.

XXV.

Unwearied yet, he sees th' assailants yield—
  The rampart's gained. High on the wall he stands,
A moment gazed upon the distant field,
  Where safety seem'd to smile with beck'ning hands
  Beneath him still he views the struggling bands,
Where death that night a plenteous harvest reap'd,
  With desperate shout, amid the clattering brands,
Harsh echoing shields and carnage spoil high heap'd—
He waved his gory blade, and from the rampart leap'd.

XXVI.

As when from wave-worn cliff of far Kilkee,
  Time-loosen'd from its immemorial hold,
Some ponderous fragment seeks the booming sea,
  Down the black steep with thundering impulse roll'd,
So stern descending came the Desmond bold,
  So shrunk around, aghast, th' affrighted foes,
  So fierce recoil'd when from the gory mould,
Beneath his burthen bow'd, the chieftain rose,
So roaring vengeance wild in mortal combat close.

XXVII.

So from thy lofty wall, O sea-girt Tyre!
　In mailed panoply descending bright,
Like launched bolt of heaven's electric fire,
　The son of Ammon left that dizzy height,
　Scattering around dismay and pale affright,
Strong in the might of his heroic mind.
　For glory he, and pow'r; but for the right,
And dear connubial love, did Desmond wind
His way that night 'mid many a biting point unkind.

XXVIII.

Still dark upon his path the foemen swarm,
　With rising anger fierce and wrathful brow,
He stirs his giant strength with combat warm,
　And shakes his crest—and, 'ware the Desmond now!
　As parts the surge before some warrior prow,
When windward bound 'gainst wave and storm she steers;
　Or stubborn bawn before the rending plough:
So yield beneath his sway the crashing spears,
And down the hill he drove 'mid yells and fruitless tears.

XXIX.

Who now shall cross the Desmond? Calm no more
　The war-soil stream'd beneath his matted hair:
Sullied with clotted dust and mingled gore,
　Foams the dragg'd lip—the starting eye-balls glare.
　Like maniac roused, he drives the withering share
With desperate fury wild—around—beneath,
　Nor measured ire nor govern'd heat was there—
At every blow a heart's blood stain'd the heath;
The very wind they cast seemed rife with pain and death

XXX.

Fight! Desmond, fight! he pants—each quiv'ring limb
    Instinct with rage high wrought, and breathing doom.
Like mower toiling in midsummer beam,
    Or smith at anvil bow'd with brow of gloom
    Out burst at once, as from volcanic womb,
The pent up fury stirr'd by contest dire,
    So chafes the downward flood with whitening spume.
So drives o'er autumn heath the scorching ire,
Wind-borne resistless on, of fast consuming fire.

XXXI.

Right on the hero drove like northern storm,
    And pass'd the bridge and gain'd the moonlit plain,
Still clasp'd with instinct dear that precious form;
    But vain his valorous toil, his fondness vain.
    Thick round his pathway hurl'd, as winter rain,
Bow, sling, and gun, their murderous death-show'r sped—
    That shriek! ah, who shall tell the Desmond's pain?
It is, it is her life-stream bubbling red;
And "husband, lay me down," the wounded lady said.

XXXII.

Soul-piercing sight! with anguish'd heart aghast,
    Upon a bank beside the lonely wave,
Gently he staunch'd the heart's blood, issuing fast,
    And pray'd high heav'n her gentle soul to save.
    Sigh after sigh the wounded Countess gave,
A year of life with every parting breath,
    Stretch'd in the nerveless posture of the grave;
Silent she lies upon the gory heath,
And sets in those sweet eyes the whitening glare of death.

XXXIII.

With grief impatient, on the darkling lea,
  The wretched chieftain cast his useless blade.
' Ye woman-slaying hinds, why spared ye me?
  And why is Desmond here, unhurt?" he said.
" My life! my love! see! Desmond guards thy head!
Look up and live!" he sigh'd in accents mild.
  Silent she hears—speech, sense, and motion fled.
He raised his clenched hands with action wild,
And lifted up his voice, and wept like infant child.

XXXIV.

Yes, Desmond wept, he who alone had gazed
  That night unmoved on all that hostile band;
Stirr'd by th' unwonted sound, the Countess raised
  Her dying frame, and pressed his succouring hand;
And " Comfort thee," she sigh'd in whisper bland;
' Comfort thee, Desmond! all that valour could
  To-night thine arm hath wrought for tow'r and land—
He who for us hath shed his saving blood,
Felt, too, the bitter pangs of man's ingratitude."

XXXV.

" Curst be the traitor!"—" Hold, my husband, hold!
  Nor let the last—last words my soul shall hear
From those kind lips before its sense is cold,
  With vengeful meaning fright my dying ear.
  Farewell! thou hast to me been true and dear,
Be so to heav'n when I am lowly laid;
  Let me not need the Christian's wonted bier,
Nor narrow tomb within the hallow'd shade,
And be above my grave the requiem duly said."

XXXVI

She said, and folded her sweet hands in pray'r,
   While reverent sate apart the sorrowing chief,
To resignation changed his heart's despair,
   Close pent within his breast the stifling grief.
   Slow came and leaden-paced Death's cold relief;
Faint in her bosom ebbs the wasting tide.
   " Receive my stained soul !" she murmured brief,
" Thou who for sinful man in torment died ;"
And forth with that last pray'r her gentle soul she sigh'd.

XXXVII.

With rending heart the chieftain saw her die—
   Awhile he knelt beside the lifeless clay ;
Then with the silver wave, that murmur'd by,
   He washed with care that gory soil away,
   That dark upon the paly features lay,
And rais'd his mournful burthen from the ground,
   And up the stream pursued his weary way,
Where, buried deep in listening woods profound,
You aged abbey casts its sacred shade around.

XXXVIII.

Sad burthen bow'd the chief !—less ponderous far
   Her living weight, or that which once of yore
From the last scene of Ilium's mighty war,
   The pious prince with filial anguish bore.
   Far distant, on some safe sequester'd shore,
He yet might watch beside his rescued sire;
   But she shall grace the Desmond's board no more,
No more shall cheer his lonely evening fire,
Nor, with persuasion soft, disarm his household ire.

XXXIX.

Slant on his path the westward moonbeam shone,
    When, still beneath his dismal burthen bow'd,
He reach'd the abbey, screen'd in woodland 'lone
    Of pines and waving yew, a sombre shroud.
"Open your gates!" the midnight summons loud
Rang mournful through the cloisters' echoing halls.
    "The harbour to the harbourless allow'd.
Your houseless ruler seeks within your walls;
Open your holy gates!—'tis Desmond's lord that

XL.

Wide gaped the convent door, revolving slow:
    The abbot knows those noble accents well.
What words can paint the old man's speechless woe,
    When on that group his wildering glances fell.
"Father! behold the wreck unspeakable
Of what was late my bosom's earthly pearl!
    The poorest monk, within his convent cell,
Who shuns the rage of life's tempestuous whirl,
Holds more of wealth to-night than Desmond's mighty
    earl."

XLI

Slow rose the requiem from the midnight choir;
    By haste compell'd, the friendly brethren lay,
Ere kindled from yon hills the eastern fire,
    In its low house, that piece of lifeless clay.
The widow'd chieftain mark'd the opening day,
And turn'd him from the holy solitude.
    Westward again he held his venturous way,
By glen untrod, and swamp, and darkling wood,
Unconquer'd at the heart—in spirit unsubdued.

XLII.

Twelve years have passed since then, nor if he dwells
    In life or death his sorrowing vassals know;
They paid the traitor with his tow'rs and dells,
    But love nor right with strong possession go—
Their hearts are still with Desmond in his woe,
Unchanged as when they saw their chieftain stand
    On yonder shore, at moonlight, lingering slow.
" Farewell!" he cried, and wrung each eager hand,
"Farewell, my faithful friends! farewell, my native land!"

XLIII.

Twelve years have pass'd—and tyranny since then
    With iron hand upon the vale hath press'd;
The roofless cot within the fertile glen,
    The blacken'd scar upon the mountain's breast,
The usurper's conscience-haunted reign attest.
Ev'n now, secure amid his archer train,
    His eye betrays his bosom's deep unrest;
With doubtful scowl he views that peopled plain,
And fears a secret foe in every injured swain.

XLIV.

See! southward borne along the shining tide,
    Finned with lithe ash, a nimble curragh flew;
'Tis but a stranger come from Thomond side
    To see the southern archers strain the yew;
And near that throng, with careless piece, he drew.
While loud appalling thunders shook the air—
    For now the chieftain's son, with action true
And steady gaze, has aim'd the arrow fair,
And sent it to the mark, and left it quivering there.

XLV.

"What fairer shot," a flattering vassal cries,
  "Hath ever eye beheld on Desmond's plains?"
"Sooth, that have mine," the stranger's voice replies,
  "When old Fitz-Gerald held these fair domains;
  And though my hair be grizzled, and my veins
With lessening current beat, and action tame,
  Enough, even yet, of force and skill remains
To bear my answer out, or I would shame
To tread the Desmond's soil, and name the Desmond's name."

XLVI.

He said, and far beyond the target set,
  Deep in the turf, a carrowe's* ashen spear;
Then backward through the silent circle paced
  Full half three hundred paces, meted clear.
  Fixed is each eye, attent is every ear;
The bolt is drawn—the parting impulse given—
  Sharp rang the string, like harp at evening cheer;
Swift sped the bolt—the ashen shaft is riv'n,
And louder thunders rise and rend the echoing heav'n.

---

* The *Carrowe* was the ancient Irish horseman.—"These," says an old writer, "when they have no staie of their own, gad and range from house to house, like Arrant Knights of the Round-table, and they never dismount till they ride into the hall and as farre as the table. There is among them a brotherhode of *Carrowes* that proffer to plaie at cards all the year long, and make it their only occupation. They plaie away mantel and all to the bare skin, and trusse themselves in straw or leaves; then wait for passengers on the highwaie, and ask no more than companions to make them sport."

XLVII.

Laughing, the stranger sought the neighb'ring shore,
    Where the spent waves on quarried granite beat;
A fragment slowly up the slope he bore,
    Massy and huge, for Druid altar meet.
    Erect he stands before the chieftain's seat—
"Since years have yet not quench'd the generous rage
    Of manhood in these limbs, and youthful heat,
With all thy band a merry war I wage,
In feat of strength or skill, and thereto cast my gage."

XLVIII.

He said, and on the sward his burden threw,
    Like meteoric rock it pierced the green;
With wondering eyes the silent circle view
    The stranger's ponderous bulk and lofty mien.
    Such forms, in radiant majesty serene,
Once on the heathen artist's slumber shone—
    When, burning with high thoughts and genius keen,
He caught the fleeting vision's heavenly tone,
And woke to hew a god from out the Parian stone.

XLIX.

Stalwart he stood amid the mountain kerne;
    Calm gleam his eyes in dignity severe;
His shoulders huge, like his the Argive stern,
    Who, one long day, upheld the heavenly sphere.
    Sallow his hue as tanned hide of steer,
Nor mark he bore of woman's gentle mould;
    His frame was knit by many a toilsome year—
His noble hair, in jetty ringlets roll'd,
Hung curling down his neck, like British seamen bold.

L.

But who the stranger's offer'd gage shall raise?
　　Some shun abash'd that glance of piercing gray;
Some view the mass inert, with curious gaze,
　　Deep-fix'd within the yawning soil that lay;
　　Some lent their mightiest force with vain essay,
'Mid many a stifled laugh and whisper'd jest,
　　To lift the fragment from its bed of clay.
Forth came, with conscious smile, the stranger guest,
And to the giant task his iron strength address'd.

LI.

With vigorous ease he raised the rocky weight,
　　And, wheeling round, upon his centre came,
With well-timed action, forceful, yet sedate,
　　Gathering the sum of motion in his frame,
　　And hurl'd the mass aloft with giant aim,
And all his strength into the impulse threw:
　　Like fragment heaved from Etna's throat of flame,
Or launch'd from ancient catapult, it flew
And smote the echoing strand, and dash'd the brine to dew.

LII.

'And who and what art thou?" the chieftain cries,
　　"With more than human skill and vigour blest?"
"One of your blood," the stranger calm replies,
　　"Though long an exile in the sunny west—
　　A landless, noteless man, my noblest crest
Is now that oft with Geraldine I bled.
　　Unmark'd I roam, the lowly shielding's guest—
My mightiest boast, that I am island bred;
My highest praise to say, I love the land I tread."

LIII.

Now sinks the sun behind the hills of Clare,
  The kerne are scatter'd to their mountain fires
And wake with many a wond'rous legend there,
  The memory of their old heroic sires—
  The weary herdsman to his shed retires.
And all is lull'd in midnight stillness soon,
  Save where the convent hymn to heaven aspires,
Or patient fisher lifts his merry tune,
And plies his weary trade beneath the smiling moon.

LIV.

Within a grove, by Shanid's lofty hill,
  A hermit held his penitential cell,
Wild herbs his food, his drink the lucid rill,
  That bubbled sweetly from a neighbouring well—
  He in the busy world had ceased to dwell;
A passion-wasted heart—a bruised reed;
  His science, suffering, and the art to quell
Each earthly wish, in hope of heavenly meed,
By following to the life the perfect Christian creed.

LV.

And heav'n received his penitence sincere;
  For when the stroke of Death had closed his race,
They said a lustre play'd around his bier,
  And precious fragrance fill'd the lonely place.
  The earth upon his tomb had healing grace,
And sickness of the mind or frame removed:
  There oft the pious pilgrim came to trace
Where heav'n with many a holy sign approved,
The holocaust of praise and purity it loved.

LVI.

Scarce in the east the ruddy daylight breaks,
   When down the secret pathway, pacing slow,
The aged nurse her tottering journey takes,
   Where by the hill the lucid waters flow,
   Faint down the vale the early sunbeams glow;
When by the crystal fount the matron stands,
   With wooden cup and pitcher, bending low,
She fills the sparkling lymph with trembling hands,
And sighs break forth between, and tears bedew the sands.

LVII.

Sudden a rustling in the shrubs she hears,
   That round the well their graceful foliage wove;
That stranger's form upon the brink appears,
   Half hid by leaves and clustering boughs above;
   And tears of gentlest tenderness and love
On that stern cheek their softening influence shed;
   His quiv'ring lips with sweet affections move;
Low o'er the bank he bow'd his noble head,
And "Dost thou know me, nurse?" in whisper soft, he said.

LVIII.

Like one whose quicken'd fancy hears at night
   Strange spectral voices in the rushing wind.
The startled matron clears her inward sight
   And seeks the lost idea in her mind.
   Beside her now, in broader light defined,
He gazed into her soul, and sweetly smiled
   Her heart awakened at the greeting kind,
aint from her bosom broke the accents wild,
As on his neck she fell. "It is—it is my child!"

LIX.

"Yes, Desmond treads again his natal land,
   To find again his castle, or a grave;
Four weeks have pass'd since on the western strand
   I came, a home-sick wanderer of the wave;
   Me, Loughill's kerns a joyous welcome gave—
But, ah, my heart is rack'd, where'er it turns,
   To hear the blood-hounds of the tyrant rave,
To see the shieling wreck'd—the roof that burns,
Where many an orphan'd child and houseless widow
   mourns.

LX.

"To-night, in Shanagolden's lovely vale,
   Two thousand kerns at midnight wait my call;
Such force as may with sure success assail
   The traitor in our own usurped hall:
   Yet loth I were that child of Desmond fall
By kindred weapon struck, in dire array;
   More meet it were to gain the lofty wall
By secret skill, than battle's loud essay,
And with his own dark art that traitor slave repay.

LXI.

"Where rests the harper?" "In the eastern keep.
   "Oh, nurse, to-night, at that unguarded hour,
When kern and galloglach are lulled in sleep,
   Be thou our friend within the embattled tow'r;
   When dull of sense, from wine's oppressive pow'r,
That drunken harper seeks our fair alcove,
   Be thou before him in the window'd bow'r,
And place a lamp upon the sill above,
And see no other hand than his the light remove."

LXII.

They part—'tis night—within that lofty hold
    Loud rung the merry sounds of festal cheer;
Slow up the east, on golden axis roll'd,
    The peaceful moon reveal'd her smiling sphere;
    Close hid, with eye intent and watchful ear,
The Desmond stands beside that narrow stream·
    Oft gazed he on the castle, frowning near,
If haply he may see the tiny beam
Of that small lamp from out the chieftain's window
    gleam.

LXIII.

It shines at length. His practised hands alert
    Poise the long musket on the ashen rest,
The burning match within the lock insert,
    And all the horrid art of death address'd.
    Yet not revenge nor hatred fired his breast,
But patriot zeal, and firmest sense of right,
    And pity for his people long oppress'd,
And land betrayed for gold. Ha! see!—the light!
It stirs—he fires—and all is dark as death and night.

LXIV.

Awake! arise! What, ho! 'tis Desmond calls;
    Sound the loud trumpet down the echoing vale!
See—fluttering from high Shanid's towering walls—
    Our ancient banner meets the western gale!"
    That well-known cry prolong'd from dale to dale,
Roused answering wood and shore and peopled hill:
    "Desmond is come again!" the rapturous tale
Woke in each listener's heart the welcome thrill
Of ecstasy return'd and old devoted zeal.

LXV.

Shanid-a-bo! the Desmond's in his hall!
   Vale answers vale along th' awaken'd shore;
With tears of love the joyous clansmen fall
   Around his feet, and press the marble floor,
   And bless the hour that did their lord restore
To his old home and plunder'd rights again.
   But carrion birds the traitor's carcase tore,
While smiling Peace return'd o'er hill and plain,
And Desmond in the Keep resumed his ancient reign.

Orange and Green.

Erin, thy silent tear never shall cease—
Erin, thy languid smile ne'er shall increase
   Till, like the rainbow's light,
   Thy various tints unite,
   And form in heaven's sight
One arch of peace!

                              THOMAS MOORE.

I.

The night was falling dreary
   In merry Bandon town,
When in his cottage, weary,
   An Orangeman lay down.
The summer sun in splendour
   Had set upon the vale,
And shouts of "No surrender!"
   Arose upon the gale.

II.

Beside the waters, laving
 The feet of aged trees,
The Orange banners waving,
 Flew boldly in the breeze
In mighty chorus meeting,
 A hundred voices join,
And fife and drum were beating
 The *Battle of the Boyne.*

III.

Ha! tow'rd his cottage hieing,
 What form is speedy now,
From yonder thicket flying,
 With blood upon his brow?
"Hide—hide me, worthy stranger!
 Though green my colour be,
And in the day of danger
 May heaven remember thee!

IV.

"In yonder vale contending,
 Alone against that crew,
My life and limbs defending,
 An Orangeman I slew.
Hark! hear that fearful warning,
 There's death in every tone—
Oh, save my life till morning,
 And heav'n prolong your own

V.

The Orange heart was melted,
 In pity to the green;
He heard the tale, and felt it,
 His very soul within.

" Dread not that angry warning,
    Though death be in its tone—
I'll save your life till morning,
    Or I will lose my own."

VI.

Now, round his lowly dwelling
    The angry torrent press'd,
A hundred voices swelling,
    The Orangeman address'd—
" Arise, arise, and follow
    The chase along the plain!
In yonder stony hollow
    Your only son is slain!"

VII.

With rising shouts they gather
    Upon the track amain,
And leave the childless father
    Aghast with sudden pain.
He seeks the righted stranger
    In covert where he lay—
" Arise!" he said, " all danger
    Is gone and past away!

VIII.

" I had a son—one only,
    One loved as my life,
Thy hand has left me lonely
    In that accursed strife.
I pledged my word to save thee,
    Until the storm should cease;
I keep the pledge I gave thee—
    Arise, and go in peace!"

F.

IX.

The stranger soon departed
    From that unhappy vale;
The father, broken-hearted,
    Lay brooding o'er that tale.
Full twenty summers after
    To silver turned his beard;
And yet the sound of laughter
    From him was never heard.

X.

The night was falling dreary,
    In merry Wexford town,
When in his cabin, weary,
    A peasant laid him down.
And many a voice was singing
    Along the summer vale,
And Wexford town was ringing
    With shouts of " Granua Uile

XI.

Beside the waters laving
    The feet of aged trees,
The green flag, gaily waving,
    Was spread against the breeze;
In mighty chorus meeting,
    Loud voices filled the town,
And fife and drum were beating,
    " *Down, Orangemen, lie Down!*"

XII.

Hark! 'mid the stirring clangour,
    That woke the echoes there,
Loud voices, high in anger,
    Rise on the evening air.

Like billows of the ocean,
  He sees them hurry on—
And, 'mid the wild commotion,
  An Orangeman alone.

XIII.

"My hair," he said, "is hoary,
  And feeble is my hand,
And I could tell a story
  Would shame your cruel band.
Full twenty years and over
  Have changed my heart and brow,
And I am grown a lover
  Of peace and concord now.

XIV.

"It was not thus I greeted
  Your brother of the Green,
When, fainting and defeated,
  I freely took him in.
I pledged my word to save him
  From vengeance rushing on;
I kept the pledge I gave him,
  Though he had kill'd my son."

XV.

That aged peasant heard him,
  And knew him as he stood;
Remembrance kindly stirr'd him,
  And tender gratitude.
With gushing tears of pleasure
  He pierced the listening train—
"I'm here to pay the measure
  Of kindness back again!"

XVI.

Upon his bosom falling,
   That old man's tears came down.
Deep memory recalling
   That cot and fatal town.
"The hand that would offend thee
   My being first shall end—
I'm living to defend thee,
   My saviour and my friend!"

XVII.

So said, and, slowly turning,
   Address'd the wondering crowd,
With fervent spirit burning,
   He told the tale aloud.
Now pressed the warm beholders,
   Their aged foe to greet;
They raised him on their shoulders,
   And chair'd him through the street.

XVIII.

As he had saved that stranger
   From peril scowling dim,
So in his day of danger
   Did Heav'n remember him.
By joyous crowds attending,
   The worthy pair were seen,
And their flags that day were blended
   Of Orange and of Green.

The Traveller and the Moon.

WRITTEN FOR A BIRTHDAY PRESENT TO A YOUNG FRIEND.

The glorious sun yet burned on high,
His light embracing earth and sky,
When, like a spectre seen at noon,
On Glenvill rose the early moon.

* * * * *

" Glory to thee, all bounteous sun !"
(A traveller thus his theme begun,
Who by Liscanor's sounding bay
To Callan took his lonely way.)
" Thou stirrest the heart to love and mirth,
Thou gladdenest heaven and quickenest earth ;
Thou callest to being, ripe and warm,
The thousand charms of hue and form.
All nature feels thy genial dower,
From lordly man to lowly flower.
How faint to thine, great lord of day,
Yon feeble moon's reflected ray !
To her we owe no fruitful plains,
But swelling seas and frantic brains."

* * * * *

He said, and onward gaily pressed,
Till darkness crept o'er all the west,
And he o'er moor and mountain gray,
Benighted, sought his trackless way.

Far o'er the loud Atlantic's wave
He hears the coming tempests rave.
The clouds have left their ocean bed—
Flash'd the blue night-bolt o'er his head;
Chorussed by winds and hissing fire,
The tempest tunes his demon lyre.
Now chilled by wind, and drenched with rain,
Our wanderer groped o'er hill and plain;
No cottage light, nor human voice,
To bid his sinking heart rejoice.
When, bursting through the stormy rack,
The midnight moon illum'd the track.
From heaven's high arch, in state serene,
Pour'd light and beauty o'er the scene;
To silver turned the flying cloud,
Hushed in the skies the quarrel loud,
And spread afar her radiance mild,
Till even the cheek of darkness smiled.

* * * * *

Thus, while prosperity is ours,
And pleasure strews our way with flowers,
Rejoicing in the glorious day,
We scorn Religion's humble ray.
'Tis only when the night draws on,
And all our worldly light is gone,
When black misfortune's clouds arise,
And vex with storms life's evening skies,
When darkling, lost, and tempest driven,
She cheers our path with light from heaven;
We blush to own the thankless slight,
And feel her power, and bless her might.

Anna Blake.

A FRAGMENT.

I.

Hark! heard ye not that stifled groan
   A wretched woman's piercing wail;
It echoes through those ruins lone,
   It died upon the meadow gale!

II.

See, see amid the ivied screen,
   That veils the cloister's column'd aisle,
What wasted form is dimly seen,
   With rapid beck and frantic smile.

III.

Some creature of abortive brain,
   Or victim of impassioned breast—
Some wreck of bliss, as bright as vain,
   Or fiend, deluded and possessed.

IV.

Perchance—for see her garb is dark,
   And hooded is her curling hair,
And girded is her waist—and mark
   The Rosary descending there.

V.

Some reason-blasted child of wrath!
   Some Dathan of the virgin choir,
Who trod uncalled the holy path,
   And tampered with celestial fire.

VI.

A sunbeam strikes that frenzied brow
   Through yonder oriel glancing down.
Alas! Alas! I know her now!—
   'Tis Anna Blake of Galway town!

VII.

See, see, with spectral haste she glides
   Through broken light and rayless gloom,
To where the funeral yew tree hides
   The wild Biscayen's early tomb!

VIII.

Poor Anna! once unknown to woe!
   A gayer heart, a happier mind
Ne'er lent to worth their social glow,
   In frame of fairer mould enshrined.

IX.

Mark, as the quivering sunbeams fall,
   She turns to shade that hooded brow,
Where moping Phrensy in the hall
   Of banished Reason riots now.

X.

Now swift she starts with warning sign;
   And now with keen heart-straining gaze,
Beside the ivy-mantled shrine,
   The wretched maiden kneels and prays.

XI.

Oft has she roamed in happier hours
   The walks where now she loiters wild,
When, blest within her natal towers,
   Her father nursed his darling child.

XII.

While yet their ancient dwelling stood,
    By Corrib's wild and gusty lake;
And many a western chieftain wooed
    The heiress of the high-born Blake.

XIII.

And Mary made the moments light,
    With friendship's soft and tranquil joy;
And Eman held her promised plight,
    The Mayor of Galway's gallant boy.

XIV.

An autumn's sun had shown the tower,
    Deep imaged in the waveless lake,
When sadly, in their secret bower,
    Young Mary questioned Anna Blake.

XV.

" 'The morn," she said, " is rosy bright—
    Ah! why art thou so pale and chill?
The flowers look up to meet the light,
    Ah, why is Anna drooping still?

XVI.

" Is this my brother's beauteous bride,
    That ere the bridal sinks forlorn!
Is Mary falser than the tide?
    Is Eman colder than the morn?"

XVII.

" Cold!" said the maiden, as she raised
    Her moistened eyes and sadly smiled:
" *Not cold*—though coldness might be praised
    Before a love so weak and wild.

XVIII.

"Mary, forgive!—I know thou art
　　His softer self from infancy;
Yet Nature's bond within my heart,
　　Is less a bond than Love's in me.

XIX.

"My sister and my friend sincere,
　　Ah, blame not one confiding sigh!
I breathe my griefs in Mary's ear,
　　As if the wind alone were nigh.

XX.

"No, though from youth the fire divine,
　　Unfading burns in either breast
I feel a warning sense in mine,
　　That tells me it shall ne'er be blest.

XXI.

"To stranger heart, to friend less dear,
　　I would not own one thought of pain;
Not Eman's self should know the fear
　　That makes this bridal splendour vain.

XXII.

"Can I not sing a mirthful song,
　　Or dance, or laugh by summer stream,
But I must hold some thought of wrong,
　　Some secret slight at heart to him?

XXIII.

"Oh, never may our Mary prove
　　The jealous glance—the doubt unjust—
The thousand pains that wait on Love
　　When watched by beetle-brow'd distrust!

XXIV.

"The veiled blame, the tone that stirs
  Even love's own sweetness into gall;
But, ah! the thought that he who errs,
  Is still the best beloved of all!

XXV.

"The eye, whose unconfiding beam
  Ne'er meets thine own with meaning free—
The temper like a maniac's dream;
  The secret step that—hush! 'tis he!"

XXVI.

A shadow falls across the leaves,
  That cluster round the arched bower,
Where close the sunbright jasmine weaves
  Its shoots through Bruge's lingering flower.

XXVII.

'Tis Eman's step—'tis Eman's form,
  In nuptial splendour all arrayed;
Yet in his greeting, fond and warm,
  There lingered still an anxious shade.

XXVIII.

"What means that quick, distrustful hush,
  When Eman's form the maidens see?
Why rises Anna's conscious blush?
  They have been whispering here of me!"

XXIX.

But soon the unworthy darkness passed,
  At Anna's smile, from that high brow,
As hills by transient gloom o'ercast,
  In light as transient brighten now.

XXX.

"Joy to my Anna!—it is come!
  The morn of long-expected bliss,
And Doubt is fled—and Fear is dumb,
  And hours are rising bright with peace.

XXXI.

"And wilt thou now forgive the pain
  That Eman's anxious thoughts have given?
That never can return again,
  Till life's new gilded links are riven!

XXXII.

"Oh, wordless joy!—the morn-beams break,
  For which my lonely heart has sighed—
Since first by Corrib's mighty lake
  I saw my young and gifted bride."

XXXIII.

"Oh, joy of joys! the blushing ray
  That smiling brings the bridal dawn!
The sweetly-wakening waves that play,
  All bright against the sunny lawn.

XXXIV.

"The fostering light—the genial air,
  That breathe in nature's morning bowers,
Brings less of rapturous promise there
  Than this arising day of ours!"

XXXV.

Even while he spoke, and Anna smiled,
  There fell a darkness on the bower,
As when on Burrin's mountain wild
  The west-winds drive the sudden shower.

XXXVI.

The rising breeze unglassed the lake,
  The far blue hills grew dark and near,
As in the autumnal blasts that break
  The beauty of the closing year.

XXXVII.

The vapoury pile, arising dun,
  Slow up the altering east is driven;
A veil obscures the distant sun,
  And darkness chills the face of heaven.

XXXVIII.

High in his airy field remote
  The skylark ends his beauteous strain,
And, with a long and warning note,
  Drops sudden on the darkening plain.

XXXIX.

The peasant rests his weary spade,
  And backward views the threatening moon;
The pedlar marks the deepening shade
  Upon his mountain track forlorn.

XL.

The boatman spreads his stinted sail,
  Safe moored beside the windward cliff,
Already hears the rushing gale,
  And closer winds the prudent reef.

XLI.

Along the shore, with rapid stroke,
  The fisher plies the bending ash;
Beneath the broad and darkening oak
  The billows break their noisier plash.

XLII.

The curlew seeks the inland moor,

My Spirit is Gay.

I.

My spirit is gay as the breaking of dawn,
As the breeze that sports over the sun-lighted lawn,
As the song of yon lark from his kingdom of light,
Or the harp-string that rings in the chambers at night;
For the world and its vapours, though darkly they fold,
I have light that can turn them to purple and gold,
Till they brighten the landscape they came to deface,
And deformity changes to beauty and grace.

II.

Yet say not to selfish delights I must turn,
From the grief-laden bosoms around me that mourn,
For 'tis pleasure to share in each sorrow I see,
And sweet sympathy's tear is enjoyment to me.
Oh! blest is the heart, when misfortunes assail,
That is armed in content as a garment of mail,
For the grief of another that treasures its zeal,
And remembers no woe but the woe it can heal.

III.

When the storm gathers dark o'er the summer's young bloom,
And each ray of the noontide is sheathed in gloom,
I would be the rainbow, high arching in air,
Like a gleaming of hope on the brow of despair.
When the burst of its fury is spent on the bow'r,
And the buds are yet bow'd with the weight of the show'r,
I would be the beam that comes warming and bright,
And that bids them burst open to fragrance and light.

IV.

I would be the smile that comes breaking serene
O'er the features where lately affliction has been,
Or the heart-speaking scroll, after years of alloy,
That brings home to the desolate tidings of joy;
Or the life-giving rose odour borne by the breeze
To the sense rising keen from the couch of disease,
Or the whisper of charity, tender and kind,
Or the dawning of hope on the penitent's mind.

V.

Then breathe ye, sweet roses, your fragrance around,
And waken ye, wild birds, the grove with your sound;
When the soul is unstained and the heart is at ease,
There's a rapture in pleasures so simple as these.
I rejoice in each sunbeam that gladdens the vale,
I rejoice in each odour that sweetens the gale;
In the bloom of the spring, in the summer's gay voice,
With a spirit as gay, I rejoice! I rejoice!

The Tie is broke, my Irish Girl.

The tie is broke, my Irish girl,
  That bound thee here to me;
My heart has lost its single pearl,
  And thine at last is free—
Dead as the earth that wraps thy clay,
  Dead as the stone above thee—
Cold as this heart, that breaks to say
  It never more can love thee.

II.

I press thee to my aching breast—
　No blush comes o'er thy brow—
Those gentle arms that once caress'd
　Fall round me deadly now;
The smiles of love no longer part
　Those dead, blue lips of thine—
I lay my hand upon thy heart,
　'Tis cold at last to mine.

III.

Were we beneath our native heaven,
　Within our native land,
A fairer grave to thee were given
　Than this wild bed of sand—
But thou wert single in thy faith,
　And single in thy worth,
And thou should'st die a lonely death,
　And lie in lonely earth.

IV.

Then lay thee down, and take thy rest!
　My last, last look is given—
The earth is smooth above *thy breast*,
　And mine is yet unriven!
No mass—no parting Rosary—
　My perished love can have;
But a husband's sighs embalm her corse,
　A husband's tears her grave.

When Love in a Young Heart.

I.

When love in a young heart his dwelling has taken,
   And pines on the white cheek, and burns in the veins,
Say, how can the reign of the tyrant be shaken—
   By absence? by poverty? sickness? or chains?

II.

No!—these have been tried, and the tempter has come
   Unmoved through the changes of grief and distress
But if you would send him at once to the tomb,
   You must poison his hope with a dose of—success.

Sleep, that like the Couched Dove.

I.

Sleep, that like the couched dove,
   Broods o'er the weary eye,
Dreams that with soft heavings move
   The heart of memory—
Labour's guerdon, golden rest,
Wrap thee in its downy vest;
Fall like comfort on thy brain,
And sing the hush-song to thy pain!

II.

Far from thee be startling fears,
   And dreams the guilty dream;
No banshee scare thy drowsy ears
   With her ill-omened scream.
But tones of fairy minstrelsy
Float like the ghosts of sound o'er thee,
Soft as the chapel's distant bell,
And lull thee to a sweet farewell.

III.

Ye, for whom the ashy hearth
   The fearful housewife clears—
Ye, whose tiny sounds of mirth
   The nighted carman hears—
Ye, whose pigmy hammers make
The wonderers of the cottage wake—
Noiseless be your airy flight,
Silent as the still moonlight.

IV.

Silent go and harmless come,
   Fairies of the stream—
Ye, who love the winter gloom,
   Or the gay moonbeam—
Hither bring your drowsy store,
Gather'd from the bright lusmore,
Shake o'er temples—soft and deep—
The comfort of the poor man's sleep.

The Sally-coop, where once I Strayed

I.

The sally-coop, where once I strayed,
   Is faded now and lonely—
The echoes in the leafless glade
   Wake to the waters only;
My early haunts are perished all,
   My early friends departed—
And I sit in my native hall
   Forlorn and broken-hearted.

II.

When last I lay beside that stream
   I dreamt of fame and splendour,
And bliss was mingled with my dream—
   Domestic, sweet, and tender;
Now I would give that fame and all,
   Were this soft starlight gleaming
On my old friends, in their old hall,
   And I an infant dreaming.

The Mie-na-mallah now is Past.

Air—"*Oh! Wirra-sthru.*"

I.

The mie-na-mallah* now is past,
   Oh, wirra-sthru! oh, wirra-sthru!
And I must leave my home at last,
   Oh, wirra-sthru! oh, wirra-sthru!

* Honeymoon.

I look into my father's eyes,
I hear my mother's parting sighs—
Ah! fool to pine for other ties—
    Oh, wirra-sthru! oh, wirra-sthru!

II.

This evening they must sit alone,
    Oh, wirra-sthru! oh, wirra-sthru!
They'll talk of me when I am gone,
    Oh, wirra-sthru! oh, wirra-sthru!
Who now will cheer my weary sire,
When toil and care his heart shall tire?
My chair is empty by the fire!
    Oh, wirra-sthru! oh, wirra-sthru!

III.

How sunny looks my pleasant home,
    Oh, wirra-sthru! oh, wirra-sthru!
Those flowers for me shall never bloom—
    Oh, wirra-sthru! oh, wirra-sthru!
I seek new friends, and I am told
That they are rich in lands and gold—
Ah! will they love me like the old?
    Oh, wirra-sthru! oh, wirra-sthru

IV.

Farewell, dear friends, we meet no more—
    Oh, wirra-sthru! oh, wirra-sthru!
My husband's horse is at the door—
    Oh, wirra-sthru! oh, wirra-sthru!
Ah, love! ah, love! be kind to me,
For by this breaking heart you see
How dearly I have purchased thee!
    Oh, wirra-sthru! oh, wirra-sthru

The Wanderer's Return.

I.

I've come unto my home again, and find myself alone,
The friends I left in quiet there are perished all and gone—
My father's house is tenantless, my early love lies low;
But one remains of all that made my youthful spirit glow—
My love lies in the blushing west, drest in a robe of green,
And pleasant waters sing to her, and know her for their queen:
The wild winds fan her face, that o'er the distant billows come—
She is my last remaining love—my own, my island home.

II.

I know I've not the cunning got to tell the love I feel,
And few give timid truth the faith they yield to seeming zeal.
The friends who loved me thought me cold, and fell off one by one,
And left me in my solitude to live and love alone.
But each pleasant grove of thine, my love, and stream my fervour know—
For there is no distrusting glance to meet and check its glow:
To every dell I freely tell my thoughts, where'er I roam,
How dear thou art to this lorn heart—my own, my island home.

III.

And when I lift my voice, and sing unto thy silent shades,
And echo wakens merrily in all thy drowsy glades,
There's not a rill—a vale—a hill—a wild wood, or still grove,
But gives again the burning strain, and yields me love for love.

Oh, I have seen the maiden of my bosom pine and die—
And I have seen my bosom friend look on me doubtingly—
And long—oh, long—have all my young affections found
 a tomb—
Yet thou art all in all to me—my own, my island home.

IV.

And now I bring a weary thing—a withered heart to thee—
To lay me down upon thy breast, and die there quietly—
I've wandered o'er, oh, many a shore, to die this death
 at last—
And my soul is glad, its wish is gained, and all my toils
 are past.
Oh, take me to thy bosom then, and let the spot of earth
Receive the wanderer to his rest that gave the wanderer
 birth—
And the stream, beside whose gentle tide a child I loved
 to roam,
Now pour its wave along my grave—my narrow, island
 home.

Old Times! Old Times!

I.

Old times! old times! the gay old times!
 When I was young and free,
And heard the merry Easter chimes
 Under the sally tree.
My Sunday palm beside me placed—
 My cross upon my hand—
A heart at rest within my breast,
 And sunshine on the land!
  Old times! Old times!

II.

It is not that my fortunes flee,
   Nor that my cheek is pale—
I mourn whene'er I think of thee,
   My darling, native vale!—
A wiser head I have, I know,
   Than when I loitered there;
But in my wisdom there is woe,
   And in my knowledge care.
          Old times! Old times!

III.

I've lived to know my share of joy,
   To feel my share of pain—
To learn that friendship's self can cloy,
   To love, and love in vain—
To feel a pang and wear a smile,
   To tire of other climes—
To like my own unhappy isle,
   And sing the gay old times!
          Old times! Old times!

IV.

And sure the land is nothing changed,
   The birds are singing still;
The flowers are springing where we ranged,
   There's sunshine on the hill!
The sally, waving o'er my head,
   Still sweetly shades my frame—
But, ah, those happy days are fled,
   And I am not the same!
          Old times! Old times!

V.

Oh, come again, ye merry times!
  Sweet, sunny, fresh, and calm —
And let me hear those Easter chimes,
  And wear my Sunday palm.
If I could cry away mine eyes,
  My tears would flow in vain —
If I could waste my heart in sighs,
  They'll never come again!
        Old times! Old times!

A Place in thy Memory, Dearest.

I.

A PLACE in thy memory, dearest,
  Is all that I claim,
To pause and look back when thou hearest
  The sound of my name.
Another may woo thee, nearer,
  Another may win and wear;
I care not though he be dearer,
  If I am remembered there.

II.

Remember me — not as a lover
  Whose hope was cross'd,
Whose bosom can never recover
  The light it hath lost;
As the young bride remembers the mother
  She loves, though she never may see;
As a sister remembers a brother,
  dearest! remember me.

III.

Could I be thy true lover, dearest,
   Could'st thou smile on me,
I would be the fondest and nearest
   That ever loved thee!
But a cloud on my pathway is glooming,
   That never must burst upon thine;
And Heaven, that made thee all blooming,
   Ne'er made thee to wither on mine.

IV.

Remember me, then!—Oh, remember,
   My calm, light love;
Though bleak as the blasts of November
   My life may prove,
That life will, though lonely, be sweet,
   If its brightest enjoyment should be
A smile and kind word when we meet,
   And a place in thy memory.

My Mary of the Curling Hair.

AIR—"*Shule, agra.*"

I.

My Mary of the curling hair,
The laughing teeth and bashful air,
Our bridal morn is dawning fair,
   With blushes in the skies,
*Shule! Shule! Shule! agra,
Shule, asucur, agus shule, aroon.**
   My love! my pearl!
   My own dear girl!
My mountain maid, arise!

---

* Come! come! come, my darling—
Come, softly, and come, my love!

II.

Wake, linnet of the osier grove!
Wake, trembling, stainless, virgin dove!
Wake, nestling of a parent's love!
  Let Moran see thine eyes.
Shule! Shule! &c.

III.

I am no stranger, proud and gay,
To win thee from thy home away,
And find thee, for a distant day,
  A theme for wasting sighs.
Shule! Shule! &c.

IV.

But we were known from infancy,
Thy father's hearth was home to me;
No selfish love was mine for thee,
  Unholy and unwise.
Shule! Shule! &c.

V.

And yet (to see what Love can do)!
Though calm my hope has burned, and true,
My cheek is pale and worn for you,
  And sunken are mine eyes!
Shule! Shule! &c.

VI.

But soon my love shall be my bride,
And happy by our own fire-side,
My veins shall feel the rosy tide,
  That lingering Hope denies.
Shule! Shule! &c.

VII.

My Mary of the curling hair,
The laughing teeth and bashful air,
Our bridal morn is dawning fair,
   With blushes in the skies.
Shule! Shule! Shule, agra,
Shule asucur, agus shule, aroon!
   My love! my pearl!
   My own dear girl!
My mountain maid, arise!

Gilli Ma Chree.

Air—"*Paddy O'Rourke's the bouchal.*"

I.

   Gilli ma chree,
   Sit down by me,
We now are joined, and ne'er shall sever
   This hearth's our own,
   Our hearts are one,
And peace is ours for ever!

II.

   When I was poor,
   Your father's door
Was closed against your constant lover;
   With care and pain
   I tried in vain
My fortunes to recover

I said, "To other lands I'll roam,
  Where Fate may smile on me, love;"
I said, "Farewell, my own old home!"
  And I said, "Farewell to thee, love!"
      Sing *Gilla ma chree, &c.*

III.

I might have said,
My mountain maid,
"Come, live with me, your own true love;
I know a spot,
A silent cot,
Your friends can ne'er discover.
Where gently flows the waveless tide,
  By one small garden only;
Where the heron waves his wings so wide,
  And the linnet sings so lonely!"
      Sing *Gilli ma chree, &c.*

IV.

I might have said,
My mountain maid,
"A father's right was never given
True hearts to curse
With tyrant force
That have been blest in heaven."
But then, I said, "In after years,
  When thoughts of home shall find her,
My love may mourn with secret tears
  Her friends thus left behind her."
      Sing *Gilli ma chree, &c.*

V.

Oh! no, I said,
My own dear maid,
For me, though all forlorn, for ever
That heart of thine
Shall ne'er repine
O'er slighted duty—never.
From home and thee, though wandering far,
A dreary fate be mine, love;
I'd rather live in endless war,
Than buy my peace with thine, love.
Sing *Gilli ma chree*, &c.

VI.

Far, far away,
By night and day,
I toiled to win a golden treasure;
And golden gains
Repaid my pains
In fair and shining measure.
I sought again my native land,
Thy father welcomed me, love;
I poured my gold into his hand,
And my guerdon found in thee, love!
Sing *Gilli ma chree*,
Sit down by me,
We now are joined, and ne'er shall sever;
This hearth's our own,
Our hearts are one,
And peace is ours for ever.

For I am Desolate.

I.

The Christmas light* is burning bright
  In many a village pane,
And many a cottage rings to-night
  With many a merry strain.
Young boys and girls run laughing by,
  Their hearts and eyes elate—
I can but think on mine, and sigh,
  For I am desolate.

II.

There's none to watch in our old cot,
  Beside the holy light,
No tongue to bless the silent spot
  Against the parting night.†
I've closed the door, and hither come
  To mourn my lonely fate;
I cannot bear my own old home,
  It is so desolate!

---

* The Christmas—a light blessed by the priest, and lighted at sun-set, on Christmas eve, in Irish houses. It is a kind of impiety to snuff, touch, or use it for any profane purposes after.

† It is the custom, in Irish Catholic families, to sit up till midnight on Christmas-eve, in order to join in devotion at that hour. Few ceremonies of the religion have a more splendid and imposing effect than the morning mass, which, in cities, is celebrated soon after the hour alluded to, and long before day-break.

LI.

I saw my father's eyes grow dim,
　And clasp'd my mother's knee;
I saw my mother follow him—
　My husband wept with me.
My husband did not long remain—
　His child was left me yet
But now my heart's last love is slain,
　And I am desolate!

The Bridal Wake.

I.

The priest stood at the marriage board,
　The marriage cake was made,
With meat the marriage chest was stored,
　Decked was the marriage bed.
The old man sat beside the fire,
　The mother sat by him,
The white bride was in gay attire;
　But her dark eye was dim.
　　　　　Ululah! Ululah!
The night falls quick—the sun is set;
Her love is on the water yet.

II.

I saw a red cloud in the west,
　Against the morning light—
Heaven shield the youth that she loves best
　From evil chance to-night.

The door flings wide! Loud moans the gale;
  Wild fear her bosom fills—
It is, it is the Banshee's wail!
  Over the darken'd hills.
            Ululah! Ululah!
The day is past! the night is dark!
The waves are mounting round his bark

III.

The guests sit round the bridal bed,
  And break the bridal cake;
But they sit by the dead man's head,
  And hold his wedding wake.
The bride is praying in her room,
  The place is silent all!
A fearful call! a sudden doom!
  Bridal and funeral.
            Ululah! Ululah!
A youth to Kilficheras'* ta'en
That never will return again.

Once I had a True Love.

ONCE I had a true love,
  I loved him well, I loved him well;
But since he's found a new love,
  Alone I dwell, alone I dwell.

* The name of a churchyard near Kilkee.

I.

How oft we've wandered lonely
　Through yon old glen, through yon old glen;
I was his treasure only,
　And true love then, and true love then;
But Mary's singing brought me
　To sigh all day, to sigh all day.
Oh, had my mother taught me
　To sing and play, to sing and play.
　　　　　　Once I had, &c.

II.

By lone Glencree, at even,
　I passed him late, I passed him late;
A glance, just sidelong given,
　Told all his fate, told all his fate;
His step no longer airy,
　His head it hung, his head it hung.
Ah, well I knew that Mary
　She had a tongue, she had a tongue.
　　　　　　Once I had, &c.

III.

The spring is coming early,
　And skies are blue, and skies are blue,
And trees are budding fairly,
　And corn is new, and corn is new;
What clouds the sunny morrow
　Of nature then, of nature then;
And turns young Hope to sorrow?
　Oh, fickle men! Oh, fickle men!
Once I had a true love,
　I loved him well, I loved him well
But since he's found a new love,
　Alone I dwell, alone I dwell.

Hark! Hark! the Soft Bugle.

I.

Hark! hark! the soft bugle sounds over the wood,
   And thrills in the silence of even,
Till faint, and more faint, in the far solitude,
   It dies on the portals of heaven!
But echo springs up, from her home in the rock,
   And seizes the perishing strain;
And sends the gay challenge, with shadowy mock,
   From mountain to mountain again!
        And again!
From mountain to mountain again.

II.

Oh, thus let my love, like a sound of delight,
   Be around thee while shines the glad day,
And leave thee, unpain'd, in the silence of night,
   And die like sweet music away.
While hope, with her warm light, thy glancing eye fills,
   Oh, say—" Like that echoing strain,
Though the sounds of his love has died over the hills,
   It will waken in heaven again.'
        And again!
It will waken in heaven again.

Farewell.

ADDRESSED TO A FRIEND.

I.

Faded now, and slowly chilling,
    Summer leaves the weeping dell,
While, forlorn and all unwilling,
    Here I come, to say —Farewell!
Spring was green when first I met thee,
    Autumn sees our parting pain;
Never, if my heart forget thee,
    Summer shine on me again!

II.

Fame invites! her summons only
    Is a magic spell to me;
For when I was sad and lonely,
    Fame it was that gave me thee.
False she is, her sland'rers sing me,
    Wreathing flowers that soonest fade;
But such gifts if Fame can bring me,
    Who will call the nymph a shade?

III.

Hearts that feel not, hearts half broken
    Deem her reign no more divine,
Vain to them are praises spoken,
    Vain the light that fills her shrine.
But in mine, those joys Elysian,
    Deeply sink and warmly breathe;
Fame to me has been no vision,
    Friendship's smile embalms the wreath.

IV.

Sunny lakes, and spired mountains,
    Where that friendship sweetly grew;
Ruins hoar, and gleaming fountains,
    Scenes of vanished joys, adieu!
Oh, where'er my steps may wander,
    While my home-sick bosom heaves,
On these scenes my heart will ponder,
    Silent, oft, in summer eves.

V.

Still, when calm, the sun down-shining,
    Turns to gold the winding tide:
Lonely on that couch reclining,
    Bid these scenes before thee glide;
Fair Killarney's sunset splendour,
    Broken crag, and mountain gray,
And Glengarriff's moonlight tender,
    Bosomed on the heaving bay.

STANZAS ADDED AT A LATER PERIOD.

VI.

Oh, farewell! these joys are ended—
    Oh, farewell! that day is done;
Passed in clouds, and darkly blended,
    Slowly sinks our wasted sun.
When shall we, with souls delighted,
    See these rosy times return;
And in blameless love united,
    View the past, yet never mourn?

VII.

Hues of darker fate assuming,
    Faster change life's summer skies;
In the future, dimly glooming,
    Forms of deadly promise rise.
See a loved home forsaken,
    Sunder'd ties and tears for thee—
And by thoughts of terror shaken,
    See an alter'd soul in me.

VIII.

Sung in pride and young illusion,
    Then forgive the idle strain;
Now my heart, in low confusion,
    Owns its sanguine promise vain.
Fool of fame! that earthly vision,
    Charms no more thy cheated youth;
And these boasted dreams Elysian
    Fly the searching dawn of truth.

IX.

Never in these tended bowers,
    Never by that reedy stream;
Lull'd on beds of tinted flowers,
    Young Romance again shall dream.
Now his rainbow pinions shaking—
    Oh, he hates the lonesome shore:
Where a funeral voice awaking,
    Bids us rest in joy no more.

X.

Yet all pleasing rise the measure,
    Memory soon shall hymn to thee:
Dull for me no coming pleasure,
    Lose no joy for thought of me.

Oh, I would not leave thee weeping
But when falls our parting day,
See thee hushed, on roses sleeping,
Sigh unheard, and steal away!

The Mother's Lament.

I.

My darling, my darling, while silence is on the moor,
And lone in the sunshine, I sit by our cabin door;
When evening falls quiet, and calm over land and sea,
My darling, my darling, I think of past times and thee

II.

Here, while on this cold shore, I wear out my lonely hours,
My child in the heavens is spreading my bed with flowers;
All weary my bosom is grown of this friendless clime—
But I long not to leave it; for that were a shame and crime.

III.

They bear to the church-yard the youth in their health away—
I know where a fruit hangs more ripe for the grave than
   they—
But I wish not for death, for my spirit is all resigned,
And the hope that stays with me gives peace to my aged
   mind.

IV.

My darling, my darling, God gave to my feeble age
A prop for my faint heart, a stay in my pilgrimage;
My darling, my darling, God takes back his gift again—
And my heart may be broken, but ne'er shall my will
   complain

Lines addressed to a Lady.

I.

A gay, shifting eye, like the swift ray of light,
The May morning shoots o'er the brow of the night,
That is veiled up in mist, like that eye in its lid,
Yet is loved for the promise of light that is hid.
Ah, trust not that eye! for though gentle it seems,
It is but the will that has shrouded its beams;
It has fire, it has love, it has smiles, it has tears,
For the world and its passions, its sorrows and fears.

II.

A voice like a sound heard in deep solitude,
Like the song of the night-bird alone in the wood
A melody struck by the finger of art,
From the small strings that tremble round nature's own heart;
But hear not that voice, for though softly it breathe,
Its tones round the trusting heart cunningly wreathe,
When chain'd through its pulses, and bound for a spoil,
It may throb at the cheat, but must pain in the toil.

III.

A brow that is built for the throne of the mind,
And curtained by dark ringlets gracefully twined,
The glance of the falcon, the gaze of the dove,
The smile that is blended of mirth and of love.
A shape soft and gliding, like those which arise,
Through the shadows of time, on the young poet's eyes,
When the cloud of the future he toils to remove,
And fancy the maiden who shall be his love.

IV.

Ah, the days of her youth are for ever gone by;
Yet the spring-tide of genius is young in her eye;
Fast over her beauties the parting years roll,
Still they bloom with the evergreen hue of the soul;
The rose leaves fall silently down from her cheek,
Still it hath the dear meaning, time never can break
And each act of her motion an impulse reveals
Of a spirit that thinks and a bosom that feels.

V.

Even such was my love, and in merrier hours
I filled the bright vase with Hope's loveliest flowers;
Young Fancy flew over my bower of peace,
And soared in the golden clouds, singing of bliss;
But vain was my dream! for these hours are fled—
That song it is silent, that bower is dead,
The gold coloured mists of life's morning are flown,
My vase it is broken, my flowers are gone!

VI.

Yet blame me not, lady, if thus, while I dwell
On a form that my memory has treasured too well;
An Idol, my faith would make all but divine,
I should breathe out one heart-broken sigh at its shrine.
I look on thy state, and I think on mine own,
And I laugh at the hope that would bid me love on—
Yet my reason asks—"Why do I love thee?" in vain,
While my heart can but echo, "I love thee" again.

Let others breathe in glowing Words.

I.

Let others breathe in glowing words
    The secret of their bosom pain,
And bid the loud harp's speaking chords
    Tell o'er the weary tale again.
From me no burning stave shall rise—
    A cold heart's answering sigh to move;
But I will gaze upon those eyes,
    And waste away in silent love.

II.

I cannot find in art a strain
    To echo forth mine inward moan;
If sighs and looks can't tell my pain,
    Oh, never shall my love be known.
Safe is the flame whose answering breath
    A tear may quench, a sigh may move;
But full of danger and of death
    Is the pent fire of silent love.

You never bade me Hope, 'tis true.

I.

You never bade me hope, 'tis true—
    I asked you not to swear;
But I looked in those eyes of blue,
    And read a promise there.

II.

The vow should bind with maiden sighs
That maiden's lips have spoken—
But that which looks from maiden's eyes
Should last of all be broken!

A Soldier—A Soldier to-night is our Guest.

I.

Fan, fan the gay hearth, and fling back the barr'd door,
Strew, strew the fresh rushes around on our floor,
And blithe be the welcome in every breast—
For a soldier—a soldier to-night is our guest.

II.

All honour to him who, when danger afar,
Had lighted for ruin his ominous star,
Left pleasure, and country, and kindred behind,
And sped to the shock on the wings of the wind.

III.

If you value the blessings that shine at our hearth—
The wife's smiling welcome, the infant's sweet mirth—
While they charm us at eve, let us think upon those
Who have bought with their blood our domestic repose.

IV.

Then share with the soldier your hearth and your home,
And warm be your greeting whene'er he shall come;
Let love light a welcome in every breast—
For a soldier—a soldier to-night is our guest.

Duet.

FROM THE DUKE OF MONMOUTH.

AQUILA.

Dewy dimmet!* silent hour!
Welcome to our cottage bow'r!
See, along the lonely meadow,
Ghost-like, falls the lengthen'd shadow,
While the sun, with level shine,
Turns the stream to rosy wine;
And from yonder busy town
Valeward hies the lazy clown.

BOTH.

Lovely dimmet! pleasing hour!
Welcome to our lonely bow'r.

TAMSEN.

Hark! along the dewy ground
Steals the sheep-bell's drowsy sound;
While the ploughman, home returning,
Sees his cheerful faggot burning,
And his dame, with kindly smile,
Meets him by the rustic stile;
While beneath the hawthorn mute
Swells the peasant's merry flute.

---

* Dimmet.—The name given to the twilight in parts of the West of England.

BOTH.

Peaceful dimmet! mirthful hour!
Welcome to our cottage bow'r!

AQUILA.

Lass, from market homeward speed;
Traveller, urge thy lagging steed—
Fly the dark woods lurking danger;
Churl, receive the 'nighted stranger—
He with merry song and jest
Will repay thy niggard feast,
And the eye of heaven above
Smile upon the deed of love.

BOTH.

Dusky dimmet! dewy hour!
Welcome to our lonely bow'r!

TAMSEN.

Hour of beauty! hour of peace!
Hour when care and labour cease;
When around her hush'd dominion
Nature spreads her brooding pinion,
While a thousand angel eyes
Wake to watch us from the skies,
Till the reason centres there,
And the heart is moved to pray'r.

BOTH.

Lovely dimmet! witching hour!
Welcome to our cottage bow'r!

Though Lonely here, by Avon's Tide.

I.

Though lonely here, by Avon's tide,
   I waste my cheerless hours,
And see its silent waters glide
   By thy forsaken bow'rs;
I'd rather bear the lasting pain
   That breaks this heart of mine,
Than pine beneath the golden chain
   That guilt has flung o'er thine.

II.

In dreams I deem thee still mine own,
   Unsullied and unchanged;
But morning shows the vision flown,
   And thee again estranged.
Oh! when from some unheeding tongue
   I hear that once-loved name,
Then, then my inmost heart is wrung
   To think upon thy shame.

III.

How lonely, when I wake at dawn,
   Each silent chamber now!
How joyless looks the sunny lawn,
   How droops each weeping bough!
For though the noontide sun shine warm,
   All cheerless falls his beams;
And lonesome now, without that form,
   The gay verandah seems.

IV.

With sinking heart and thoughtful pace
 I pass our garden door,
And 'mid the leafy stillness trace
 Each haunt of rapture o'er.
The scents that rise, the flowers that blow,
 The breeze that wanders free,
My alter'd sense can hardly know—
 All breathe of death and thee.

V.

Ah, once I thought that mind was thin,
 And void of inward blame;
Old age, I said, and hoary hair,
 Will find our hearts the same.
Now soon—oh, soon!—the churchyard lone
 Shall hide those cares from me—
Ah! may that turf and cold, gray stone
 Rest lightly yet on thee!

VI.

But not with old affection's slight,
 And love's forgotten day,
I charge thee in my song to-night,
 Or pleasures past away.
No—pledged on yonder sacred sod,
 Thy vows were heard above;
And thou wert falser to thy God,
 Than e'en to Edmund's love.

Monmouth's Address.*

I.

"Up! ye who have the hands to fight,
    Who have the hearts to feel!
Up, up! for merry England's right,
    With musket and with steel!
Oh, brightly streams on summer's gale
    The gilded mist on high;
But brighter soon in Taunton vale
    Shall Freedom's ensign fly!
        Then up! who have, &c.

II.

"For Liberty and Monmouth! ho!
    For liberty, arise!
There's mercy in the conquering blow
    When grim Oppression dies.
There's music in the mustering feet
    That marked the daisied green,
When the gallant friends of Freedom meet
    In lovely Taunton Dene!
        Up! ye who have, &c.

III.

"Who basely shuns a glorious death,
    Dishonour haunt his tomb!
Who nobly wins a victor wreath,
    Long may he see it bloom!

* Taken from the novel of "The Duke of Monmouth."

Who freely sheds his gen'rous blood,
  His children long shall tell
How he for England bravely stood,
  How he for England fell!
      Then up! who have the hands to fight
        Who have the hearts to feel!
      Up, up! for merry England's right,
        With musket and with steel!"

Like the Oak by the Fountain.

I.

Like the oak by the fountain,
  In sunshine and storm;
Like the rock on the mountain,
  Unchanging in form;
Like the course of the river,
  Through ages the same;
Like the mist, mounting ever
  To heaven, whence it came.

II.

So firm be thy merit,
  So changeless thy soul;
So constant thy spirit,
  While seasons shall roll;
The fancy that ranges,
  Ends where it began;
But the mind that ne'er changes
  Brings glory to man.

Falta Volla! Falta Volla!

SONG FROM THE INVASION.

I.

Falta volla! falta volla! welcome to the mountains!
Falta volla! welcome to your native woods and fountains!
To hear the harper play again—and the shouts that greet thee;
Falta volla! how it glads the widow's heart to meet thee;
  Falta volla! falta volla!
  Welcome to Rath-Aiden.

II.

Shule a volla! shule a volla! through our parted island,
Many a friend and foe hast thou in valley and in highland;
But where'er the friends are false—when the foes distress thee—
Shule a volla! here are ready weapons to redress thee.
  Shule a volla! shule a volla!
  Shelter in Rath-Aiden.

III.

Ire a volla! ire a volla! far in Corca's vallies,
When round the Bloody Hand the routed Dal Gas rallies;
When the groans of dying friends filled the air above thee—
Ire a volla! there are hands to help and hearts to love thee
  Ire a volla! ire a volla!
  Hasten to Rath-Aiden.

Cead Millia Falta! Elim.

SONG FOR THE INVASION.

I.

Cead millia falta! child of the Ithian!
Cead millia falta, Elim!
Aisneach, thy temple in ruins is lying,
In Druim na Druid the dark blast is sighing;
Lonely we shelter in grief and in danger,
Yet have we welcome and cheer for the stranger.
Cead millia falta! child of the Ithian!
Cead millia falta, Elim!

II.

Woe for the weapons that guarded our slumbers,
Tambreach, they said, was too small for our numbers
Little is left for our sons to inherit,
Yet what we have thou art welcome to share it.
Cead millia falta! child of the Ithian!
Cead millia falta, Elim!

III.

Cormac, thy teachers have died broken-hearted;
Voice of the trilithon, thou art departed!
All have forsaken our mountains so dreary,
All but the spirit that welcomes the weary.
Cead millia falta! child of the Ithian!
Cead millia falta, Elim!

IV.

Vainly the Draithe, alone in the mountain,
Looks to the torn cloud or eddying fountain;
The spell of the Christian has vanquished their power,
Yet he is welcome to rest in our bower.
    Cead millia falta! child of the Ithian!
      Cead millia falta, Elim!

V.

Wake for the Christian your welcoming numbers!
Strew the dry rushes, to pillow his slumbers;
Long let him cherish, with deep recollection,
The eve of our feast, and the Druids' affection.
    Cead millia falta! child of the Ithian!
      Cead millia falta, Elim!

The Isle of Saints.

I.

FAR, far amid those lonely seas,
    Where evening leaves her latest smile,
Where solemn ocean's earliest breeze
    Breathes, peaceful, o'er our holy isle.

II.

Remote from that distracted world,
    Where sin has reared his gloomy throne,
With passion's ensign sweetly furl'd,
    We live and breathe for heaven alone.

III.

For heaven we hope, for heaven we pray,
    For heaven we look, and long to die;
For heaven—for heaven, by night by day,
    Untiring watch, unceasing sigh.

IV.

Here, fann'd by heavenly temper'd winds,
    Our island lifts her tranquil breast;
Oh, come to her, ye wounded minds!
    Oh, come and share our holy rest!

V.

For not to hoard the golden spoil
    Of earthly minds we bow the knee—
Our labour is the saintly toil,
    Whose hire is in eternity.

VI.

The mountain wild, the islet fair,
    The corrig bleak, and lonely vale;
The lawn that feels the summer air,
    The peak that splits the wintry gale.

VII.

From northern Ulladh's column'd store,
    To distant Clair's embosom'd nest;
From high Benhedir's summit hoar,
    To Ara in the lonely west.

VIII.

Through all, the same resounding choir,
    Harmonious pours its descant strong,
All feel the same adoring fire,
    All raise the same celestial song.

IX.

When sinks the sun beyond the west,
  Our vesper hymn salutes him there ;
And when he wakes the world from rest,
  We meet his morning light with prayer.

X.

The hermit by his holy well,
  The monk within his cloister gray,
The virgin in her silent cell,
  The pilgrim on his votive way.

XI.

To all, the same returning light,
  The same returning fervour brings ;
And, thoughtful in the dawning bright,
  The spirit spreads her heaven-ward wings.

XII.

From hill to hill, from plain to plain,
  Wherever falls his fostering ray,
Still swells the same aspiring strain,
  From angel souls, in shapes of clay.

XIII.

The echoes of the tranquil lake,
  The clifted ocean's cavern'd maze,
The same untiring music make,
  The same eternal sound of praise.

XIV.

Oh, come, and see our Isle of Saints,
  Ye weary of the ways of strife ;
Where oft the breath of discord taints
  The banquet sweets of joyous life

XV.

Ye weary of the lingering woes
　That crowd on Passion's footsteps, pale—
Oh, come and taste the sweet repose
　That breathes in distant Inisfail.

XVI.

Not ours the zeal for pomp—for power—
　The boastful threat—the bearing vain—
The mailed host—the haughty tower—
　The pomp of war's encumbered plain.

XVII.

Our strifes are in the holy walk
　Of love serene and all sincere;
Our converse is the soothing talk
　Of souls that feel like strangers here.

XVIII.

Our armies are the peaceful bands
　Of saints and sages mustering nigh;
Our towers are raised by pious hands
　To point the wanderer's thoughts on high.

XIX.

The fleeting joys of selfish earth
　We learn to shun with holy scorn;
They cannot quench the inward dearth
　With man's immortal spirit born.

XX.

Yet while my heart within me burns
　To hear that still resounding choir;
To days unblest it fondly turns;
　When dies that heaven-descended fire?

XXI.

How long shalt thou be thus divine,
   Fair isle of piety and song?
How long shall peace and love be thine,
    Oh, land of peace—how long? how long?

XXII.

Hark! echoing from each sainted tomb
   Prophetic voices sternly roll—
They wrap my thoughts in sudden gloom,
   Their accents freeze my shuddering soul.

XXIII.

Ha! say ye that triumphant hell
   Shall riot in these holy grounds?
Shield, shield me from those visions fell,
   Oh, silent be those fearful sounds!

XXIV.

They tell of crime, of contest sharp,
   Of force and fraud, and hate and wrong—
No more, no more, my venturous harp,
   Oh, trembling close thine altered song.

XXV.

Oh, let thy thoughtful numbers cease,
   Ere yet the touch of frenzy taints
The land of love and letter'd peace,
   The Isle of Sages and of Saints.

Ho! not for the Glories of Days that are Flown.

I.
No, not for the glories of days that are flown,
For the fall of a splendour that was but our own
No, not for the dust of our heroes that sleep,
Should the bard of the Coom in his melody weep.

II.
For the thought of that glory remains in each breast,
Though we see them no longer, the dead are at rest,
And gay is the face of the Druids' lone vale;
But dark is the bosom of wide Inisfail.

III.
The demon of discord has breathed on the land,
And her sons on her mountains meet hand against hand;
The children who fought for her welfare are slain,
And her bosom is trampled by those who remain.

IV.
Wild blast of the trompa! that, echoing far,
Hast summoned Leath Mogha with Cuin to war,
Far westward of Ara die over the main,
And never be heard in our vallies again.

V.
Arise on the mountains, O spirit of peace;
Let the sons of the Riada hear thee, and cease;
Too late for their country, oh, let them not prove!
That the strength of the island is union and love.

VI.
Oh, spread not thy strife-quelling pinions aloft
Till the calm on our country fall sunny and soft;
From Rechrin's cold islet and Ulladh the green,
To woody Glengariff and fair Ibherseeine.

Come to Glengariff! Come

Air—"Ours is a Merry Land."

I.

Come to Glengariff! come!
　Close by the sea;
Ours is a happy home,
　Peaceful and free.
There, there, far away,
Happy by our sunny bay,
We live, from day to day,
　Blithe as the bee;
For ours is a sunny home,
　Joyous and free.
Come to Glengariff! come!
　Close by the sea.

II.

Thine is a mountain hoar,
　Frowning and wild;
Ours is a lowland shore,
　Fertile and mild.
There, there, loud and strong,
Sudden tempests drive along;
Here, their gentle song
　Scarce moves the tree!
For ours is a lowland home,
　Peaceful and free.
Come from the mountain!
　Come to the sea!

The Phantom City.

I.

A STORY I heard on the cliffs of the west,
    That oft, through the breakers dividing,
A city is seen on the ocean's wild breast
    In turretted majesty riding.
But brief is the glimpse of that phantom so bright,
    Soon close the white waters to screen it,
And the bodement, they say, of the wonderful sight,
    Is death to the eyes that have seen it.

II.

I said, when they told me the wonderful tale,
    My country, is this not thy story?
Thus oft, through the breakers of discord, we hail
    A promise of peace and of glory.
Soon gulphed in those waters of hatred again
    No longer our fancy can find it,
And woe to our hearts for the vision so vain;
    For ruin and death come behind it.

While the Stars of Heaven are Shining.

AIR—"*Ar hyd a nos.*"

I.

WHILE the stars of heaven are shining,
    Ar hyd a nos,
Here at midnight lone, reclining,
    Ar hyd a nos,

Fancy flies to those wild bowers,
Sunny fields and springing flowers,
Where I passed my infant hours,
    Ar hyd a nos.

II.

To my own beloved mountains,
    Ar hyd a nos,
Rushing streams and quiet fountains,
    Ar hyd a nos,
Sleepless still my thoughts returning,
Leave my lonely bosom mourning,
And my heart within me burning,
    Ar hyd a nos.

III.

There light slumbers blessed my pillow,
    Ar hyd a nos,
There, beside the starlit billow,
    Ar hyd a nos,
Visions soft to me were given,
Pure as mountain winds at even,
Peace for earth and hope for heaven,
    Ar hyd a nos.

IV.

Still that Sabbath bell is ringing,
    Ar hyd a nos,
Still that Sabbath choir is singing,
    Ar hyd a nos,
Sounds beloved! Oh, restore me,
With the scenes ye bring before me,
Hopes that then hung blooming o'er me,
    Ar hyd a nos.

War! War! Horrid War

I.

War! War! Horrid war!
  Fly our lovely plain,
Guide fleet and far,
  Thy fiery car,
And never come again,
  And never,
Never come again!

II.

Peace! Peace! smiling Peace!
  Bless our lonely plain,
Guide swiftly here,
  Thy mild career,
And never go again!
  And never,
Never go again!

War Song of O'Dristol.

I.

From the shieling that stands by the lone mountain river,
Hurry, hurry down with the axe and the quiver,
From the deep-seated Coom, from the storm-beaten highland
Hurry, hurry down to the shores of your island.
    Hurry down, hurry down!
    Hurry, hurry, &c.

II.

Galloglach and Kern, hurry down to the sea—
There the hungry Raven's beak is gaping for a prey;
Farrah! to the onset! Farrah! to the shore!
Feast him with the pirate's flesh, the bird of gloom and gore
   Hurry down, hurry down
   Hurry down, &c.

III.

Hurry, for the slaves of Bel are mustering to meet ye,
Hurry by the beaten cliff, the Nordman longs to greet ye
Hurry from the mountain! hurry, hurry from the plain!
Welcome him, and never let him leave our land again!
   Hurry down, hurry down!
   Hurry down, &c.

IV.

On the land a sulky wolf, and in the sea a shark,
Hew the ruffian spoiler down, and burn his gory bark!
Slayer of the unresisting! ravager profane!
Leave the White sea-tyrant's limbs to moulder on the plain.
   Hurry down, hurry down!
   Hurry down, &c.

Fare thee Well, my Native Dell.

Air—"*Fare thee well, Sweet Killarne.*"

I.

Fare thee well, my native dell,
 Though far away I wander;
With thee my thoughts shall ever dwell,
 In absence only fonder

Farewell, ye banks, where once I roved
　To view that lonely river—
And you, ye groves so long beloved,
　And fields, farewell for ever!
　　　Fare thee well, &c.

II.

Here once my youthful moments flew,
　In joy like sunshine splendid,
The brightest hours that e'er I knew
　With those sweet scenes were blended—
When o'er those hills, at break of morn,
　The deer went bounding early,
And huntsmen woke with hounds and horn
　The mountain echoes cheerly,
　　　Fare thee well, &c.

III.

Fare ye well, ye happy hours,
　So bright, but long departed!
Fare ye well, ye fragrant bow'rs,
　So sweet, but now deserted!
Farewell each rock and lonely isle,
　That make the poet's numbers;
And thou, oh, ancient holy pile,*
　Where mighty Bryan slumbers!
　　　Fare ye well, &c.

* The cathedral in which is the monument of the celebrated Brian Boroimhe.

IV.

Farewell, thou old, romantic bridge,
　Where morn has seen me roaming,
To mark across each shallow ridge,
　The mighty Shannon foaming.
No more I'll press the bending oar,
　To speed the painted wherry;
And glide along the woody shore,
　To view the hills of Derry.
　　　　　Fare thee well, &c.

V.

There's many an isle in Scariff Bay,
　With many a garden blooming;
Where oft I've passed the summer day,
　Till twilight hours were glooming.
No more shall evening's yellow glow
　Among those ruins find me;
Far from these dear scenes I go,
　But leave my heart behind me.
　　　　　Fare thee well, &c.

VI.

Fast, fast we ride by bridge and tree,
　Fast fade my loved bow'rs;
Still through the bursting tears I see
　Thy hills and hoary towers.
'Tis past! my last faint glimpse is o'er,
　My last farewell is spoken;
I see those loved scenes no more—
　My heart—my heart is broken.
Fare thee well, my native dell,
　Though far away I wander,
With thee my thoughts shall ever dwell—
　In absence only fonder.

Aileen Aroon.

I.

When like the early rose,
    Aileen aroon!
Beauty in childhood blows,
    Aileen aroon!
When like a diadem,
Buds blush around the stem,
Which is the fairest gem?
    Aileen aroon!

II.

Is it the laughing eye?
    Aileen aroon!
Is it the timid sigh?
    Aileen aroon
Is it the tender tone,
Soft as the stringed harp's tune?
Oh, it is truth alone,
    Aileen aroon!

III.

When, like the rising day,
    Aileen aroon!
Love sends his early ray,
    Aileen aroon!
What makes his dawning glow
Changeless through joy or woe
Only the constant know,
    Aileen aroon!

IV.

I know a valley fair,
      Aileen aroon!
I knew a cottage there,
      Aileen aroon!
Far in that valley's shade
I knew a gentle maid,
Flower of the hazel glade,
      Aileen aroon!

V.

Who in the song so sweet,
      Aileen aroon!
Who in the dance so sweet,
      Aileen aroon!
Dear were her charms to me,
Dearer her laughter free,
Dearest her constancy,
      Aileen aroon.

VI.

Were she no longer true,
      Aileen aroon!
What should her lover do?
      Aileen aroon!
Fly with his broken chain
Far o'er the sounding main,
Never to love again,
      Aileen aroon!

VII.

Youth must with time decay,
      Aileen aroon!
Youth must fade away,

Castles are sacked in war
Chieftains are scattered far
Truth is a fixed star,
    Aileen aroon!

Gone! Gone! for ever

I.

Gone gone, for ever gone
  Are the hopes I cherished,
Changed like the sunny dawn,
  In sudden showers perished.

II.

Wither'd is the early flower,
  Like a bright lake broken,
Faded like a happy hour,
  Or Love's secret spoken.

III.

Life! what a cheat art thou!
  On youthful fancy stealing,
A prodigal in promise now;
  A miser in fulfilling!

Ancient Lullaby.

I.

Darkness o'er the world is creeping,
Slumber while the heavens are weeping,
While the kerns their watch are keeping,
And all eyes beside are sleeping.

II.

Heaven's dark curtains now are closing
The wild winds in peace reposing;
Now the harper old is prosing,
While his chieftain's eyes are dozing.

III.

Heavy is the humming number:
Let the witch that scatters slumber,
In her passage halt and murmer,
Till her dews thy lids encumber.

IV.

Dull and dim the moon is gleaming,
Drowsy is the owlet's screaming,
Sullen sounds and gloomy seeming
Soon shall mingle in thy dreaming,

Know ye not that Lovely River.*

Air—"Roy's wife of Aldivalloch."

I.

Know ye not that lovely river?
Know ye not that smiling river?
　　Whose gentle flood,
　　By cliff and wood,
With wildering sound goes winding ever.
　Oh! often yet with feeling strong,
　On that dear stream my memory ponders,
　And still I prize its murmuring song,
For by my childhood's home it wanders.
　　　　Know ye not, &c.

II.

There's music in each wind that flows
　Within our native woodland breathing;
There's beauty in each flower that blows
　Around our native woodland wreathing,
The memory of the brightest joys
　In childhood's happy morn that found us,
Is dearer than the richest toys,
　The present vainly sheds around us.
　　　　Know ye not, &c.

* These verses were written at the request of his sister, who wrote to him from America for new words for the old Scotch air of Roy's wife of Aldivalloch.

III.

Oh, sister! when 'mid doubts and fears,
    That haunt life's onward journey ever,
I turn to those departed years,
    And that beloved and lonely river;
With sinking mind and bosom riven,
    And heart with lonely anguish aching;
It needs my long-taught hope in heaven
    To keep this weary heart from breaking!
        Know ye not, &c.

I Love my Love in the Morning.

I.

I LOVE my love in the morning,
    For she like morn is fair—
Her blushing cheek, its crimson streak,
    It clouds her golden hair.
Her glance, its beam, so soft and kind;
    Her tears, its dewy showers;
And her voice, the tender whispering wind
    That stirs the early bowers.

II.

I love my love in the morning,
    I love my love at noon,
For she is bright, as the lord of light,
    Yet mild as autumn's moon:
Her beauty is my bosom's sun,
    Her faith my fostering shade,
And I will love my darling one,
    Till even the sun shall fade.

LI.

I love my love in the morning,
   I love my love at even;
Her smile's soft play is like the ray
   That lights the western heaven:
I loved her when the sun was high,
   I loved her when he rose,
But best of all when evening's sigh
   Was murmuring at its close.

Merrily Whistles the Wind on the Shore.

I.

Merrily whistles the wind on the shore
   Through the little willow,
But wearily drops the boatman's oar
   On the calm billow:
'Tis silent there—although it sing
   So freshly on the land;
The feather shook from the wild duck's wing
   Scarce finds the strand!
Then do not fear—up, maiden, and hear
   The gushing billow;
In the deep* silent of the night
   Lie on your pillow,
But wake with the waking of the daylight—
As fresh and as fair, and as blushing and bright

---

* "Dead night—dun night—the silent of the night."—*Shakspeare.*

II.

It is not pleasanter thus to steal
    O'er the water—than on a dull bed,
To toss in the wasting sun, and to feel
    The heavy air over your head—
For this keen, elastic wind? Look back!
    Ha! how fleetly
St. Mary's turrets fade from our track—
    And how sweetly
The chime of its bells come o'er the ear
With the rush of the Shannon's waters here!

III.

Oh! it is pleasant to mark the lark,
    When the dark brow of night is clearing,
Give greeting to the dawn—and—hark!
Waked by the dashing of our bark,
    Through the green waves careering,
The plover and the shrill curlew
    Round us screaming—
Startle thy silent shore, Tervoe!
    Where the beaming
Of the unshrouded, morning sun
Finds pleasant scenes to smile upon!

IV.

'Tis noon! The Race* is past! 'Tis even—
    Ha! see St. Sinon's isle—
With its high round towers and churches eleven,
    Bathed in the evening's smile—

---

* The Race—a narrow part of the lower Shannon, between Tarbo and Clonderlaw, where the tide runs rapidly.

And deeper—and fainter—and fainter still
        That smile is growing;
And now the last flush is on the hill—
        Wasting and glowing;
And now in the west there's a flickering bright—
'Tis the triumph of Darkness! the death of Light.

v.

Now steal we under the drowsy shore—
Our toil is done—our sailing o'er!
How lovely thou lookest, young maiden, now
Thy cheek is flushed—and on thy brow,
        White—soft—and sleek—
One purple vein is faintly seen,
        Like a thin streak
Of the blue sky, shown through a silver cloud,
Where the dim sun lies in his morning shroud!

When Filled with Thoughts of Life's Young Day.

I.

When filled with thoughts of life's young day,
  Alone in distant climes we roam,
And year on year has roll'd away
  Since last we view'd our own dear home,
Oh, then, at evening's silent hour,
In chamber lone or moonlight bow'r,
How sad, on memory's listening ear,
Come long lost voices sounding near—
Like the wild chime of village bells
Heard far away in mountain dells

II.

But, oh! for him let kind hearts grieve,
    His term of youth and exile o'er,
Who sees in life's declining eve,
    With alter'd eyes, his native shore!
With aching heart and weary brain,
Who treads those lonesome scenes again!
And backward views the sunny hours
When first he knew those ruin'd bow'rs,
And hears in every passing gale
Some best affection's dying wail.

III.

Oh, say, what spell of power serene
    Can cheer that hour of sharpest pain,
And turn to peace the anguish keen
    That deeplier wounds because in vain?
'Tis not the thought of glory won,
Of hoarded gold or pleasures gone,
But one bright course, from earliest youth,
Of changeless faith—unbroken truth.
These turn to gold the vapours dun
That close on life's descending sun.

Hark, Erin! the Blast is Blown.

I.

Hark, Erin! the blast is blown on the heath,
That summons thy sons to conquest or death;
The lines are all set in fearful array,
And thou must be saved or ruin'd to-day

Like the flood of the winter, resistless and grand,
Forth rushed to the shock the strength of the land;
And hearty and free was the ready halloo
That answered the call of Brian Boru.

II.

"Oh, trust not that form, so aged and dear,
Amid the wild crush of target and spear:
Bright star of the field and light of the hall,
Our ruin is sure if Brian should fall."
Like the waves of the west that burst on the rock,
The hosts at the morning rushed to the shock,
But ere his last beam was quench'd in the sea,
The Raven was quell'd and Erin was free.

III.

Yet hush'd be the sound of trumpet and drum,
And silent as death let victory come;
For he, at whose call the chieftains arose,
All bleeding and cold was found at the close.
And Erin is sad, though burst in her chain,
And loud was the wail that rose o'er the plain;
For victory cost more tears on that shore
Than ever defeat or ruin before.

The Merriest Bird on Bush or Tree.

I.

The merriest bird on bush or tree
  Was Robin of the grove,
When, in the jocund spring-time, he
  Sang to his nestling love.

Unknowing he the art to frame
   Methodic numbers vain,
But as each varied feeling came
   He wove it in his strain.
     With freedom gay
     He poured his lay,
While heaved his little breast of fire,
To rival all the woodland choir.

II.

Upon a day, a luckless day,
   When drove the wintry sleet,
Some urchins limed a willow spray
   To catch poor Robin's feet.
They sought, by measured rule and note,
   To change his woodland strain,
Do, re, mi, fa, he heeded not,
   He never sung again!
     His joy is o'er,
     He sings no more,
Nor knows the genial kindling thrill,
That only freedom's children feel.

III.

You, who would dull the poet's fire,
   With learning of the schools,
Gay Fancy's feet with fetters tire,
   And give to Genius rules.
Had bounteous Nature's counsel hung
   Upon your will severe,
Tom Moore had ne'er green Erin sung,
   Nor Burns the banks of Ayr.
     O'er awed I ween
     Both bards had been;
Nor dared to strike the simple lute
In your majestic presence mute.

'Tis, it is the Shannon's Stream.

I.

'Tis, it is the Shannon's stream
   Brightly glancing, brightly glancing,
See, oh, see the ruddy beam
   Upon its waters dancing!
Thus returned from travel vain,
Years of exile, years of pain,
To see old Shannon's face again,
   Oh, the bliss entrancing!
Hail our own majestic stream,
   Flowing ever, flowing ever,
Silent in the morning beam,
   Our own beloved river!

II.

Fling thy rocky portals wide,
   Western ocean, western ocean,
Bend ye hills, on either side,
   In solemn, deep devotion;
While before the rising gales
On his heaving surface sails,
Half the wealth of Erin's vales,
   With undulating motion.
Hail, our own beloved stream,
   Flowing ever, flowing ever,
Silent in the morning beam,
   Our own majestic river!

III.

On thy bosom deep and wide,
   Noble river, lordly river,
Royal navies safe might ride,
   Green Erin's lovely river!
Proud upon thy banks to dwell,
Let me ring Ambition's knell,
Lured by Hope's illusive spell
   Again to wander, never.
Hail, our own romantic stream,
   Flowing ever, flowing ever,
Silent in the morning beam,
   Our own majestic river!

IV.

Let me from thy placid course,
   Gentle river, mighty river,
Draw such truth of silent force
   As sophist uttered never.
Thus, like thee, unchanging still,
With tranquil breast and ordered will,
My heaven-appointed course fulfil,
   Undeviating ever!
Hail, our own majestic stream,
   Flowing ever, flowing ever,
Silent in the morning beam,
   Our own delightful river!

I am Alone! I am Alone!

I.

My soul is sick and alone,
   No social ties its love entwine,
A heart upon a desert thrown
   Beats not in solitude like mine:

For though the pleasant sunlight shine,
  It show'd no form that I may own,
And closed to me is friendship's shrine:
  I am alone!—I am alone!

II.

It is no joy for me
  To mark the fond and eager meeting
Of friends whom absence pined—and see
  The love-lit eyes speak out their greeting,
For then a stilly voice repeating
  What oft hath woke its deepest moan,
Startles my heart and stays its beating:
  I am alone!—I am alone!

III.

Why hath my soul been given
  A zeal to soar at higher things
Than quiet rest—to seek a heaven,
  And fall with scathed heart and wings?
Have I been blest? The sea-wave sings
  'Tween me and all that was mine own;
I've found the joy ambition brings
  And walk alone!—and walk alone!

IV.

I have a heart:—I'd live
  And die for him whose worth I knew—
But could not clasp his hand and give
  My full heart forth as talkers do—
And they who loved me—the kind few—
  Believed me changed in heart and tone
And left me, while it burned as true,
  To live alone!—to live alone!

V.

And such shall be my day
 Of life—unfriended, cold, and dead.
My hope shall slowly wear away
 As all my young affections fled—
No kindred hand shall grace my head
 When life's last flickering light is gone
But I shall find a silent bed
 And die alone!—and die alone

Sonnet.

ADDRESSED TO FRIENDS IN AMERICA, AND PREFIXED TO CARD-DRAWING OR THE TALES OF THE MUNSTER FESTIVALS.

I.

Friends far away—and late in life exiled—
 Whene'er these scattered pages meet your gaze,
Think of the scenes where early fortune smiled—
 The land that was your home in happier days—
The sloping lawn, to which the tired rays
 Of evening, stole o'er Shannon's sheeted flood—
The hills of Clare that in its soft'ning haze
 Looked vapour-like and dim—the lonely wood—
The cliff-bound Inch—the chapel in the glen,
 Where oft, with bare and reverent locks, we stood,
To hear th' Eternal truths—the small dark maze
Of the wild stream that clipp'd the blossom'd plain,
 And toiling through the varied solitude,
 Upraised its hundred silver tongues and babbled praise.

II.

That home is desolate! our quiet hearth
  Is ruinous and cold—and many a sight
And many a sound are met of vulgar mirth,
  Where once your gentle laughter cheered the night.
It is as with your country. The calm light
  Of social peace for her is quenched too—
Rude Discord blots her scenes of old delight,
  Her gentle virtues scared away—like you.
Remember her when in this tale you meet
  The story of a struggling right—of ties
  Fast bound and swiftly rent—of joy—of pain—
Legends which by the cottage fire sound sweet,
  Nor let the hand that wakes those memories
  (In faint but fond essay) be unremembered then.

ADDRESSED TO HIS NATIVE GLENS, AND PREFIXED TO THE HALF SIR.

I.

Glens of the West! the days are past and gone,
  Since while the north wind howled amidst your bowers,
  And hurrying through its course of frequent showers,
Sped, pale, 'mid winter showers, the southern sun;
When the vext Shannon, rid by ruffian gales—
  That whipped his foaming sides with tireless hand—
  Shook his white mane along the darkening strand,
And bounded fiercely by the leafless vales;
Since when our turfen fire made glad the hearth,
  And shone on merry faces gathered near,
  With untaught song—light jest—and drowsy story,
We blessed the winter eve, with gentle mirth—
  Or in soft sorrow lent a pensive ear,
  To tales of Erin's elder strength and faded glory.

II.

Ambition, absence, death, have thinned the number
   Of those who met beside your evening fires;
   Some, gathered to the ashes of our sires,
On yonder sacred mount in silence slumber;
Some, scattered far, extend their longing hands
   Towards those loved shades and lonely walks, in vain,
   For never shall your sun behold again
Their early footprints on your dewy lands—
And never more, within that ruined gate,
   Shall their blithe voices cheer the hush'd domain
   Yet some are left to pace your dreary ways—
Some cherished friends, in whose sweet circle late,
   Old joys came hovering round my heart again—
   Faint echoes of the bliss we knew in early days.

ADDRESSED TO A FRIEND AND PREFIXED TO SUIL DHUV.

I.

I HOLD not out my hand in grateful love,
   Because ye were my friend, where friends were few;
Nor in the pride of conscious truth, to prove
   The heart ye wronged and doubted, yet was true—
It is that while the close and blinding veil
   That youth and blissful ignorance had cast
   Around mine inward sight, is clearing fast
Before its strengthening vision—while the scale
   Falls from mine eye-balls—and the gloomy stream
Of human motive, whitening in my view,
Shows clear as dew showers in the gray morn beam—
While hearts and acts, whose impulse seemed divine,
   Put on the grossness of an earthlier hue—
I still can gaze, and deeply still can honour thine.

II.

Judge not your friend by what he seemed, when Fate
   Had crossed him in his chosen, cherished aim—
When spirit-broken—baffled—moved to hate
   The very kindness that but made his shame
More self-induced—he rudely turned aside
   In bitter, hopeless agony from all
     Alike—of those who mocked or mourned his fall,
And fence his injured heart in lonely pride.
   Wayward and sullen as suspicion's soul;
     To his own mind he lived a mystery;
But now the heavens have changed—the vapours roll
Far from his heart, and in his solitude,
   While the fell night-mares of his spirit flee,
He wakes to weave for thee a tale of joy renewed.

The Future.

Here by the shores of mine own sunny bay—
   Here in the shadow of my native bowers,
   Let me wear out in sweet content those hours
That bear me gently toward my dying day,
Warring with earth's affections, till the gray
   Of age hath touched my hair, and passion fled
   Leaves hope and stingless memory by my bed.
And thoughts of danger quelled, and passed away;
But there's a whispering fear within my breast
   That fills my mind with many a sad presage—
That breaks hope's morning dream of peace and rest—
That tells me I must never reach that time,
   Of reverend virtue, of victorious age,
But early die in youth, and stained by sudden crime.

A Fragment.

I.

A LONELY wanderer in the haunts of song,
   Unloved, unknown, I held my course forlorn,
   While sighing Echo on the soft wings borne,
With shivering pinions bore my strains along.
And, distant as they heard, the listening throng
   Cheered on the unseen bard, but sad was I;
   For none there was to hear my pensive sigh,
And passion in my heart was deep and strong;
I did not sigh for love—for I had given
   For some brief date, my tender vows to fame;
But yet I sighed for something like to love,
For I was young, and summer lit the heaven,
   And gentle longings filled my anxious frame,
As I sate all alone within that tuneful grove.

II.

Even in that time of song-born loneliness.
*   *   *   *   *

In Remembrance of his Sister.

I.

OH, not for ever lost! though in our ear
   Those uncomplaining accents fall no more,
   And Earth has won and never will restore
That form that well-worn grief made doubly dear.

Oh, not for ever lost!—though Hope may rear
  No more sweet visions in the future now,
  And even the memory of thy pallid brow
Grows unfamiliar with each passing year.
Though lonely be thy place on earth, and few
  The tongues that name thee on thy native plains,
  Where sorrow first thy gentle presence crossed,
And dreary tints o'er all the future threw;
  While life's young zeal yet triumph'd in thy veins;
  Oh, early fallen thou art!—but not for ever lost.

II.

If in that land where hope can cheat no more,
  Lavish in promise—laggard in fulfilling—
  Where fearless love on every bosom stealing,
And boundless knowledge brighten all the shore
If in that land—when life's cold toils are done
  And my heart lies as motionless as thine,
  I still might hope to press that hand in mine—
My unoffending—my offended one!
I would not mourn the health that flies my cheek,
  I would not mourn my dissappointed years—
  My vain heart mock'd, and worldly hopes o'erthrown,
But long to meet thee in that land of rest,
  Nor deem it joy to breathe in careless ears
  A tale of blighted hopes, as mournful as thine own.

Benevolence.

A YOUTHFUL pair by virtuous love made one,
  Two fond hearts yoked by that sweet unseen chain
  That doubles every joy—divides each pain,
Doth the sun look a lovelier sight upon?
  Ay, let them laud love's holiness as they will,
    Its infelt thrill to heavenly bliss allied,
    In the wrapt visions of poetry purified;
It is earth-born, cold, selfish, sensual still.
Oh, it is in the wide, benevolent feel,
  The limitless expanse of heart, embracing
Within its undistinguishing circle, all,
From the insect to the fellow-pilgrim, chasing
    Each lonely affection from the heart, we steal
Of heavenly love some faint memorial.

Friendship.

A WEARY time hath pass'd since last we parted;
  Thy gentle eye was filled with sorrow, and
  I did not speak, but pressed thy trembling hand,
Even in that hour of rapture, broken hearted.
I have not seen thee since—for thou art changed
  There sits a coldness on thy lip and brow—
  The look, the tone, the smile, are altered now
And all about, within thee, quite estranged.
I have not seen thee since—although perchance
  Among the heartless and the vain, on me
All coldly courteous lights thy lovely glance,
  Yet art thou happier? Oh, if such may be
The love that Friendship vows—give me again
My heart, my days of peace, my lute, and listening plain.

Fame.

Why hast thou lured me on, fond muse, to quit
  The path of plain dull worldly sense, and be
  A wanderer through the realms of thought with thee
While hearts that never knew thy visitings sweet,
  Cold souls that mock thy quiet melancholy,
Win their bright way up Fortune's glittering wheel;
And we sit lingering here in darkness still,
  Scorned by the bustling sons of wealth and folly?
Yet still thou whisperest in mine ear, "the day—
  The day may be at hand when thou and I,
  (The season of expectant pain gone by),
Shall tread to Joy's bright porch a smiling way,
And rising, not as once, with hurried wing,
To purer skies aspire, and hail a lovelier spring."

Mitchelstown Caverns.

Gaudly it frown'd when first with shuddering mind
  We saw the far-famed Cavern's darkling womb,
  And for that vault of silence and of gloom
Left the fair day and smiling world behind.
But what bright wonder hail'd our eyes ere long!
  The chrystal well—the sparry curtained dome—
  The sparkling shafts that propp'd that cavern'd home,
And vaults that turn'd the homeliest sounds to song.
  Oh, this, I thought, is sure a symbol plain
Of that undreaded death, the holy die,
  Stern at the first and withering to the view;
But past that gate of darkness and of pain,
  What scenes of unimagined rapture lie—
  Rich with elysian wealth and splendour ever new.

Written in Adare in 1820.

I LOOKED upon a dark and sullen sea
   Over whose slumbering wave the night's mists hung,
   Till from the morn's gray breast a fresh wind sprung
And sought its brightening bosom joyously;
Then fled the mists its quickening breath before;
   The glad sea rose to meet it—and each wave
   Retiring from the sweet caress it gave,
Made summer music to the listening shore.
So slept my soul, unmindful of thy reign;
   But the sweet breath of thy celestial grace,
   Hath risen—oh, let its quickening spirit chase
From that dark seat, each mist and secret stain,
Till, as in yon clear water, mirror'd fair,
Heaven sees its own calm hues reflected there.

On Remembering an Inadvertent Jest on Lord Byron's Poetry.

I.

FORGIVE me, Thou who formed that wondrous mind,
   Where shone Thy works with fairly mirrored gleam,
If thoughtlessly my lips with jest unkind,
   Have dared to slight Thy handy-work in him.
   For what of pure delight the quickening beam
Of genius from his potent numbers cast,
   Our grateful praise we owe; and if its dim
And wavering flame not heavenward burned at last,
In truth, we should not judge, but wait in silence fast.

II.

Oh, blessed Charity! Religion mild!
  Thy gentle smiles are never meant to wound;
No jest hast thou for Error's helpless child,
  But holy tears and love without a bound—
  Thy constant votaries!—they are seldom found
With barbed censure on their lips, but those
  Who newly enter on thy sacred ground,
With little heed the thoughts of blame unclose
And deem they love thee, when they only wound thy foes.

Lines to a Departed Friend.

When May with all her blooming train
Came o'er the woodland and the plain—
When mingling winds and waters made
A murmuring music in the shade,
I loved to hear that artless song—
I loved to stray those groves among,
And every sound of rustic pleasure,
Waked in my heart an answering measure.

But now no more that gentle scene,
Of mellow light and freshening green,
Seems lovely to my altered eye;
And that soft west wind, hastening by,
Seems breathing near me faint and low—
Some warning dirge, some song of woe.

How have I loved at early morn
When the dew topp'd the glistening thorn—

When o'er the hill the day-beam broke,
And nature's plumed minstrels woke—
To praise with them the will divine
That bade that glorious sun to shine!

That day-beam burns as brightly still,
The wild birds charm the echoing hill;
But light and song alike are vain
To soothe a heart that throbs in pain;
And pale disease that scene surveys
Without one languid smile of praise.

Thine was the gift, Almighty power!
That brighten'd many a youthful hour;
Found joys in Winter's havoc drear,
When heaven was dark and earth was bare,
And raised the heart on secret wing
To rapture in the bloom of spring.
That blessing Thou hast claimed again,
And left me wrapped in lingering pain.
Almighty power! the will was Thine,
And this weak heart shall ne'er repine.
In joy or grief, in good or ill,
This tongue shall praise Thy mercies still!
But may that feeble praise be blest,
And deeply felt, though ill confessed—
Blest in my own awakened heed,
Felt in the hearts of those who read!

Lost days of youth! Oh, holy days,
When joy was blent with prayer and praise!
When this sad heart, now deeply dyed
With many a thought unsanctified,
Trembled at every venial stain,
And shrunk from sin, as now from pain!

Oh! not that even in that hour
Of early reason's dawning power,
My soul was pure from thoughts of sin,
But now so dark the past has been,
That those first stains of young offence
Wear the light hue of innocence!

Departed spirit! often then,
By peaceful fire in lonely glen,
Did thy maturer reason shine,
A guidance and a light to mine;—
Did thy maturer piety
Awake some holy thoughts in me.
Late, wandering in those silent ways,
I thought upon our early days;
Ah! may I never feel again,
The pain that touched my spirit then!
For every shrub and every tree,
Spoke with a still reproach to me;
And even the scene of boyish crime,
Seem'd hallow'd by the light of time!

What could my heart, in passion tried,
If it could err, when by thy side?
Ambitious, there it would not dwell,
We parted—and the faithless fell;
We parted—and the world since then
Has learned the lesson o'er again,
That Virtue, humble, simple, fair,
Is all the knowledge worth our care;
That heavenly wisdom is a thing
Above the flight of reason's wing;
That human genius cannot sound
The depths in which her truth is found;

While a poor peasant's simple prayer,
Will find her always watching there;
That hearts untaught can learn her rules,
While far she flies from human schools;
That learning oft is but a rod—
That he knows all who loves his God,
And every other eye is dim,
Save theirs who hope and trust in Him.
Willing to serve is truly free;
Obedience is best liberty;
And man's first power—a bended knee.

'Twere vain to hope, if I could part
Upon this page my bleeding heart,
And to the young enquirer show
How often knowledge ends in woe.
Hearts would no more by earth be riven,
And souls no longer lost to heaven.
No! human pride and passion still
Will hold the reins of human will;
And, even in passion's fierce excess,
Find argument of haughtiness!
Youth's budding virtues will be blighted,
The law of heaven forgot and slighted,
Age follow age, yet, hurrying on,
Trust no experience but its own.
Yet it is something if we steal
One spirit from the dizzy reel,
A few may wake, when thousands sleep,
Millions may scoff, but one may weep!

'Tis something, too, to think that, now,
While I renew my infant vow,
Thy gentle shade may wander near,
And smile on each repentant tear;

To find, as thus, I glance mine eye
Over those pages mournfully,
Something that might in former days,
Have won that blameless spirit's praise.
Ah, it were all, if now at last
This offering for evil past,
Might pierce the ear of heaven and win
Oblivion for that faithless sin;
If thy pure, saintly, fervent prayer,
Might find a sweet acceptance there,
And from that sacred home, on me
Draw down the fire of charity!
That I might scatter, wide and far
My Maker's praise, from star to star,
And joyous sing how He had smiled,
Forgiveness on His erring child!

That all who heard that grateful song
Might learn to grieve for secret wrong,
And turn their hearts from joys of sense,
To holy praise and penitence!
Ah, sanguine hope! not in an hour
Can zeal from passion wrest his power,
Nor former scandals be removed,
Though those we teach be dearly loved.
All the repentant soul can do,
Is still to toil and labour through
The remnant of life's shortening day,
And for the rest to hope and pray.

Sweet Taunton Dene.

I.

Sweet Taunton Dene! thy smiling fields
   Once more with merry accents ring;
Once more reviving nature yields
   Her tribute to the smiling spring.
The small birds in the woodland sing,
The ploughman turns the kindly green,
   And pleasure waves her restless wing
Among thy groves, Sweet Taunton Dene.

II.

But peace abides with Him alone
   Who rules with calm, resistless pow'r.
Through all creation's boundless zone,
   From rolling sphere to garden flow'r,
Nor falls in Spring the welcome show'r
Unwill'd of Him, nor tempest blows,
   Nor wind within the fragrant bow'r
Can rend a leaf from summer rose.

III.

Sweet Taunton Dene! oh, long abide
   In thy fair vale delights like these!
And long may Tone's smooth waters glide
   By smiling cots and hearts at ease!
   Be thine the joy of rustic peace,
Each sound that haunts the woodland scene
   And blithe beneath thy bowering trees
The dance at eve, Sweet Taunton Dene!

Adieu to London.

COMPOSED ON THE COACH, ON HIS WAY FROM LONDON.

I.

Adieu! thou pestilential air,
  Where death and pain reside—
Where every brow is dark with care,
  And every eye with pride!
Where vapours change the maiden hue
  Of winter's cloudless moon,
And man's unwinking eye may view
  The burning sun at noon!

II.

And welcome! welcome, O ye hills!
  Bright skies and varied plain!
A rushing joy my bosom fills
  To see your tints again.
Here no deceitful ruin lurks
  Beneath the splendid show,
But God unrols His glorious works
  Around me as I go.

III.

Health breathes in every passing gale
  That shades my parted hair;
I bid the western breezes hail
  With laughing forehead bare.
They tell me of my native plains—
  They whisper of my home,
And the freshening blood within my veins
  Runs gaily while I roam.

IV.

Away, away, fair Taunton Dene
    Lies nearer to the West;
Now fast o'er Hounslow's fading scene
    Night draws his gloomy vest.
Now, while I watch the tiny beam
    Shot from each beauteous star,
I think of Ireland and of him
    Who reads their lore afar.

V.

'Tis morn—and I am far away
    From London's smoky den,
And mark the light of breaking day
    'Mid Nature's haunts again;
I hear her hedge-notes sweetly trilled
    Still hurrying swift along,
And like an organ newly filled
    My bosom swells with song.

VI.

For who can see the morning shine
    And view these blushing skies,
Nor think of Him whose love divine
    Still bids that sun arise?
'Tis eve—and for the noisy town
    'Mid walks of silent green,
I turn to see that sun go down
    On lovely Taunton Dene.

VII.

There, gazing on the smiling West
    I stay my wandering feet,
And gentlest feelings fill my breast
    And sweetest pulses beat.

For far beyond that woodland scene—
  Beyond that grassy lea,
I think of all that lies between
  That setting star and me.

VIII.

O, absence! that like death doth make
  The friends you take more dear;
How sad were life for their sweet sake,
  But Hope stays whispering near.
Still pointing to the exiled heart
  That heavenly-promised shore,
Where friends shall meet "no more to part—
  To mingle tears no more."

My Spirit is of Pensive Mould.

I.

My spirit is of pensive mould,
I cannot laugh as once of old,
When sporting o'er some woodland scene
A child I trod the dewy green.

II.

I cannot sing my merry lay,
As in that past unconscious day;
For time has laid existence bare,
And shown me sorrow lurking there.

III.

I would I were the lonely breeze
That mourns among the leafless trees,
That I might sigh from morn till night
O'er vanished peace and lost delight.

IV.

I would I were the heavy show'r,
That falls in spring on leaf and bow'r,
That I might weep the live-long day
For erring man and hope's decay.

V.

For all the woe beneath the sun,
For all the wrong to virtue done,
For every soul to falsehood gain'd,
For every heart by evil stain'd.

VI.

For man by man in durance held,
For early dreams of joy dispell'd,
For all the hope the world awakes
In youthful hearts and after breaks.

VII.

But still, though hate, and fraud, and strife
Have stain'd the shining web of life,
Sweet Hope the glowing woof renews,
In all its old, enchanting hues.

VIII.

Flow on, flow on, thou shining stream!
Beyond life's dark and changeful dream,
There is a hope, there is a joy,
This faithless world can ne'er destroy.

IX.

Sigh on, sigh on, ye gentle winds!
For stainless hearts and faithful minds,
There is a bliss abiding true,
That shall not pass and die like you.

X.

Shine on, shine on, thou glorious sun!
When Day his latest course has run,
On sinless hearts shall rise a light
That ne'er shall set in gloomy night.

Lines on a Lady's Seal Box.

I.

Read ye the casket's history,
Lay not the simple trinket by,
But see those various signets met,
O'er the enamelled surface set:
    For hearts that feel
    In every seal
Can find a theme of grief or glee
That careless eyes may never see.

II.

Read ye the casket's history,
Let Fancy turn the leaf for thee—
Here is a seal that brought afar
Tidings of joy from scenes of war;
    A mother sighed
    For her perished pride,
A maiden mourned her idle truth,
And this brought sudden bliss to both.

III.

This tells a tale of drearier mood—
A bride beside the altar stood;
What force compell'd his cold delay
The bridegroom never came to say.
    This signet came
    To clear his fame,
Its hue was blasting to her sight,
For it was black as death and night!

IV.

Here is a crest and here a shield
With honours throng'd upon its field,
Both in heraldic lustre bright,
Both boasting high of princely right,
    Their owner's claim
    A bloody fame;
One fell in fight on Cressy's plain,
And one—cut steaks in Warwick-lane.

V.

How many hearts these toys have chill'd—
Or with a sudden rapture fill'd—
What tales of joy or sorrow spoken—
What misery healed or bright hopes broken!
    My song should dwell
    O'er long to tell,
Though many a passion deep might be,
Awakened in their history!

VI.

I know a casket, (guess you where?)
Filled with sweet thoughts and feelings rare,
A richer and a simpler one
For poet's thoughts to dwell upon

A meeter theme
For minstrel dream,
Upon whose glowing surface yet
(Or do I err?) no seal is set.

VII.

Oh, bid me name a hand to place
On that soft heart the first deep trace
And his it shall be in whose eye
A soft and gentle dignity;
   A healthful cheek,
   And smiles that speak;
A voice whose memory haunts the ear,
And full deep flashing eyes are dear.

VIII.

Let joys that time may never dim
Share like thine own kind looks for him
Who first the dear impression makes,
And withered be the hand that breaks;
   Let life glide by
   All peacefully,
Till on that sinless brow of thine
The signet of the blest shall shine.

A Portrait.

I.

Merry honrs will fleet,
   Friends that love must sever,
Oft in joy we meet,
   To part in tears for ever

Many a word is said,
  And changed as soon as spoken;
Many a vow is made
  Only to be broken.

II.

Life is like a glass
  O'er whose surface gleaming,
Brilliant shadows pass,
  But vain as childhood's dreaming.
Could we find the art
  To fix the flying splendour,
One I know my heart
  Never would surrender.

III.

'Tis a lovely shade!
  Paint it while it lingers,
Ere it fail and fade,
  Ere the wasting fingers
Of the haggard Time,
  The blasting and consuming,
Touch its tender prime,
  And wither all its blooming.

IV

Paint a fitting form
  In royal halls to wander,
With woman's softness warm,
  With dignity beyond her;
Think a youthful Queen
  Tarries while you trace it,
'Tis a shape and mien,
  To fill a throne and grace it.

V.

Paint a blushing cheek
　Filled with healthful beauty,
Ready smiles that speak
　Of peace and cherished duty:
Eyes that shift and shine
　With a full, deep meaning,
Clouded curls that twine,
　A sunny forehead screening.

VI.

Paint a blooming lip
　With blushing softness swelling,
Where mirth and kindness keep
　An undivided dwelling.
The charm is wanting still
　That on that soft lip lingers,
And the ready skill
　That haunts those taper fingers.

VII.

Merry hours will fleet,
　Friends that love must sever,
Oft in joy we meet
　To part in tears for ever.
But in absence, warm,
　Upon this heart reclining
I will keep that form
　Of memory's fond designing.

VIII.

Oft in lonesome eves,
　When the light is dying,
And the shivering leaves
　In all the woods are sighing;

Fancy will restore,
    Those well-remembered hours,
That romantic shore,
    And those forsaken bowers.

IX.

Fate may frown her worst.
    I no more will fear it,
Let her thunder burst,
    I will smile to hear it;
If, when life shall fleet,
    A sinless death be given,
And a hope to meet
    Hearts like thine in heaven.

LINES ADDRESSED TO A YOUNG LADY ON READING A POEM OF HERS ADDRESSED TO DEATH.

Oh, may the burden of thy song
Forbear the gentle minstrel long,
But when all joys for which we live,
Save those alone which guilt can give—
When all thine early hopes are won,
And love and friendship long thine own;
Then, with those love-knots softly riven,
With all thy virtues ripe for heaven;
Then, looking calm to joys above,
And leaving peace with all you love,
Pass gently like an evening wind,
And leave no broken hearts behind.

Inscription for a Cup

It was not dug from charnel deep,
It was not hewn from quarried steep,
But sweetly fill'd its covering dun
Beneath warm India's burning sun;
That Lydia might the shell receive,
In memory of that parted eve.

Ah, still when each returning May,
Restores sweet friendship's opening day,
Remember those descending showers,
And lovely Richmond's drooping bowers;
And welcome then to thee and thine
The May-day guest of twenty-nine.

By lonely Dunloh's echoing lakes,
By wild Glengariff's rocky brakes,
By old Askeyton's cloister still,
By sweet Ringmoylan's leafy hill,
And by that wild and clifted shore
That hears the roused Atlantic roar,
Remember him who gives the shell,
And keep it long and guard it well,
Devote—in Friendship's name to thee,
And thine—oh, fair Fidelity

Impromptu,

ON SEEING AN IRIS FORMED BY THE SPRAY OF THE OCEAN AT MILTOWNMALBAY.

Oh, sun-coloured breaker! when gazing on thee
  I think of the eastern story,
How beauty arose from the foam of the sea—
  A creature of light and of glory.
But, hark! a hoarse answer is sent from the wave,
  "No—Venus was never my daughter—
"To golden-haired Iris her being I gave,
  "Behold where she shines o'er the water."

The Wake without a Corpse.*

I.

The dismal yew and cypress tall,
  Wave o'er the church-yard lone,
Where rest our friends and fathers all,
  Beneath the funeral stone.
Unvexed in holy ground they sleep,
  Oh, early lost! o'er thee
No sorrowing friend shall ever weep,
  Nor stranger bend the knee.
    Mo chuma! lorn am I!
Hoarse dashing rolls the salt sea wave,
Over our perished darling's grave.

---

* It is a custom among the peasantry in some parts of Ireland, when any member of a family has been lost at sea (or in any other way which renders the performance of the customary funeral rite impossible), to celebrate the "wake," exactly in the same way as if the corpse were actually present.

II.

The winds the sullen deep that tore
  His death song chaunted loud,
The weeds that line the clifted shore
  Were all his burial shroud;
For friendly wail and holy dirge
  And long lament of love,
Around him roared the angry surge,
  The curlew screamed above.
        Mo chuma! lorn am I,
My grief would turn to rapture now,
Might I but touch that pallid brow.

III.

The stream-born bubbles soonest burst,
  That earliest left the source:
Buds earliest blown are faded first,
  In Nature's wonted course;
With guarded pace her seasons creep,
  By slow decay expire,
The young above the aged weep,
  The son above the sire:
        Mo chuma! lorn am I,
That death a backward course should hold,
To smite the young and spare the old.

To a Young Friend on his Birth-day.

I.

The world has run one chequered round
  Within its airy ring,
Since thou, unfolding flower! hast found
  The light of life's soft spring.

II.

Thy parents were my friends in joy,
   My friends in sadness long,
And now, to greet their rosy boy,
   I bring my birth-day song.

III.

By many a shore and mountain wild,
   Lone lake and cheerful bower,
We wove a tie, beloved child,
   To bless a distant hour.

IV.

We staid not on the threshold cold,
   Of strange and lingering form,
But pressed to friendship's inmost hold,
   With trusting hearts and warm.

V.

Perhaps—because I wrote of truth,
   They deem'd I loved her too,
And painting forms of generous youth,
   I was the thing I drew.

VI.

For soon their hearts were bound to me,
   In feeling deep and sure,
Like old friends lost in infancy,
   And found in life mature.

VII.

The light of earth's uncertain skies,
   Not yet its quickening flood,
Had sent into those gentle eyes,
   Dark, unexpanded bud!

VIII.

When, in an hour of joy serene,
    A kindly promise came,
That now, my young and loved Eugene,
    Is broken in thy name.

IX.

Yet ne'er for that unheeding turn,
    Of friendship's first excess,
More faintly mine to them shall burn,
    Nor thou be loved the less.

X.

Whene'er thine altered name I hear,
    My heart may mourn, 'tis true;
A keen reproach must grieve mine ear,
    And wholesome warning too.

XI.

For oft I think, 'mid lonesome hours,
    By night and silence stirred—
Whene'er I think on those lost hours,
    And that forgotten word.

XII.

That had they found this heart when tried,
    The heart their fancy dreamed,
And had long knowledge justified,
    What trusting friendship deemed.

XIII.

That pledge might be remembered now,
    That confidence the same,
And, sign of altered feeling thou,
    Had'st borne another name.

XIV.

But far let waking reason keep
  Each indolent regret;
And while she hoards the lesson deep
  The useless grief forget.

XV.

Now many a month has rolled away,
  Dear boy, for us and you,
And closed are all those scenes so gay,
  And changed their actors too!

XVI.

But let me turn from thoughts like these,
  And change my song to joy,
And rhyme for thee a prayer of peace,
  Oh, sinless, angel boy!

XVII.

Fair virtue guide my young Eugene,
  With footing firm and true,
And keep his breast from sorrow keen;
  His feet from wandering too!

XVIII.

Mercy divine!—if changing fate
  Rave in his pathway wild;
Make strong thine arm to shield his state!
  Oh, save this infant child!

Addressed to a Friend.

I.

What! passed away! those happy hours
  When sunny friendship yet was new,
When love's own music filled those bowers
  And joy's bright sun broke dazzling through.

II.

Ah, no! the spirit is not fled
  That woke that brief, admiring rhyme,
Nor feeling cold—nor memory dead—
  Though changed, alas! are place and time.

III.

Ah, no! if vivid dreams at night,
  If keen remembrances by day,
Can fetter Time's untiring flight,
  Those moments are not passed away.

IV.

Dear scenes! where oft my spirit quaffed
  Life's social joy from genial springs;
Sweet time! when Pleasure round us laughed,
  And freely waved his golden wings.

V.

Ah, does this worthless heart forget
  Those moments now so sadly sweet,
Nor musing on their memory yet,
  With lonesome feelings wildly beat?

VI.

I know the thoughts that die unsung
    To many speak a heart untrue,
They think when silence chains the tongue
    The soul must be forgetful too.

VII.

Yet, trust me, Memory's warmest sighs
    Are often breathed in moments lorn—
And many a feeling thought will rise
    And in the bosom die unborn.

VIII.

No—Friendship does not always sleep,
    Though sometimes she may mourn alone,
Nor sympathy less kindly weep,
    Though oft her tears have fallen unknown.

On Pulling some Campanulas in a Lady's Garden.

I.

Oh, weeds will haunt the loveliest scene
    The summer sun can see,
And clouds will sometimes come between
    The truest friends that be.
And thoughts unkind will come perchance,
    And haply words of blame,
For pride is man's inheritance,
    And frailty is his name.

II.

Yet while I pace this leafy vale,
  That nursed thine infancy—
And hear in every passing gale
  A whispered sound of thee.
My 'nighted bosom wakes anew,
  To Feeling's genial ray,
And each dark mist on Memory's view
  Melts into light away.

III.

The flowers that grace this shaded spot—
  Low, lovely and obscure—
Are like the joys thy friendship brought—
  Unboasted, sweet, and pure.
Now withered is their autumn blow,
  And changed their simple hue,
Ah! must it e'er be mine to know
  Their type is faded too?

IV.

Yet should those well-remembered hours
  Return to me no more,
And—like those culled and faded flowers,
  Their day of life be o'er—
In memory's fragrant shrine concealed,
  A sweeter joy they give,
Than aught the world again can yield
  Or I again receive.

They speak of Scotland's Heroes

I.

They speak of Scotland's heroes old,
    Struggling to make their country free,
And in that hour my heart grows cold,
    For Erin! then I think of thee!

II.

They boast their Bruce of Bannockburn,
    Their noble knight of Ellerslie;
To Erin's sons I proudly turn—
    My country, then I smile for thee.

III.

They boast, tho' joined to England's power;
    Scotland ne'er bowed to slavery;
An equal league in danger's hour—
    My country, then I weep for thee.

IV.

And when they point to our fair Isle,
    And say no patriot hearts have we;
That party stains the work defile—
    My country, then I blush for thee.

V.

But Hope says, "blush or tear shall never
    Sully approving Fame's decree."
When Freedom's word her bond shall sever—
    My country, then I'll joy in thee.

VI.

But oh! be Scotland honoured long,
Be envy ever far from me,
My simple lay meant her no wrong—
My country, it was but for thee!

O'Brazil, the Isle of the Blest.

A SPECTRE ISLAND, SAID TO BE SOMETIMES VISIBLE ON THE VERGE
OF THE WESTERN HORIZON, IN THE ATLANTIC,
FROM THE ISLES OF ARRAN.

I.

On the ocean that hollows the rocks where ye dwell,
A shadowy land has appeared, as they tell;
Men thought it a region of sunshine and rest,
And they called it O'Brazil, the Isle of the Blest.
From year unto year, on the ocean's blue rim,
The beautiful spectre showed lovely and dim;
The golden clouds curtained the deep where it lay,
And it looked like an Eden, away, far away!

II.

A peasant who heard of the wonderful tale,
In the breeze of the Orient loosened his sail
From Ara, the holy, he turned to the west,
For though Ara was holy, O'Brazil was blest.
He heard not the voices that called from the shore—
He heard not the rising wind's menacing roar;
Home, kindred, and safety he left on that day,
And he sped to O'Brazil, away, far away!

III.

Morn rose on the deep, and that shadowy Isle,
O'er the faint rim of distance reflected its smile;
Noon burned on the wave, and that shadowy shore,
Seemed lovelily distant, and faint as before:
Lone evening came down, on the wanderer's track,
And to Ara again he looked timidly back;
Oh! far on the verge of the ocean it lay,
Yet the Isle of the Blest was away, far away!

IV.

Rash dreamer, return! O ye winds of the main,
Bear him back to his own peaceful Ara again;
Rash fool! for a vision of fanciful bliss,
To barter thy calm life of labour and peace.
The warning of reason was spoken in vain,
He never re-visited Ara again;
Night fell on the deep, amidst tempest and spray,
And he died on the waters, away, far away!

V.

To you, gentle friends, need I pause to reveal,
The lessons of prudence my verses conceal;
How the phantom of pleasure seen distant in youth,
Oft lures a weak heart from the circle of truth.
All lovely it seems like that shadowy Isle,
And the eye of the wisest is caught by its smile;
But, ah! for the heart, it has tempted to stray,
From the sweet home of duty, away, far away!

VI

Poor friendless adventurer! vainly might he
Look back to green Ara, along the wild sea;
But the wandering heart has a guardian above,
Who, though erring, remembers the child of his love.

Oh, who at the proffer of safety would spurn
When all that he asks, is the will to return ;
To follow a phantom, from day unto day,
And die in the tempest, away, far away !

Lines addressed to a Seagull,

SEEN OFF THE CLIFFS OF MOHER, IN THE COUNTY OF CLARE.

WHITE bird of the tempest ! oh, beautiful thing,
With the bosom of snow, and the motionless wing
Now sweeping the billow, now floating on high,
Now bathing thy plumes in the light of the sky ;
Now poising o'er ocean thy delicate form,
Now breasting the surge with thy bosom so warm ;
Now darting aloft, with a heavenly scorn,
Now shooting along, like a ray of the morn ;
Now lost in the folds of the cloud-curtained dome,
Now floating abroad like a flake of the foam ;
Now silently poised o'er the war of the main,
Like the spirit of charity, brooding o'er pain ;
Now gliding with pinion, all silently furled,
Like an Angel descending to comfort the world !
Thou seem'st to my spirit, as upward I gaze,
And see thee, now clothed in mellowest rays ;
Now lost in the storm, driven vapours that fly,
Like hosts that are routed across the broad sky !
Like a pure spirit true, to its virtue and faith,
'Mid the tempests of nature, of passion, and death !

Rise ! beautiful emblem of purity ! rise
On the sweet winds of heaven, to thine own brilliant skies
Still higher ! still higher ! till lost to our sight,
Thou hidest thy wings in a mantle of light ;

And I think how a pure spirit gazing on thee,
Must long for the moment—the joyous and free—
When the soul, disembodied from nature, shall spring,
Unfettered at once to her maker and king;
When the bright day of service and suffering past,
Shapes, fairer than thine, shall shine round her at last,
While the standard of battle triumphantly furled,
She smiles like a victor, serene on the world!

Past Times.

I.

Yes, there is the dwelling, the warmth of the year
Still lives in each blossom that flourishes here;
Yes, there is the dwelling, but lonely it seems,
As a land in which fancy stalks silent in dreams,
The door-way that welcomed the guest to the hall,
The creepers that whispered along the white wall;
Each sweet of the summer smiles tenderly there,
But where are the fingers that dress'd them? oh where?

II.

Ah, true to remembrance! Ah, true to the thought,
Deep hid in my heart, of that love-lighted spot;
Ay, there are the flower-bordered paths where we walked,
And there are the groves where we listened and talked;
All lonesomely blooming! I look, but in vain,
For a symbol of light in the quiet domain;
The lawn where the children have gamboll'd is there,
But where are the innocent faces? oh where?

III.

Yes, there is the window that looked to the flood;
But where are the friends by the casement that stood,
And told me how sweet as he sunk to his rest,
Was the smile of the sun from the clouds of the west?
How bright on the river his blushing light falls,
How spectral in distance those time-shattered walls,
And the hearts that to mine turned fervently there,
And the minds that to mine were an echo—oh where?

IV.

True!—Life is but short and possession unsure;
Religion may teach us that we should endure;
But oh! there are moments when feeling will speak,
When nature is mighty and reason is weak;
When selfishly sinking our bosoms will mourn
O'er joys that are gone and can never return;
And whisper in ignorance, fearful and drear,
Where now are the days that have left us?—oh where

V.

May He in whose keeping are sorrow and joy,
The kindly to save, and the just to destroy,
Give light to our spirits in moments so dim,
For those are the trials that turn us to Him.
There may be a time, when the bosoms that here,
Let sigh o'er the wrecks of the vanishing year.
Say whisper in joy round the foot of His throne,
'Twas well that our dwelling looked dreary and lone!

The Wreck of the Comet.

I.

Darkness is on the wave—
  The sea heaves sluggishly,
The winds are in their cave,
  Slumbering silently.
Dim is the seaman's track,
  Uncheered by starry glow,
And all above is black—
  And lightless all below.

II.

Two ships are on the sea—
  No need of wind have they,
To speed them rapidly
  Forth on their watery way.
Like creatures of the deep,
  They ply their forward course,
Breaking old Ocean's sleep
  With heavy sounds and hoarse.

III.

Look through the darkling veil—
  Night hangs upon the wave—
Death's own eternal pale—
  The universal grave!
Mark you tall bark—the din
  Of life that is about her—
Love, Hope, and Mirth are in,
  And Ruin is without her.

IV.

Youth is slumbering there,
  And Age—as beautiful—
Hush'd is the heart of Care—
  Beauty's love looks are dull—
Here young Hope's honey breath,
  The waking lover quaffs—
And yonder, see where death
  Sits on the wave, and laughs!

V.

The vessels near!—they ply—
  They meet—that fate hath caught her:
A sudden crash—a cry!
  A wail above the water—
A hiss of quenching flame—
  A rush of billows on her—
The hungry waves are tame—
  The sea is smooth upon her.

VI.

A voice is on the deep—
  Hoarse is the whirlwind's lungs—
The sea starts from her sleep,
  And lifts her billowy tongues—
'A sorrow for the dead!
  Friend—countryman—and stranger—
And a curse for him who fled
  His fellow-men in danger!"

The Sister of Charity.

I.

She once was a lady of honour and wealth,
Bright glow'd on her features the roses of health,
Her vesture was blended of silk and of gold,
And her motion shook perfume from every fold:
Joy revell'd around her—love shone at her side,
And gay was her smile, as the glance of a bride;
And light was her step, in the mirth-sounding hall,
When she heard of the daughters of Vincent de Paul.

II.

She felt in her spirit the summons of grace,
That call'd her to live for the suffering race;
And, heedless of pleasure, of comfort, of home,
Rose quickly, like Mary, and answered "I come!"
She put from her person the trappings of pride,
And passed from her home, with the joy of a bride;
Nor wept at the threshold, as onward she moved,
For her heart was on fire, in the cause it approved.

III.

Lost ever to fashion—to vanity lost,
That beauty that once was the song and the toast
No more in the ball-room that figure we meet,
But, gliding at dusk to the wretch's retreat.
Forgot in the halls is that high-sounding name,
For the Sister of Charity blushes at fame;
Forgot are the claims of her riches and birth,
For she barters for heaven, the glory of earth.

IV.

Those feet that to music could gracefully move,
Now bear her alone on the mission of love;
Those hands that once dangled the perfume and gem,
Are tending the helpless or lifted for them;
That voice that once echo'd the song of the vain,
Now whispers relief to the bosom of pain;
And the hair that was shining with diamond and pearl,
Is wet with the tears of the penitent girl.

V.

Her down-bed a pallet—her trinkets a bead,
Her lustre—one taper that serves her to read;
Her sculpture—the crucifix nail'd by her bed,
Her paintings—one print of the thorn-crowned head
Her cushion—the pavement that wearies her knees,
Her music—the psalm, or the sigh of disease;
The delicate lady lives mortified there,
And the feast is forsaken for fasting and prayer

VI.

Yet not to the service of heart and of mind,
Are the cares of that heaven-minded virgin confined:
Like Him whom she loves, to the mansions of grief,
She hastes with the tidings of joy and relief.
She strengthens the weary—she comforts the weak,
And soft is her voice in the ear of the sick;
Where want and affliction on mortals attend,
The Sister of Charity *there* is a friend.

VII.

Unshrinking where pestilence scatters his breath,
Like an angel she moves, 'mid the vapour of death;
Where rings the loud musket, and flashes the sword,
Unfearing she walks, for she follows the Lord.

How sweetly she bends o'er each plague-tainted face
With looks that are lighted with holiest grace
How kindly she dresses each suffering limb,
For she sees in the wounded the image of Him.

VIII.

Behold her, ye worldly! behold her, ye vain!
Who shrink from the pathway of virtue and pain;
Who yield up to pleasure your nights and your days,
Forgetful of service, forgetful of praise.
Ye lazy philosophers—self-seeking men—
Ye fireside philanthropists, great at the pen,
How stands in the balance your eloquence weighed,
With the life and the deeds of that high-born maid?

Nano Nagle,

FOUNDRESS OF THE PRESENTATION AND URSULINE ORDERS OF NUNS
IN IRELAND, WHICH ARE DEVOTED CHIEFLY TO THE
EDUCATION OF THE POOR.

I.

'Twas the garden of Christendom, tended with care
Ev'ry flowret of Eden grew peacefully there;
When the fire of the spoiler on Lombardy blazed,
And the Moslemin shout in the desert was raised,
And high o'er the wreck of a fear-stricken world,
The standard of hell to the winds was unfurled,
Faith, bleeding returned to the land of the west,
And with Science, her handmaid, sought shelter and rest.

II.

With a warm burst of welcome that shelter was given;
Her breast open'd wide to the envoy of heaven;
In the screen of her bowers was the stranger conceal'd,
Till her pantings were hushed and her bruises were heal'd
From the hall of the Righ, to the sheiling afar,
All echoed her glory, all greeted her star;
In the depth of our glen, were her secrets adored,
And our mountain shone out in the light of the Lord.

III.

Ye ivy-clad relics, resounding no more
With the swell of the anthem from shore unto shore
Ye crags of the ocean, ye caves, in whose gloom
The saint found a home, and the martyr a tomb:
Ye arrows of vengeance, forgot in the quiver,
Ye death-shouts of enmity silenced for ever,
Ye roods of the wilderness hoary with years,
Ye knew of her triumph—ye know of her tears.

IV.

Ye speak of that time when the cells of the west
Gave voice after voice to the choir of the blest;
When a breathing of pray'r in the desert was heard,
And the angel came down, and the waters were stirr'd
When the church of the isles saw her glories arise—
Columba the dove-like, and Carthage the wise;
And the school and the temple gave light to each shore,
From clifted Iona to wooded Lismore.

V.

There's a mist on the eye—there's a wail on the ear—
My doves of the temple!—the falcon is near!
There's a change in the heavens—there's a rushing of gloom,
And the mountains are black with the hue of the tomb,

There's a ringing of steel, there's a voice in the bower
'Tis the death-shriek of Charity striving with Power;
With finger inverted rude Ignorance smiled,
And grim Passion exulted when mind was exiled.

VI.

Woe, woe, for the ruin that broods o'er thy towers
Fair garden of Christendom where are thy flowers!
Oh, say, when that thunder-cloud burst on thy shore,
Stood thy Faith as the Skellig when Ocean is hoar?
Say, smiled she undaunted when Hope look'd aghast,
And when Learning lay prostrate, stood Piety fast?
Oh, answer ye mountains that witnessed the zeal,
When the faith of our sires dared the dungeon and steel

VII.

Ev'n still though the tempest is hushed on our plains.
On the minds of our Country the havoc remains;
Peace grieves o'er her temples, on mountain and shore,
Sad History's witnesses, vocal no more.
Shall no sabbath arise on our week-day of care?
Is no waking reserved for our sleep of despair?
Ha, see!—there's a shooting of light in the gloom,
And the spirit of Nagle replies from the tomb.

VIII.

Hail, star of the lowly! apostle of light,
In the glow of whose fervour the cottage grew bright!
Sweet violet of sanctity, lurking conceal'd,
Till the wind lifts the leaf and the bloom is reveal'd;
By the light of that glory which burst on thy youth,
In its day-dream of pleasure, and woke it to truth,
By the tears thou hast shed, by the toils thou hast borne,
Oh, say, shall our night know a breaking of morn?

IX.

"As the dawn on the lingering night of the north,
To the hills of the west has the mandate gone forth:
In the desolate aisles there's a murmur of praise,
And the lost lamp of science rekindles its rays.
The voice of lament in our island shall cease,
And her cities rejoice in the sunlight of peace;
From her sleep of enchantment young Erin shall rise,
And again be the home of the holy and wise."

To Memory.

I.

Oh, come! thou sadly pleasing power,
Companion of the twilight hour—
Come, with thy sable garments flowing,
Thy tearful smile, all brightly glowing—
Come, with thy light and noiseless tread
As one belonging to the dead!
Come, with thy bright, yet clouded eye,
Grant me thine aid, sweet memory!

II.

She comes, and pictures all again,
The "wood-fringed" lake—the rugged plain—
The mountain flower—the valley's smile,
And lovely Inisfallen's isle.
The rushing waters roaring by,
Our ringing laugh—our raptur'd sigh,

The waveless sea—the varied shore—
The dancing boat—the measur'd oar,
The lofty bugle's rousing cry,
The awakened mountains deep reply.
Silence resuming then her reign,
In awful power, o'er hill and plain.

She paints, and her unclouded dyes,
Can never fade, in feeling's eyes,
For dipp'd in love's immortal stream—
Through future years they'll brightly beam

Oh, prized and loved, though lately known,
Forget not all, when we are gone—
Think how our friendship's well-knit band
Waited not time's confirming hand.
Think how despising forms control,
Heart sprung to heart, and soul to soul—
And let us greet thee, far or near—
As cherished friend—as brother dear.

To * * * *

I.

In the time of my boyhood I had a strange feeling,
    That I was to die in the noon of my day;
Not quietly into the silent grave stealing,
    But torn, like a blasted oak, sudden away.

II.

That, even in the hour when enjoyment was keenest,
   My lamp should quench suddenly hissing in gloom,
That even when mine honours were freshest and greenest,
   A blight should rush over and scatter their bloom.

III.

It might be a fancy—it might be the glooming
   Of dark visions taking the semblance of truth,
And it might be the shade of the storm that is coming,
   Cast thus in its morn through the sunshine of youth

IV.

But be it a dream or a mystic revealing,
   The bodement has haunted me year after year;
And whenever my bosom with rapture was filling,
   I paused for the footfall of fate at mine ear.

V.

With this feeling upon me, all feverish and glowing
   I rushed up the rugged way panting to fame,
I snatched at my laurels while yet they were growing.
   And won for my guerdon the half of a name.

VI.

My triumphs I viewed from the least to the brightest,
   As gay flowers pluck'd from the fingers of death,
And whenever joy's garments flowed richest and lightest,
   I looked for the skeleton lurking beneath.

VII.

O, friend of my heart! if that doom should fall on me,
   And thou should'st live on to remember my love—
Come oft to the tomb when the turf lies upon me,
   And list to the even wind mourning above.

VIII.

Lie down by that bank where the river is creeping
  All fearfully under the still autumn tree,
When each leaf in the sunset is silently weeping,
  And sigh for departed days—thinking of me.

IX.

By the smiles ye have looked—by the words ye have spoken
  (Affection's own music—that heal as they fall,)
By the balm ye have poured on a spirit half broken,
  And, oh! by the pain ye gave, sweeter than all.

X.

Remember me * * *, when I am departed,
  Live over those moments when they, too, are gone;
Be still to your minstrel the soft and kind-hearted,
  And droop o'er the marble where he lies alone.

XI.

Remember how freely that heart, that to others
  Was dark as the tempest-dawn frowning above,
Burst open to thine with the zeal of a brother's,
  And showed all its hues in the light of thy love.

XII.

And, oh, in that moment when over him sighing,
  Forgive, if his failings should flash on thy brain,
Remember the heart that beneath thee is lying
  Can never awake to offend thee again.

XIII.

And say while ye pause o'er each sweet recollection,
  "Let love like mine own on his spirit attend—
For to me his heart turned with a poet's affection,
  Just less than a lover and more than a friend.

XIV.

" Was he selfish?   Not quite—but his bosom was glowing
  With thronging affections—unanswered—unknown;
He looked all round the world for a heart overflowing,
  But found not another to love like his own.

XV.

' Yet how?   Did the worthy avoid or forsake him?
  Ah, no—for heaven blessed him with many a friend
But few were so trusting that might not mistake him,
  Oh, none were so dear that he could not offend !

XVI.

" Yet, peace to his clay in its dreary dominion;
  I know that to me he was good and sincere,
And that Virtue ne'er shadowed with tempering pinion
  An honester friendship than Death covers here."

The Nightwalker.

I.

'TWAS in the blooming month of May,
  When woods and fields are green;
When early, at the dawn of day,
  The sky-lark sings, unseen;
A gallant brig, with swelling sails,
  Weigh'd anchor by our strand,
With convicts from poor Erin's vales,
  Bound for Van Diemen's Land.

II.

Slow down old Shannon's silent tide,
  By favouring breezes borne,
I saw the royal fabric glide,
  Dim in the twilight morn;
When sadly o'er the shining flood
  Those accents reached the shore,
" Adieu, adieu! my own green wood.
  I ne'er shall see thee more!

III.

" Ye furze-clad hills, and briery dells,
  Now waking to the dawn—
Ye streams, whose lonesome murmur swells
  Across the silent lawn—
Ye snow-white cots that sweetly smile
  Along the peaceful shore,
Adieu, adieu! my own green isle,
  I ne'er shall see thee more.

IV.

" Oh, had my tongue a trumpet's force,
  To rouse yon slumbering vale,
That I might make the echo hoarse,
  With my unhappy tale;
That I might wake each sleeping friend,
  To hear my parting moan,
And, weeping o'er my luckless end,
  Be watchful for his own.

V.

" From infancy, a blissful life
  In yonder vale I led;
There, first I met my faithful wife,
  There, first I woo'd and wed;

Long time with blithesome industry
  We met each coming dawn,
Or closed each eve with gentle glee,
  Beside the dark Ovaan.

VI.

"Oh! give again my humble lot,
  My garden by the mill,
The rose that graced our clay-built cot,
  The hazel-tufted hill;
The sweets that fill'd each grateful sense
  From dawn to dewy night;
And more than these—the innocence
  That gave the landscape light.

VII.

"For daily there the nesting lark
  Sang to my spade at morn;
The red-breast there, at fall of dark,
  Hymn'd lonely from her thorn.
Ah! must I leave that happy dell,
  Where all my youth was pass'd,
And breathe to each a sad farewell,
  My fondest, and my last?

VIII.

"When far Van Diemen's sunbeams soon
  Upon my head shall fall,
How shall I miss at toilsome noon
  My Mary's cheerful call!
When, standing on the distant stile,
  She pour'd her summons clear,
Or met me with that happy smile
  That made our threshold dear!

IX.

"What hand shall trim the rushlight now
    That glads my cabin floor?
Or raise the turf with bended bough,
    When wintry tempests roar?
Ah! never shall that lightsome hearth
    Again be swept for me;
Nor infant there, with fondling mirth,
    Come climbing to my knee.

X.

"Ah, happy days! what Mary now
    Along the hedge shall steal,
With dark blue cloak and hooded brow,
    To bring my noontide meal?
The plenteous root of Erin's fields,
    To toil-worn peasant sweet;
And that fair draught the dairy yields,
    Not whiter than her feet.

XI.

"Dream on—dream on, my happy friends
    Oh! never may you know
The hopeless, helpless grief that rends
    My bosom as I go!
But when, at merry dance or fair,
    The sportive moments flee,
Let old remembrance waken there
    One pitying thought on me.

XII.

"Yet hear my tale—the bursting sigh
    That leaves the sufferer's heart,
The tears that blind each fixed eye
    When old affections part;

The wail, the shriek, each sound of fear,
    That scares the peopled glen,
Might yet, would they the lesson hear,
    Teach wisdom unto men.

XIII.

" Twas night—the black November blast
    Howl'd fierce through shrub and briar,
We heard the demon as he pass'd,
    And stirr'd our scanty fire;
Our babes by sweetest slumber lull'd
    In rosy silence lay,
Like buds to grace a garland cull'd
    Upon a summer day.

XIV.

' A knock!—hark!—hush!—twas but the hail,
    That smote our single pane—
Still fiercer beat the ruffian gale—
    Still heavier drove the rain;
Again!—the latch is raised—the storm
    Dash'd back the opening door,
And light'ning show'd the unknown form
    That press'd our cabin floor.

XV.

" O Satan, prince of darkness! thou—
    Wert thou in presence there,
Thou could'st not wear a subtler brow,
    Nor loftier seeming bear;
Dark hung the drenched tresses wild
    Around his sallow cheek;
Nor e'er did lady, whispering mild,
    With sweeter accent speak.

XVI.

"It was, it was some friendly pow'r
  That saw my coming doom,
And warned me of that fatal hour,
  Amid the stormy gloom:
When loud I heard the thunders roll
  Prophetic in mine ear,
And something shook my secret soul
  With sense of danger near!

XVII.

"Now quickly Mary's dext'rous hand
  The simple meal prepared;
And soon, by rapid apron fann'd,
  The ruddy hearth-stone glared;
Soon by its social, quick'ning light
  We talk'd, with bosoms free,
And Mary left the long, long night
  To ruin and to me.

XVIII.

"The sound of waters gushing sweet
  Upon a summer noon,
Of winds that stir the green retreat,
  Or harvest songs in June,
Were like the soul-ensnaring words
  That from the stranger fell,
But while they sounded heavenly
  They had the spleen of hell.

XIX.

He spoke of faded martial zeal
  Before the sun was set,
That blood-red hail'd the victor star
  Of old Plantagenet.

He talked of Erin's injured plains,
  Of England's galling yoke,
And a subtle fire within my veins
  Was kindling while he spoke.

XX.

"He marked my neat:—'And if thou hast
  A pulse for Ireland still—
If thou canst wind a merry blast
  Upon a moonlight hill—
If selfish hopes and craven fears
  Have left thy courage free,
And thou canst feel thy country's tears,
  Arise and follow me!'

XXI.

We left the cot—The storm had sunk
  Upon the midnight wild,
And, bright against each leafless trunk,
  The flitting moon-beam smil'd.
We hurried down by copse and rill,
  By cliff and mountain gorge,
Till, close by Shanid's lonesome hill,
  We reached the village forge.

XXII.

" Dark, silent, lone, the hovel seem'd,
  And cloak'd each tiny pane,
Yet oft from chinks a red ray stream'd
  Across the gloomy plain;
And smother'd voices heard within
  Came doubtful on the ear,
As when a merry festal din
  Is hush'd in sudden fear.

XXIII.

"The stranger paus'd—'Within are those
　The bravest of the land,
With heart to feel her countless woes,
　And ever ready hand.
If thou for home and manhood's right
　Can mock at danger too,
Come, pledge us at our board to-night,
　And join our gallant crew!'

XXIV.

"He knocked—'Who's there?' 'My voice alone
　May answer for my name.'
Quick, from the op'ning doorway shone
　A glow of ruddy flame—
The wicket closed—the anxious blood
　Forsook my pallid face,
When, like a wild bird snared, I stood
　Within that hideous place.

XXV.

"Around a board, whose dingy plano
　Was stained by long carouse,
Sat grim Rebellion's horrid train,
　With fierce suspicious brows.
Crouch'd by the hearth, a wrinkled hag
　The fading embers blew—
Old Vauria of the river crag—
　The Hebe of the crew.

XXVI.

"Here Starlight (name of terror!) quaff'd,
　Unmix'd, the liquid fire—
Here Blink-o'-dawn, with milder draught,
　Inflamed his easy ire;

And Lard-the-back, and Death's-head gaunt
  Their murderous vigil keep,
And many a name whose echoes haunt
  The village parson's sleep.

XXVII.

"Here Moonshine (name to outrage dear)
  Told how at even close
He cropp'd the 'nighted proctor's ear,
  And slit the gauger's nose;
And how some hand, at dusk or dawn,
  Had fired the bishop's hay,
And headless by the mountain bawn,
  The base informer lay.

XXVIII.

"'Hush! hush!—'tis he!' A silence came
  Upon that guilty band,
Like mastiffs roused with glance of flame,
  The stranger form they scann'd:
'Fear not,' the chieftain said; 'he bears
  A bosom like your own;
A heart to right the orphan's tears
  And soothe the widow's moan.

XXIX.

"'Well met, my friends! Oh, glorious night,
  It glads my heart to see
That you can feel poor Erin's slight,
  And strike for liberty!
Within this hour yon castle walls
  Shall blacken in the flame,
And havoc on those painted halls
  Shall burn her ghastly name.'

XXX.

"And now, beneath the gathering cloud
    That shadow'd vale and wood,
With hasty pace the rebel crowd
    Their secret track pursued;
They reach'd a hill with waving larch
    And mingled poplar crown'd,
Where, tow'ring o'er one ivied arch,
    An ancient castle frown'd.

XXXI.

"All dark! all silent! not a light
    Gleams from a window there·
Knew they the councils of the night
    Less sound their slumbers were.
'Tis time!—the torch! but where is he
    Who led the daring band?
Why darts he by that sheltering tree?
    Why waits the lighted brand?

XXXII.

"'Fly, comrades, fly!—see yonder flame
    That rises from the hill—
Fly!—heard ye not the wild acclaim
    That hail'd that whistle shrill?'
'Twas late! A hundred bayonets gleam'd
    Around them in the toil—
And many a heart's blood hotly streamed
    Upon that fatal soil.

XXXIII.

"What, snared! betray'd!—and there he stood,
    The traitor and the slave,
Who purchased with their reeking blood
    The life his judges gave.

Still red with gore, each streaming hilt
 Against the moonlight glows—
Oh! thus shall all who sow in guilt
 Reap treason at the close.

XXXIV.

"Oh, you who bless these dawning skies
 In yon receding vales,
Take warning from my parting sighs,
 And from those swelling sails!
To answer crime with crime is worse.
 Than tamely to endure;
And ev'n for black oppression's curse
 Dark treason is no cure.

XXXV.

"Farewell, farewell! ye distant hills
 With many a garden gay!
Ye waving groves and gushing rills
 That hail the rising day!
Ye hills of Clare, with vapours hoar,
 Ringmoylan's leafy dells;
And thou, oh, wild, sea-beaten shore,
 Where many a kinsman dwells!"

XXXVI.

He sung, while o'er the darkening stream
 Fresh came the wakening gale,
And, fading like a morning dream,
 I heard his parting wail:—
"Farewell, ye cots, that sweetly smile
 Along the peaceful shore!
Farewell, farewell, my own green isle!
 I ne'er shall see thee more."

The Danish Invasion.

I.
Why weepest thou, Erin? Why droop thy green bowers.
  Why flows all in purple the wave of Cullain?
Why sink thy young maidens like rain-laden flowers?
  Why hush'd are their songs on the desolate plain?
Ruin and sorrow are o'er them spread—
Revel, and freedom, and mirth are fled.

II.
Hath the demon of pestilent airs been out
  To taint the sweet breath of thy mountain gales?
To scatter his death-breathing vapours about,
  And wave his dark wings o'er thy blooming vales?
Like the wind that mourns in the winter bowers,
Blasting the fairest of health's young flowers.

III.
No; poison and pestilence have no share
  In the ruin that moulders our strength away—
Happy are those who breathe that air,
  And die at the sight of their hopes' decay.
But the ocean's breezes fan our skies—
The plague spirit tastes their breath and dies.

IV.
But a demon more deadly—the Norman has flown
  From his lonely hills*—so chilling and gray;
He has left his rude mountains of heath and stone,
  For the fairest that bloom in the light of day—
And Erin has dropp'd her shield and sword,
And wears the yoke of a heathen lord.

* Men of the hills: the ancient epithet given to the Danes.

V.

The blood of the royal—the blood of the brave—
   Are blent with the willows of dark Cullain—
Our king is a gay and a gilded slave—
   And ours are the ruins that blot the plain.
The Ravens of Denmark are seen on our walls,
And the shout of the spoiler is loud in our halls.

VI.

Weep on, then, lost island! thy honours have fled
   Like the light on a lake that is troubled and br
Thy Suake* hath hid his coward head—
   The words of thy grief and shame are spoken.
Thou hast not left one lingering light,
To bless with a promise thy cheerless night.

The Joy of Honour.

I.

The tears from these old eyelids crept,
   When Dermod left his mother-land—
And I was one of those who wept
   Upon his neck, and pressed his hand.
He did not grieve to leave us then,
He hop'd to see his home again—
With honours twined in his bright hair
He could not hope to gather there.

   * Harp and Snake—the national standard.

II.

Year after year rolled fleetly on,
   Lost in the grave of buried time,
And Dermod's name and praise had won
   Their way into his parent clime;
But all his youthful haunts were changed,
The wild woods perished where he ranged—
And all his friends died one by one,
Till the last of Dermod's name was gone.

III.

I sat one eve in Curra's glade,
   And saw an old man tottering down,
Where the first veil of evening's shade
   Had given the heath a deeper brown.
His cheek was pale—his long hair now
Fell in white flakes o'er his aged brow,
But the same young soul was in his eye,
And I knew the friend of my infancy.

IV.

He gazed upon the silent wood—
   He passed his hand across his brow;
The hush of utter solitude
   Slept on each breathless birchen bough.
"That lake with flowering islets strewed—
   That skirts the lawn and breaks yon wood—
I knew in youth a valley green,
The seat of many a merry scene.

V.

"The youths that graced the village dance,
   Beneath the turf they trod are sleeping—
The maidens in whose gentle glance
   Their spirits lived, are o'er them weeping—

Sorrow, and blight, and age have come,
Where mirth once reigned, and youth and bloom,
And the soft charms of Nature's prime
Are blasted by the breath of Time.

VI.

" And hath the joy that honour gives
    No power o'er memories like this ?
Ah ! witless is the man who lives
    To soar at fame and spurn at bliss !
That hath been mine—*this* might have been,
Had I but held the humble mean—
And passed upon my parent soil
A life of peace and quiet toil.

VII.

' And is it thus that *all* who gain
    The phantom glory of a name,
That, ere it grace their brow, the pain
    Of their long search hath quenched the flame
That young ambition lit—and those
Whose praise they sought are at repose—
And they stand in a world unknown—
Admired—revered—unloved—alone !

VIII.

" I want my early playmates back,
    My friends, long-lost, but ne'er forgot—
Are these old men who haunt my track
    My school-day friends ? I know them not
Alas ! I grieve and call in vain,
Their youth will never come again—
But it is sad my heart should feel
Its first affections youthful still "

Would you Choose a Friend?

I.

Would you choose a friend? Attend, attend
I'll teach you how to attain your end.
He on whose lean and bloodless cheek
The red grape leaves no laughing streak;
On whose dull white brow and clouded eye
Cold thought and care sit heavily;
   Him you must flee,
   'Tween you and me,
That man is very bad company.

II.

And he around whose jewelled nose
The blood of the red grape freely flows;
Whose pursy frame as he fronts the board
Shakes like a wine sack newly stored,
In whose half-shut, moist, and sparkling eye
The wine god revels cloudily,
   Him you must flee,
   'Tween you and me,
That man is very bad company.

III.

But he who takes his wine in measure,
Mingling wit and sense with pleasure,
Who likes good wine for the joy it brings,
And merrily laughs and gaily sings:
With heart and bumper always full,
Never maudlin, never dull,
   Your friend let him be,
   'Tween you and me,
That man is excellent company.

When some Unblest and Lightless Eye.

I.

When some unblest and lightless eye,
   With lid half droop'd, and moist, and meek,
Tells silent tales of misery,
   The trembling lip could never speak,
   What is it wets the listener's cheek,
What fills with love his answering voice,
   And bids the suffering heart not break,
And bids that trembling eye rejoice?
When the heart wavers in its choice,
   What is it prompts the generous part?
Oh! spring of all life's tender joys!
   Oh, sun of youth! 'tis heart! 'tis heart!

II.

When the advancing march of time,
   With cheering breath, has roll'd away
The mists that dull'd her morning prime,
   And beauty steps into her day;
   What gives those eyes that conquering play
That aching bosoms long confess?
   And lights those charms with quickening ray
That else had charmed and conquered less;
A sweet light unto loveliness,
   A meaning breathing o'er the whole,
That else might charm, but could not bless,
   Win, but not fix? 'Tis soul! 'tis soul!

III.

When youth and youthful friends are gone,
   When disappointment glooms the brow,
And early loves leave us alone,
   To walk in friendless sorrow now.

And chill'd is young rapture's glow,
And hoary grown the raven hair,
  And age its paly tinge of woe
Hangs over all youth fancied-fair,
What guards our home from chill despair?
  And bids joy linger, loth to part?
Oh, balm of grief and pining care!
  Oh, stay of age! 'tis heart! 'tis heart!

IV.

When beauty feels the touch of years,
  When the round voice grows faint and small,
And that bright eye is dimmed by tears,
  That once held many a heart in thrall,
What makes that voice still musical?
That sunken eye still seeming bright?
  And beauty, even in beauty's fall,
As full of witching life and light,
As when the hue of young delight
  Over its blushing spring-time stole?
Oh, star of love's approaching night!
  Oh, shield of faith! 'tis soul! 'tis soul!

V.

Seldom they shine in worlds like this,
  Seldom their favouring light we see,
For passion taints earth's purest bliss
  With spots of dark mortality;
  But once a sweet dream came to me,
A vision of a glorious land,
  Where sounds of gentle revelry
Rose on the soft air, making bland
And rapturous music to a band
  Of nymphs that o'er the green path stole,
Where beauty and youth walked hand in hand,
  Lock'd in love's faith with Heart and Soul.

The Song of the Old Mendicant.

I.

A man of threescore, with the snow on his brow,
   And the light of his aged eye dim,
Oh, valley of sorrow! what lure hast thou now,
   In thy changes of promise for him?
Gay Nature may smile, but his sight has grown old—
   Joy sound, but his hearing is dull;
And pleasure may feign, but his bosom is cold,
   And the cup of his weariness full.

II.

Once warm with the pulses of young twenty-three,
   With plenty and ease in thy train,
Thy fair visions wore an enchantment for me
   That never can gild them again.
For changed are my fortunes, and early and late
   From dwelling to dwelling I go:
And I knock with my staff at our first mother's gate,
   And I ask for a lodging below.*

III.

Farewell to thee, Time! in thy passage with me,
   One truth thou hast taught me to know,
Though lovely the past and the future may be,
   The present is little but woe;
For the sum of those joys that we find in life's way,
   Where thy silent wing still wafts us on,
Is a hope for to-morrow—a want for to-day,
   And a sigh for the times that are gone.

* This beautiful sentiment occurs in Chaucer.

Mary-le-Bone Lyrics.

MR. GRAHAM TO MISS DAWSON IN THE CLOUDS.

Mr Graham now handed Miss Dawson into the car, and, in a few minutes, the aëronaut and his accomplished and beautiful fellow-voyager were lost to the gaze of the admiring multitude.
KENDAL PAPER.

Here we go up, up, up,
  And now we go down, down, down—
Now we go backward and forward,
  And heigh for London town!
DEAN SWIFT.

I.

Who says the moon is made of cheese?
  The sky a sheet of paper?
The little stars so many peas—
  The sun a mere gas* taper?
That all the clouds are chimney smoke
  The sun's attraction draws on?
'Tis clear as noon, 'tis all a joke
  To you and me, Miss Dawson.

II.

The secrets of the sky are ours—
  The heaven is opening o'er us—
The region of the thunder-showers
  Is spreading wide before us.

---

* It will be recollected that this was actually asserted, a short time since by a celebrated professional gentleman.

How pleasant, from this fleecy cloud,
　To look on ancient places,
And peer upon the pigmy crowd
　Of upturn'd gaping faces!

III.

Oh! what a place were this for love!
　Nay, never start, I pray;
Suppose our hearts could jointly move,
　And in a lawful way.
Like Ixion I should scorn the crowds
　Of earthly beauties to know,
And love a lady in the clouds—
　And you should be my Juno.

IV.

Speed higher yet—throw out more sand—
　We're not the last who'll rise,
By scattering, with lavish hand,
　Dust in our neighbours' eyes.
Away! away! the clouds divide—
　Hish! what a freezing here!—
And now we thread the mist-hill side,
　And now the heavens appear.

V.

"How blest!" (so Tommy Moore might sing
　"Did worldly love not blind us,
Could we to yon bright cloud but wing,
　And leave this earth behind us:
There feed on sunshine—safe from woe—
　We'd live and love together!"
Ah, you and I, Miss Dawson know,
　'Tis very foggy weather

VI.

Suppose some future act made void
  And lawless Gretna marriages,
The snuff-man joiner's trade destroy'd,
  And nullified post carriages:
What think you if a Gretna here,
  With post-balloons were given?
Such marriages (we all could swear)
  At least were made in heaven.

VII.

How small, Miss Dawson, from the sky
  Appears that man below—
The Triton of the *nabbing* fry,
  The sadler-king of Bow!
A fig for Dogberry, say we!
  For leathern bench and "watches!"
A fig for law! I'd like to see
  What Bishop's here could catch us?

VIII.

Suppose we smash the stars for fun?
  Have with the larks a *lark?*
Or hang a cloak upon the sun,
  And leave the world all dark?
Or upwards still pursue our flight,
  Leave that dull world at rest,
And into Eden peep—and fright
  The banquet of the blest?

IX.

Whiz! whiz! the fatal word is spoken,
  The sprites are round our car—
Our gas is spent—our pinion broke,
  And, like a shooting star,

Down, down we glide—the clouds divide;
  They close above our head—
Now, safe and sound, we touch the ground,
  And now——we go to bed.

Mary-le-Bone Lyrics.

TO CLAUDE SEURAT* ON LEAVING LONDON.

Prithee—see there! behold! look! lo! how say you?
If charnel houses and our graves must send
Those that they bury back—our monuments
Shall be the maws of kites.
                              MACBETH.

I.

Gaunt symbol of the doom
  All mortals must inherit,
Finger-post of the tomb—
  Half corse—half shade—half spirit!
Walking burlesque on man!
  Still warmer! living knell;
Dangler in life's last span,
  All hail! and fare ye well!

II.

If, as the Spaniard† says,
  At mankind's day of doom—
When starting through the blaze
  Of crackling worlds they come—

---

* A man so wasted that he was exhibited as a living skeleton.
† Queredo—visions.

Each spirit to its frame;
   All wrangling for the fairest;
What ghost, O Claude! will claim
   That wither'd trunk *thou wearest*.

III.

Say wilt thou then arise,
   A skeleton as now—
Soaring the peaceful skies
   With that pale, ghastly brow?
Oh, ere thou wanderest there,
   Just step to Curtis' shrine
He's flesh enough to spare,
   For forty shanks like thine.

IV.

I've marked that wasted trunk—
   Those fleshless bones—and thought,
While my sick spirit shrunk,
   "Is this our common lot?"
Shall the ripe cheeks—bright curls—
   And eyes that round me shine—
Must " golden boys and girls"
   To this at last " consign?"

V.

Shall Garcia cease to charm?
   Shall Chester pine and dwindle?
A drumstick Pasta's arm?
   And Vestris' leg a spindle?
Shall love's light dimple grow,
   Into a hideous wrinkle?
Burn's cheek no longer glow?
   And Foote's eye cease to twinkle?

VI.

Away—the sight that heaven
　For passing pleasures gave,
Was ne'er to mortals given
　To peer beyond the grave.
What beauty *is*—we all
　Can feel—what it *will* be
A grim memorial;
　We find, Seurat, in thee!

VII.

Thy bones are marrowless!
　Thy blood is cold! thine air,
Like his whose gory tress
　Shook blood on Macbeth's chair:
Yet no! for who'll deny—
　When first thou sought'st our nation—
Thou hads't got in that eye
　Of thine, "*some speculation?*"

VIII.

Art thou the wretch of old,
　By mammon pined to death?
Or him, the shipman bold,
　We read of it in Macbeth?
By the weird hag consumed,
　The slayer of the swine—
For thy wife's chesnuts doom'd
　To dwindle, peak, and pine!

IX.

Whate'er thou art, O Claude!
　When thou—though made of bone—
Hast ta'en at last the road,
　All flesh goes—and has gone—

The worm, who gluts his maw,
  On wreck'd humanity,
Will make, O Claude Seurat,
  A meager meal on thee!

The Prayer of Dulness.

I.

When dulness, friend of peers and kings—
  Sworn enemy (alas!) to *me*—
Last shook her flagging, dingy wings
  O'er the first island of the sea,
She fixed on London as a place
  Where she might find some friends—or so;
And travelling up at mud-cart pace,
  She hired a cellar in Soho.

II.

But sad reverse, since her last visit
  A novel rage had seized the nation;
"Sure!" the goddess cried, "how is it?
  Genius, my foe, grown into fashion."
In vain she railed; her ancient friends,
  The booksellers, had burst her trammels,
And in the new league found their ends,
  And left her for the Moores and Campbells.

III.

An unknown lawyer in the north
  Shook her Minerva press to splinters
Her favourite children sunk to earth,
  And hateful light profaned her winters.

If she took up a rhyme—'twas Byron's;
   If to the stage she turned her sight
Kean scared her from its loved environs,
   And Fanny Kelly kill'd her quite.

IV.

Despairing thus—despised, decried—
   Dulness put up her ardent prayer:—
"Grant me, O mighty Jove," she sighed,
   "Some ally in my hour of care;
Look on my votaries' sunken jaws,
   My ragged file of thin Lampedos;
Have mercy on their yearning craws:
   Send some bad taste on earth to feed us."

V.

Her prayer was heard—the rafters o'er her
   Sunder'd—and through the fissure came
A pale, white form; he stood before her,
   Lanky and gawky in his frame.
Over one bony shoulder hung
   A pot of coarse paint, with a brush in't;
His front was like white parchment strung;
   The devil couldn't have raised a blush in't.

VI.

A brazen trumpet hung beside him,
   On which he blew a thrilling blast;
With doubt and hope the goddess eyed him;
   "Fat Madam," he exclaimed at last,
"I am your servant—sent by Jove
   To bid you never be cast down—
By me your reign shall prosperous prove,
   By me you yet shall sway the town.

VII.

"My name is puff—the guardian sprite
   And patron of the dull and shameless;
Things born in shades I bring to light,
   And give a high fame to the nameless.
Me modest merit shuns to meet,
   His timid footsteps backward tracking;
The worthless all my influence greet,
   From ——'s books to Turner's blacking.

VIII.

"Receive me, goddess, in thy train,
   And thou shalt see a change ere long;
The stage shall be thine own again,
   Thine all the sons of prose and song.
———— shall delight the wenches,
   Where Richard shook the tragic scene once;
Fat Chester shall draw crowded benches,
   And Fanny Kelly play to thin ones."

IX.

The prophecy was registered,
   The prophecy has been fulfill'd;
The brazen trumpet's boast is heard
   Where once the voice of genius thrilled.
Reader, before your hopes are undone,
   This axiom you will bear in mind,
That puffing has been proved in London
   The only way to raise the wind.

Matt Hyland.*

PART I.

Thou rushing spirit, that oft of old
   Hast thrilled my veins at evening lonely,
When musing by some ivied hold,
   Where dwell the daw and marten only.
That oft has stirred my rising hair,
   When midnight on the heath has found me,
And told me potent things of air
   Were haunting all the waste around me.

Who sweep'st upon the inland breeze,
   By rock and glen in autumn weather,
With fragrance of wild myrtle trees,
   And yellow furze and mountain heather.
Who seaward on the scented gale,
   To meet the Exile coursest fleetly,
When slowly from the ocean vale
   His native land arises sweetly.

---

* This tale is an amplification of a rude, popular ballad on the same subject, called "Young Matt Hyland." The story is little altered, and is obviously made use of, as a medium for the expression of many beautiful poetical reflections, rather than for any interest it contains. The Author himself was so little satisfied with the poem, that he burned the manuscript along with many others, a day or two before he retired to a convent. Fragments of an original copy were, however, found among some untouched papers, and the restoration of the poem to its present state was afterwards, in a great degree, accomplished from the recollections of a very attached friend, who was familiar with it, and to whose fine taste and judgment the Author, had he been living, would most willingly have committed it.

That oft hast thrilled with creeping fear
   My shuddering nerves at ghostly story.
Or sweetly drew the pittying tear,
   At thought of Erin's ruined glory.
A fire that burns—a frost that chills,
   As turns the song to woe or gladness,
Now couched by wisdom's fountain rills,
   And skirting now the wilds of madness.

Oh, spirit of my island home!
   Oh, spirit of my native mountain!
Romantic fancy quickly come,
   Unseal for me thy sparkling fountain.
If e'er by lone Killarney's wave,
   Or wild Glengariff's evening billow,
My opening soul a welcome gave
   To thee beneath the rustling billow.

Or rather who, in riper days,
   In ruined aisles at solemn even,
My thoughtful bosom wont to raise,
   To themes of purity and heaven,
And people all the silent shades,
   With saintly forms of days departed,
When holy men and votive maids
   Lived humbly there and heavenly-hearted.

Oh thou, the minstrel's bliss and bane,
   His fellest foe and highest treasure,
That keep'st him from the heedless train,
   Apart in grief—apart in pleasure.
That, chainless as the wandering wind,
   Where'er thou wilt unbidden blowest.
And o'er the unexpectant mind,
   All freely com'st and freely goest.

Come, breathe along my trembling chords,
　　And mingle in the rising measure,
Those burning thoughts and tinted words
　　That pierce the inmost soul with pleasure.
Possess my tongue—possess my brain,
　　Through every nerve electric thrilling,
That I may pour my ardent strain,
　　With tuneful force and fervent feeling.

Among the groves of sweet Adare,
　　There lived a lord in days departed,
And Helen was his daughter fair,
　　The blooming and the gentle hearted.
How loved she was in all the vale
　　The village maids can still remember,
When round the fire, with many a tale
　　They cheer the eves of bleak November.

A ruin now the castle shows,
　　The ivy clothes its mouldering towers,
The wild rose on the hearthstone blows,
　　And roofless stands its secret bowers.
Close by its long abandoned hall,
　　The narrow tide is idly straying,
While ruin saps its tottering wall,
　　Like those who held it, fast decaying.

Peaceful it stands, the mighty pile,
　　By many a heart's blood once defended,
Yet silent now as cloistered aisle,
　　Where rung the sounds of banquet splendid.
Age holds his undivided state,
　　Where youth and beauty once were cherished,
And loverets pass the wardless gate,
　　Where heroes once essayed and perished.

Oh, sweet Adare! oh, lovely vale!
   Oh, soft retreat of sylvan splendour.
Nor summer sun, nor morning gale
   E'er hailed a scene more softly tender
How shall I tell the thousand charms,
   Within thy verdant bosom dwelling,
When lulled in Nature's fostering arms,
   Soft peace abides and joy excelling?

Ye morning airs, how sweet at dawn
   The slumbering boughs your song awaken:
Or, lingering o'er the silent lawn,
   With odour of the harebell taken.
Thou rising sun, how richly gleams
   Thy smile from far Knockfierna's mountain
O'er waving woods and bounding streams,
   And many a grove and glancing fountain,

Ye clouds of noon, how freshly there,
   When summer heats the open meadows,
O'er parchèd hill and valley fair,
   All coolly lie your veiling shadows.
Ye rolling shades and vapours gray,
   Slow creeping o'er the golden heaven,
How soft ye seal the eye of day,
   And wreathe the dusky brow of even.

Apart among her maidens sate
   Fair Helen, formed with grace excelling
Though first in wealth and princely state,
   The humblest heart in all the dwelling.
If ever truthful maiden's breast,
   For virtue burned with warm affection,
In Helen's heart, that influence blest,
   Had made its fixed and pure election

Not as by modern maids profaned,
  The cross adorned her vesture only,
But, deep within her heart it reigned,
  With hidden influence ruling lonely;
While that clear brow and tranquil eye,
  And plain unbraided locks of amber,
Told tales of meek humility,
  And vigils of the midnight chamber.

Endued with all the power to please,
  With wealth at will and amplest leisure,
The boor took more of sensual ease,
  The outcast slave of sensual pleasure.
Perchance even he, whose sword and shield,
  Rang loud on plain or moated tower,
Lived easier in the bannered field,
  Than Helen in her father's bower.

Oh, ye to sure destruction doomed,
  Whirled in the vortex gulf of fashion,
more unblest, who lie entombed,
  Within the living graves of passion.
Say, could it wake your slumbering fears,
  Had you beheld that tender maiden,
More deeply mourn her blameless years,
  Than hearts with blackest memories laden?

Ne'er through self-love with inmost shame,
  A weak excuse she seeks to borrow,
Nor e'er with superstitious flame,
  She played the enthusiast's part in sorrow.
But clear her speech as gliding stream,
  Each pebble in its depth revealing,
While in her soft eyes' tender gleam,
  Lay taintless truth, and childish feeling.

Some surely deemed the duteous girl
    Would soon, within some convent tower
Resign for truth's immortal pearl
    The pomp of rank and earthly power.
And, doubtless, had high heaven assigned,
    As Helen's lot such high vocation,
She then had lived, with cheerful mind,
    Obedient in an altered station.

But Heaven decreed the maiden's life
    Should pass with constant heart, unswerving,
Amid the cares of vulgar strife,
    Her purity of soul preserving.
'Mid wealth and splendour—poor in will,
    Though high in rank—in spirit lowly;
Amid the world unworldly still—
    Amid the unbelieving—holy.

Not hers the venomed tongue that feels
    Small joy in social conversation,
Save when its spite destruction deals
    On some unhappy reputation.
Not hers the doomed minds unblest,
    To mirth devote and senseless laughter,
Who waste the hours in sinful rest,
    And leave to chance—the dread hereafter.

Each eve the parting day reviewed,
    With lowly penitential feeling;
Each morn the maiden's zeal renewed,
    Fresh grace within her heart instilling
Each Sabbath eve when twilight falls,
    Its lingering light around diffusing,
Within the still, dim cloistered walls,
    O'erawed, she knelt, herself accusing.

Yet, not to outward sense exposed,
  Young Helen wore her heart's devotion,
In tone or studied mien disclosed,
  In serious or affected motion;
For, joy in all her glances shone,
  Gay rang her laugh, like music flowing,
The conscious power of duty done,
  In all her bright demeanour glowing.

And fervent heart she has to feel
  Fair Virtue's warmth, when time shall light it,
And changeless truth and fearless zeal,
  And hope that scents the winds that blight it.
For love was Helen's hourly theme,
  And some undying deep devotion,
The promise of her nightly dream,
  And spirit of her daily motion.

Not love like that whose selfish aim,
  From earthly bliss to bliss is ranging,
But such as burns with generous flame,
  In hearts devoted and unchanging,
That constant wife, and patient bride,
  Hath oft embalmed in deathless story—
The love for which the Decii died,
  And mild Camillus lives in glory.

Firmly, the pious maid designed
  That none should share her heart's affection,
Save one whose pure and stainless mind
  Might vindicate such high election.
Nor rank, nor fame, nor deeds of arms,
  Should win her mind to love unheeding—
Nor genius high, nor youthful charms,
  Of voice, or mien, or grace exceeding.

No, he should gain her hand alone,
   Whate'er his claim to wealth or station,
Whose heart had treasured like her own,
   For heaven, its warmest aspiration.
For, well she thought a rustic hind,
   To love divine, aspiring tender,
Far nobler in the heart and mind,
   Than kings who live for earthly splendour.

And who, at sober dusk had seen
   This nobly-born and beauteous maiden,
Arrayed in garb of ocean green,
   With gems of purest lustre laden.
Or lovelier still upon the lawn,
   Where morn's awakening light had found her,
Would marvel that her love had drawn
   The first of Erin's sons around her.

Full oft the Earl his daughter pressed,
   That soon in holy bonds united,
His aged years might yet be blessed,
   To hear her children's voice delighted;
Lest, buried in his own dark tomb,
   His household, name, and ancient glory,
Like lamps unfed, should quench in gloom,
   Lost ever to the eye of story.

But Helen, with evasive wile,
   Unanswered, left the fond suggestion,
With playful jest or ready smile,
   Avoiding still th' unwelcome question.
For who among the nobles there,
   Within her father's hall acquainted,
Could reach the ideal standard rare,
   Her own believing hope had painted.

For when the music merriest played,
   When dancers trod the blithest measure,
Her thoughts in calm reflection strayed,
   Far distant from these scenes of pleasure.
Where many a soul was mourning now,
   That e'er it shared such haunts of danger—
Where many a worn and fevered brow,
   Slow pining lay, to peace a stranger.

Such thoughts, in still succession brought,
   Like amulets of holiest power,
Sweet safety in her bosom wrought,
   E'en in enjoyments echoing bower.
Thus holy themes of peace and rest,
   Even in her buoyant mirth were reigning,
The hermitage within her breast,
   Inviolate still, and pure remaining.

* * * *

* * * *

Where glides the Mague as silver clear,
   Among the elms so sweetly flowing,
There fragrant in the early year,
   Wild roses on the banks are blowing,
There, wild ducks sport on rapid wing,
   Beneath the alder's leafy awning,
And sweetly there the small birds sing,
   When daylight on the hill is dawning.

There mirrored in the shallow tide,
  Around his trunks so coolly laving,
High towers the grove in vernal pride,
  His solemn boughs majestic waving.
And there beside the parting flood,
  That murmured round a lonely island,
Within the sheltering woodland stood,
  The humble roof of poor Matt Hyland.

Though now, amongst the village swains,
  Young Hyland tilled the lands surrounding.
All regal in his youthful veins,
  The blood of Erin's king's was bounding.
Yet lowly were his heart and mien,
  Nor pride he knew, nor nursed ambition,
Content, upon an humble scene,
  That Heaven had cast his low condition.

To keep his mind from sinful stain,
  In humble hope serene and lowly,
To guard his breast from fancies vain,
  That stir the heart to thoughts unholy.
For this he shunned the thoughtless crowd,
  The village dance and nightly revel,
With frequent laughter echoing loud,
  And strains that smooth the way to evil.

For this, before the early lark,
  His prayers arose, to heaven ascending.
For this he knelt at twilight dark,
  Within his lowly cottage bending;
For this, amid his daily toil,
  He poured his warmest aspirations,
And kept his heart from sinful soil,
  With force of holy meditations.

When, sounded in the silent air,
    The convent bell with tuneful motion,
He turned with thoughtful forehead bare,
    And stilly bent in low devotion.
Like miser, heaping gold on gold,
    He stored his mind with holiest treasure,
For, strong, he knew, must be the hold
    That guards the soul from guilty pleasure.

He heard in youth the wondrous tale,
    How man was first created purely,
Awhile to walk earth's flowering vale,
    Then rest in lasting joy, securely.
He learned by what accursed art
    His race had lost that high vocation,
And found within his opening heart,
    The witness of the revelation.

Each evil wish that turned his thoughts
    From thirst of pure and heavenly glory,
Unholy attestation brought
    Of that sublime and awful story.
The strife with passion—dark, intense—
    The erring will that still betrayed him;
And plain it seemed unto his sense
    That man was not as heaven had made him.

Yet strong he walked, with guarded mind,
    A thing of pure unearthly feeling;
With reverend eye the village hind
    Beheld him in the chancel kneeling;
And grateful blessed high heaven above
    To see that youth, with mind believing,
The sacred feast of fire and love,
    With seraph heart on fire, receiving.

Though scant was Hyland's humble store,
　　Yet never wandering child of sorrow
At evening sought his open door
　　In vain to ask, in vain to borrow.
The orphan's sigh, the widow's prayer,
　　To him appealed with mightier power,
And found a kindlier welcome there
　　Than oft within the lordly tower.

And Hyland had his raptures, too,
　　When darkly sunk the silent even,
And lone beneath the solemn yew
　　He lent his soul to dreams of heaven.
Till all the glorious concave seemed
　　That clime revealed in saintly story,
And every winking star that gleamed,
　　An angel shining in its glory.

Nor frown, ye grave, at thoughts like this,
　　That lend to virtue lovelier beauty,
And sweet imagined sights of bliss,
　　That cheer the toils of sterner duty.
For holiest hearts with earthly things
　　Have blended themes of deep devotion,
Heard seraphs in the minstrel's strings,
　　And seen eternity in ocean.

One evening, wrapt in thoughts like these,
　　With tears of heavenly sweetness flowing,
He stood beneath the moonlit trees,
　　His fervent heart divinely glowing.
"Thou power," he said "whose kindly hand
　　Has fashioned all this fair creation,
Oh! aid me still, secure to stand
　　Amid the snares of dark temptation.

" Still sweetly fill my yielding breast,
  With boundless hope and love unmeasured—
Still lift my soul to thoughts of rest,
  And lasting joys securely treasured.
Oh! not for all the senseless glee
  Of worldly souls would I surrender,
The joy my lonely thoughts of thee,
  Wake in my bosom purely tender.

" I see thee in the winter's snow,
  The echoing bolt and roaring thunder,
And waves that foam, and fires that glow,
  And sounds of awe, and sights of wonder.
I hear thee in the rustling woods,
  When darkness rests on grove and fountain;
I see thee in the rushing floods,
  I read thee in the lonely mountain.

" From household love—from friendship's tie—
  Though sweet the transient bliss we borrow,
Soon, soon the frail enchantments fly,
  And leave us wrapp'd in lonely sorrow.
For thee alone our love was made,
  In thee alone it centres purely;
There lives in light that ne'er can fade—
  There rests its tired wings securely.

" Whate'er of sanctioned rapture chaste,
  Whate'er of blameless pure emotion,
Thou will'st my heart in life should taste,
  Be thou its first and last devotion!
Like birds that seek a distant home,
  O'er ocean's waste and wide dominion,
And only touch the heaving foam,
  To rise again with stronger pinion.

"Oh thou! the wretch's surest friend,
  First source of blessing and of beauty,
Be still my being's aim and end,
  Chief mark of worship and of duty.
Like sailors on a stormy sea,
  Like wandering exiles homeward hasting,
So turn my constant thoughts to thee,
  Oh, unbeginning, everlasting!

"Yes, since to thee, alone our sighs,
  Arise with certain hope ascending,
Still keep my heart from guilty ties,
  And wandering loves and quickly ending.
Still turn my spirit's eagle gaze,
  From joys like marsh lights widely straying,
To that unchanging crown of rays—
  The boundless and the undecaying.

"Here lone within this sacred grove
  Beside those banks and listening river,
To thee I pledge my youthful love,
  My loyalty and faith for ever.
Whate'er of earthly bliss be mine,
  Of joy fulfilled or blest affection,
Let heavenly hope and love divine,
  Be still my spirit's first election!"

Dark hovering in the midnight air,
  A demon heard the prayer ascending,
And saw beneath the moonlight there,
  The fervent youth devoutly bending.
Grimly he smiled to hear that word,
  With deep confiding ardour spoken,
From feeble man so often heard,
  By faithless man so often broken.

Like ocean bird that downward views
    His prey within the summer billow,
The fiend with baleful wing pursues,
    Young Hyland to his nightly pillow.
With many a wile he haunts the cot,
    And deep suggestion darkly tainted,
And now he seems a sinful thought,
    Or sight-alluring fancy painted.

But firmly stood the holy youth,
    By many a guardian bright attended,
Unshrinking zeal and spotless truth,
    In holy rapture calmly blended.
Each sacramental rite of love,
    With reverent heed devout to render,
He felt his prayer received above,
    Far dearer than whole mines of splendor.

Nor when by ills like these oppressed,
    Turned he his mind to daring question,
Nor fed within his simple heart,
    The demon tempter's dark suggestion.
But placed on God his trust aright,
    Without whose wise according power,
Not e'en the tempest's fiercest might,
    Can rend a leaf from slend'rest flower.

PART II.

Oh, fatal power of human love,
    The swift-enthralling—swifter cloying,
For earth below and heaven above,
    The all-confounding—all destroying.

With visions wild it cheats the brain,
   And steals its peace and leaves it lonely;
It whispers hope that must be vain,
   And joys in hearts ill sorted only.

Alas! within the youthful breast,
   When holy thoughts arise sincerest,
And when the heart is most at rest,
   Temptation oft is lurking nearest.
Confiding high in purpose pure,
   To fear and guilt alike a stranger,
It steps within the fatal lure
   And falls, before it sees the danger.

'Tis vain to say, in youthful ears,
   Time flies—earth fades with all its pleasures—
The ardent heart attentive hears,
   But nought of transient counsel treasures.
'Tis heavenly grace—pure, undefiled,
   The voice of prayer ascending duly,
Can firmly stem the tumult wild,
   Of earthly passion rising newly.

Upon a day—a summer's day,
   When calmly broke the dewy morning,
Young Helen sought the woodland gay,
   With rosy buds her brows adorning;
And joyous as the early bird,
   She sung along the green wood bounding,
And rock and cliff the soft notes heard,
   And answered from the hill surrounding.

Her golden hair the rising breeze
   Around her laughing face was blowing,
While gliding fleet beneath the trees,
   She seemed a star, through thin clouds going

What eye that saw her tripping light
  Along each laurel-shaded alley,
But must have deemed a form so bright,
  Some fairy of the leafy valley.

Hark, far within the silent wood,
  What sounds are those that softly linger?
Beneath the stream fair Helen stood,
  With lips apart and listening finger.
They ceased——she leaves the sunny spot
  Through brake and covert swiftly hieing,
Till stretched beside his lonely cot
  She saw the youthful minstrel lying

Fly, Helen! fly that fatal sight!
  Oh, hast thou seen the rose-bud fading,
When sudden breathes the eastern blight,
  Its tender bloom with death invading;
Or wounded bird that turns to pine,
  And die in some sequestered bower?
More woe awaits that heart of thine
  Than wounded bird or blighted flower.

Black flowed his hair as moonless night,
  His eyes like midnight stars unclouded.
Of many hues the vesture bright,
  His peaceful form that lightly shrouded.
And Genius on his youthful face,
  And o'er his ample forehead stealing,
With strong expression's thoughtful grace,
  Habitual, noble thoughts revealing.

Deep hid within that tangled screen,
  The lady saw him lone reclining,
While reason's light was faint within,
  found fancy's only round her shining.

Oh, woe! that e'er a heart so light
    Should feel the gloom of early sadness—
That cankering sorrow e'er should blight
    The healthful glow of blameless gladness!

*   *   *   *

*   *   *   *

One of the lesser sprites, who keep
    Amongst the blest their radiant station,
Saw from the far empyrean steep
    The subtle tempter's sly temptation.
And upward sought in higher air,
    Bright hovering o'er the sunny water,
That angel whose protecting care
    Kept watch around the chieftain's daughter.

"Terrible brightness!" thus it said,
    "See'st thou yon fiend with wings extended,
Malign, above that simple maid,
    Dark, lowering in the moonbeam splendid?
Hast thou thy tender charge resigned;
    Dost thou no more her safety cherish,
That thus, with heedless impulse blind,
    Thou leav'st her in the snare to perish?"

Smiling, the essence pure replied,
    "Peace with thee be, blest one!—thee only—
Who tempt their fate in curious pride,
    On their own strength presuming lonely;
Or strongly tried, who fail to use
    With vigorous will their free endeavour,
Shall in the internal conflict lose
    The banner of their hope for ever.

"The dead who weaves that web malign,
　　Sees not, with finite vision bounded,
He doth but aid the high design,
　　In deep unerring wisdom founded.
Thus oft, the accursed slaves of ill
　　Are instruments of good, unknowing,
And hate, with undesigning will,
　　Can set the founts of mercy flowing."

* * * *

* * * *

"Is this the youth," fair Helen said,
　　"Of whom my maidens have been telling—
A holy life who long has led,
　　Devout, within this humble dwelling?
Oh! if a pure and lofty mind,
　　And generous thoughts, and high endeavour
Be in such noble form enshrined,
　　I'd listen to his song for ever.

"But how comes he a village swain,
　　A youth from noble race descended,
Whose sires, in Desmond's knightly train,
　　In field and banquet hall attended;
When far in Shanid's western keep,
　　The Desmond trod his leaguered towers,
And saw around the guarded steep
　　The Butler led his battled powers?

"There is a pride in lofty birth,
　　But honour is the meed of merit,
And nobler is the living worth
　　Than aught which thriftless heirs inherit.
The gem may deck the lordly vest,
　　With wrought adornments richly twining,
But brighter in the lowly breast,
　　The lamp of goodness purely shining.

"Fain would I leave the crowded halls,
　　Where pride meets pride in fierce emotion,
And place me where the sunlight falls
　　On sweet content and meek devotion;
There let me find the only joys
　　That leave no griefs to those who share them,
And give, oh, give these golden toys
　　To any maid that cares to wear them."

Hush! silent be the breezy plain;
　　Hush! silent be the small birds singing.
He wakes again, that rustic strain,
　　His gentle cruit* sweetly stringing.
He sung of Erin's golden day,
　　Ere native faith and trust were shaken,
And pleasant was his simple lay,
　　As when the morning winds awaken.

And then, with bosom beating strong,
　　And upraised eyes and pale lips quivering,
He sadly changed his tuneful tongue
　　To notes like sounds of soft leaves shivering:
So sweet his strains that violets there,
　　Awakening from their odorous slumbers,
Looked up into the stilly air,
　　To catch the spirit of his numbers.

* A small harp.

He sung of Love serene and high,
　　Though o'er an earthly bosom swaying
That love that bids all tumult die,
　　The silent and the undecaying.
How, in a peasant's humble breast,
　　Confined to toil and labour lowly,
That noiseless passion deep did rest,
　　The mute, the stainless, and the holy.

How oft, at hoary-vestured morn,
　　Or in the hour of fragrant even,
The bright mien of the nobly born
　　Mingled amid his dreams of heaven.
And how, when in the whispering woods,
　　At Sabbath noon he wandered lonely:
The brightest leaves and stateliest buds
　　Were types of her, and of her only;

And how, upon the fruitful plain,
　　Low bending o'er the sweeping sickle,
He started when the golden grain
　　Shook, rustling in the breezes fickle.
Hoping in vain 'twas her loved step,
　　Her silken scarf the winds caressing,
Or murmer of her balmy breath,
　　That poured upon his toil a blessing.

Fondly forgetting that in vain
　　The spirit spells of love were spoken;
For maiden high, to lowly swain,
　　Ne'er bent e'en though a heart were broken.
What though he came of noble birth,
　　Of high-born race long famed in story?
His lot was now to till the earth—
　　Forgotten all that ancient glory

"Alas!" he said, while frequent sighs
  Rose from his young heart's depths of feeling,
And sad tears dimmed his gentle eyes,
  His strong emotion all revealing.
"Alas!" he said, "it must be so ;
  The high-born may not leave their station,
Though lowlier hearts be rent with woe,
  And worn with helpless adoration.

"Yes, it must ever, ever be
  In this frail world of abject mortals ;
The iron hand of poverty
  Closeth for aye the golden portals!
But Thou—great watcher of the mind—
  Though sad and dark thoughts there are swelling,
Bid it in meekness be resigned,
  Through sorrow's dim and clouded dwelling."

Like winds that fall on perfumed flowers,
  Wearied of wandering o'er the meadows,
So died the lay, and those green bowers
  Were left in silence to their shadows.
Fair Helen stood with beating heart,
  And spirit wakening from its slumbers,
While through her soul strange passions dart,
  Respondent to the breathing numbers.

Within her heart a hidden sense
  Told her that his was that affection—
The high, the holy, the intense—
  And she was that pure heart's election.
Tears, burning tears of joy and pain,
  Upon her cheek were wildly gleaming,
He rose—her spirit woke again,
  And swift dispelled its wayward dreaming.

She looked along the sunny vale,
  She heard the joyous lark ascending,
She felt the soft persuasive gale,
  She heard the stream its murmur blending:
She marked the cot—the smiling tide,
  She gazed upon the lonely island,
She trembling turned, and wept aside,
  For, oh! she loved the young Matt Hyland.

Like one beside a fountain clear,
  His fever thirst impatient slaking,
She stands with fixed eye and ear,
  At every sense the rapture taking.
He stirs—O pleasure!—quickly o'er,
  Ah! dream of bliss how briefly ended!
She sees him pass that cottage door,
  And gloom upon the scene descended.

With drooping head and downcast eyes,
  And hands entwined in thoughtful seeming,
Young Helen through the greenwood hies,
  No more with infant rapture beaming:
Unlike, alas! the laughing child
  That left those halls at dawning early,
With sportive action bounding wild,
  And voice that woke the echoes cheerly.

A dew-drop from the daisy brushed,
  A happy fancy dashed with sorrow,
A woodland song untimely hushed,
  A sunny eve and clouded morrow:
A gilded barge that sinks at sea,
  Upon a summer noon o'erladen;
A falling star—a blighted tree,
  Are types of thee, O, wounded maiden!

* * * * *

* * * *

"Thou sister of my reason's choice,
    In heart as young, in counsel older,
Oh! let me hear thy friendly voice,
    And lay my head upon thy shoulder
Thy counsel quick!—for in my heart
    A shaft is sped—a fire is lighted,
And thou and I in death shall part,
    For fast I sink, and fancy blighted.

"Unhappy day!—at break of dawn
    I left my room when thou wert sleeping;
I passed the wood—the bridge—the lawn:
    Through tangled copse and thicket creeping.
And joyful in the glowing morn
    I onward roved with thoughts unheeding,
Now watching 'neath the perfumed thorn,
    The timid rabbit swiftly speeding.

"Or seeking for the sky-lark's nest,
    Within the dewy-scented meadow,
Or tracing o'er its waving breast
    The morn-cloud's dark and fitful shadow.
Sudden upon the breezy air
    Such thrilling strains of song awake
Entranced I stood, attentive there,
    My very bosom's breathing taken.

Beside the quiet stream I stood,
  And fondly gazed and eager listened,
While all the roused and quivering wood
  With rosy morning's dew-drop glistened.
And there, where winds and wavelets played,
  Harmonious round the lonely island,
Beneath the cool, embowering shade,
  Reclining lay the young Matt Hyland.

"With thrilling notes ascending slow,
  Like tuneful sound of falling water,
He sung how simple peasant low
  Had dared to love a chieftain's daughter
O Nora! in my bosom's core,
  A voice, a spell, a breath of heaven,
Told me he was that peasant poor,
  And I for whom that heart was riven.

"Yes, he's a simple village swain,
  Yet claims descent from bold O'Connor!
And though content to till the plain,
  His soul is high and full of honour,
And I am come of high degree,
  From Desmond's noble race descended;
But, oh! a village maid I'd be,
  If with his lot my fate were blended.

"Hushed was the song—within the shade
  He sat in pensive mood reclining,
His silent cruit near him laid,
  His tranquil eye divinely shining.
Deep silence o'er the garden hung,
  His modest brow was bending lowly,
When now the morning hymn he sung,
  His strains ascending soft and holy.

"I gazed upon his humble cot,
    I gazed upon his lonely island,
And rank and state were all forgot,
    While I beheld the young Matt Hyland!
Oh! Nora, ease my bosom's pain;
    Oh! Nora, soothe this bitter anguish,
Which fires my heart, and heats my brain,
    Oh give me comfort, or I languish!"

With startled horror Nora hears
    The story of the noble maiden,
Her heart too deeply wrung for tears,
    Her soul with bitter memories laden.
For since when first in early prime
    She trod the sunny path of childhood,
She loved, with strength increased by time,
    The dweller in the lonely wild-wood.

No words escape her faltering tongue,
    Her pale hands press her beating bosom;
The dirge of all her hopes is rung,
    The bolt hath fallen—and she must lose him.
"For this," she thought, "he scorned my love,
    For this alone my heart he slighted;
But time may be he'll dearly prove
    The feelings of a bosom slighted!"

She started—on her arm upraised
    Helen had laid her finger gently,
And up into her eyes had gazed,
    With eager questioning glance intently.
"Alas! I see thou deem'st me wrong,
    All sudden fallen, and lowly-hearted;
With reckless passion borne along,
    With pride, and shame, and honour parted!"

Soft gleams the light in Nora's eye,
    A gentle smile her pale lip flushing,
While evil thoughts are brooding nigh,
    And vengeance o'er her spirit rushing.
"Have I not, lady, watched by thee,
    In festal hall, or wild-wood bower,
From earliest years of infancy,
    Companion of each passing hour?

"Then wonder not I now should shrink,
    To see the boding storm of anguish,
To see thy gentle spirit sink,
    All rudely pressed, and droop and languish.
Like dew upon the wild wind's path,
    Like slender leaves by tempests shaken,
Thou'lt fall before a father's wrath,
    By friends, and fame, and pride forsaken.

"Thy sire is lord of all this land,
    And thou'rt his loved and only daughter,
And many a suitor seeks thy hand,
    From far Ciar to Corrib water.
Think not the Desmond's pride will bow,
    For even his loved and fondly cherished;
Rather than see her bending low,
    He'd mourn above her, fallen and perished.'

Young Helen's cheek hath brightly flushed,
    Affection's fire her eye hath lighted.
"Oh! rather let my heart be crushed,
    Its hopes denied—its wishes blighted!
Oh! rather let my head be laid
    Silent beneath the grave's cold shadow,
While sunshine glads the flowery glade,
    And fragrant winds o'ersweep the meadow.

"Than that one ingrate thought should bring;
   A sorrow o'er his age declining,
Or disobedience taint the spring
   Where holiest love was ever shining.
No! Peace shall hallow Desmond's years,
   Unknown his daughter's hapless story,
Till Hyland's name in Desmond's ears
   Sound sweet as songs of knightly glory.

Yet, Nora, yet I fain would test
   His famed worth and stainless merit,
And should they fail—why, peace and rest
   May soothe again my troubled spirit.
My soul, perhaps, in fancy vain,
   Is worshipping a vision only,
Which lures me on, through grief and pain,
   At last to leave me dark and lonely.

"I'd know if that which tempts my heart
   Be worthless of the pain 'tis bringing,
And burning thoughts might then depart,
   Now round my inmost feelings clinging.
'Tis wooing fate—yet, Nora, go,
   And seek him in his lonely island,
When dewy winds are whispering low,
   Say I would speak with young Matt Hyland."

PART III.

Oh, spotless purity of mind!
   Majestic grace of youthful beauty!
Who lov'st, within the heart refined,
   To house with peace and simple duty.

Pure as the gale whose viewless wings
  The wind harp sweeps with mournful fleetness
Oh, come and teach the eager strings
  To blend their fires with heavenly sweetness.

First grace of virgin souls! to thee—
  To thee I pour my minstrel story;
Oh! let the descant rising free,
  From thee receive its saving glory.
Few, few for thee awake the strain,
  Few tune for thee the pleasing measure,
For first amongst the slothful train
  The poet haunts the gates of pleasure.

Then quickly come, oh, angel maid!
  In robe of purest white descending!
Who lovest to haunt the sacred shade
  Where sounds of choral praise are blending;
The banquet late and grossly stored,
  And tipsy dance who flies affrighted,
But lovest the spare and simple board,
  By sweet religion calmly lighted.

Without thee, life were all a waste;
  Without thee, vile were rank and power;
Without thee, science sinks debased,
  And beauty lies a soiled flower.
The monarch's crown—the conqueror's arms—
  The poet's artful strains enchanting—
The sage's love—the maiden's charms,
  Are shorn of praise when thou art wanting.

How wide they err who deem thee chill,
  And hard of heart to human feeling,
Because thou loath'st the hateful thrill,
  In passion's bosom darkly stealing.

They know who filled with heavenly zest,
   All earthly love, for thee surrender,
How pure within the lonely breast
   Thy spirit burns divinely tender.

No more, no more, ye feeble minds
   Who early cross'd in young affection,
Lie bare to passion's stormy winds,
   Make bleak despair your fell election.
The suicidal draught refrain,
   And learn your Nature's loftier tending,
Nor change an hour of fancied pain
   For grief unknown, and never ending.

*   *   *   *

*   *   *   *

Come down with more than wonted fires,
   And burst my spirit's sensual slumbers,
And light my heart to high desires,
   And kindle in my rising numbers,
For mighty is the theme I sing,
   Though by a feeble voice repeated,
And strong shall be the sounding string,
   That tells a tale of love defeated

In sweet Adare, o'er hill and plain,
   The summer moon is softly gleaming:
What finger taps the cottage pane,
   And breaks the youthful peasant's dreaming?
He hears in accents murmuring sweet,
   "Matt Hyland, wake! and rise and follow;"
He leaves the cot and courses fleet,
   A flying form o'er hill and hollow.

They enter at a garden gate;
    "Hush, soft! my lady's in her bower;"
Above them flapped in gloomy state
    The flag from each embattled tower.
Still thridding soft in cautious guise,
    Through grassy walk and covert shady,
With wonder in his heart and eyes,
    He stands before that beauteous lady.

*   *   *   *

*   *   *   *

"Oh! scorn me not!" she said and sighed,
    And trembling paused, and deeply blushing,
For e'en the midnight could not hide,
    The shame o'er all her forehead rushing.
"Oh! blame me not!—but kindly hear,
    And kindlier feel my wretched story;
And lend at least a pitying ear,
    For state despised and hated glory!

"My sire is lord of all this land,
    And I his loved and only daughter,
And many a lord has sought my hand,
    From far Ciar to Corrib water.
Oh! vain is now their suit to me,
    I've marked the worth that shines about thee;
And I had rather toil with thee,
    Than live and reign a queen without thee

"Oh! take me from a rank I hate,
   Oh! take me from this joyless splendour,
And let me share thy lonely state,
   A dowerless bride—but true and tender.
The Kernes are hushed—my father sleeps—
   My steed is on the 'nighted heather,
And drowsy watch the warder keeps,
   And safe will be our flight together!"

Matt Hyland was a village swain,
   Nor tower, nor land may he inherit,
Yet honour fired each bounding vein,
   And princely worth and regal spirit.
He knelt before the lady's feet,
   Her sandall'd shoes with tears bedewing,
Like doomed serf with action meet,
   To Northern Empress lowly suing.

"O grief!" he said, " for him who knows
   And feels the force of worth and beauty,
Whose heart with youthful ardour glows,
   Yet owns the tie of loyal duty!—
Oh, do not say my heart is cold,
   But mingle pity while thou blamest,
Though not for mines of hoarded gold
   Would I become the wretch thou namest!

'Thy sire is Lord of all Adare;
   From Desmond's noble chiefs descended,
And true to them my fathers were
   In battle stern and banquet splendid.
What kinder chief can peasant hail,
   From far Ciar to Corrib water,
And how would sound the thankless tale,
   If I should steal his only daughter?

" And would'st thou be Matt Hyland's bride!
    And would'st thou share his lowly station!—
Though wooed by all the wealth and pride
    That lives in Erin's regal nation?
O Lady, nursed in fortune's arms,
    Life's flowers around thee ever blooming,
Thou little knowest the countless harms,
    That o'er the peasant's cot are glooming.

" The scanty meal—the raiment thin—
    Uncertain health and certain labour—
The sick-bed lone—where rarely's seen,
    And fearful comes the timid neighbour.
When fierce and sudden tempests burst,
    Beside a cheerless hearth he freezes,
For him the winter blows its worst,
    And fever taints the summer breezes.

" Yet I were blest—the tempest hoarse
    On me might waste its lungs for ever,
On me the winter bend its force,
    And ruin wreak its worst endeavour.
But, oh! to think, young blushing one!
    Thy tender cherished frame should bear it;
Full bitter is the draught alone,
    But, oh! 'twere death with thee to share it.

And, ah! for love—its golden veil
    Falls quick at dark misfortune's greeting;
All earthly love is earthly frail,
    All earthly passion doubly fleeting.
The hope, to fancy only bright,
    Would nearer lose its witching power,
And thou would'st mourn the hapless night
    That led thee from thy father's tower.

"Yet take a peasant's humble thanks,
 For trust or love so kindly rendered ;
And still, amid the shining ranks
 Of Erin's daughters highly tendered,
Remember him to whom thy peace
 Was dearer than the love within thee,
Who held it far the nobler bliss
 To live without than basely win thee."

"Farewell," she sighed, "thou faultless youth,
 Mine art has wrought mine own undoing ;
I did but try thy loyal truth,
 And find it stainless—to my ruin.
Here, wear for me this clasp of gold :
 Farewell, for see the dawn is breaking !"
Matt Hyland leaves that lordly hold,
 Like one from blissful dreams awaking.

She passed her father at the gate :
 Why changed is Helen's mirthful greeting?
Why shun each mark of wealth or state,
 Through hall and chamber sadly fleeting?
"Woe ! woe for me ! though in these dells
 The summer sun is brightly shining,
Black midnight in my bosom dwells :
 My peace is gone—my heart is pining!

"Ye woods and lawns of sweet Adare;
 Ye ruined aisles and shining river,
Ye dreams of childhood, falsely fair,
 And faded now, farewell for ever.
Take, take away this gorgeous train,
 Whose splendour mocks my sadness only,
For, oh ! how sad ! for oh ! how vain
 Is grandeur, when the heart is lonely

"Oh! had I been a village lass,
　　In yonder lowly cottage dwelling,
At vesper late, or early mass,
　　My humble beads devoutly telling.
Then blameless might young Helen share
　　His cot beside that murmuring water,
The happiest heart in all Adare,
　　Though reared a lowly peasant's daughter.

"Now merry harp and song adieu!
　　And dance at eve and music sounding;
I'll roam in groves of dismal yew,
　　And funeral cypress all surrounding.
Soon, soon an early tomb shall hide
　　This frame, already faint and dying;
Some village maid shall be his bride,
　　When I am in the churchyard lying.

"Yet blessed be they! and safe from ill,
　　When day for me no more is shining;
Let better thoughts my bosom fill,
　　Than fruitless sighs and vain repining.
Since duty mars life's only bliss,
　　With higher hopes my sighs I'll smother,
And, oh! for all we lose in this,
　　May heaven reward us in another!"

Now, slow amid the closed buds,
　　Soft hung with dew-drops pale and quivering,
Matt Hyland treads the silent woods,
　　'Neath gleaming moon-beams coldly shivering.
'How comes it thus! what dream is this!
　　And have I stood in Helen's bower?
Oh! let me dwell upon the bliss
　　No more, of that enchanting hour.

"No more of each angelic tone,
   That like unearthly music flowing
Still fell upon my ear alone,
   'Midst sounds of leaves and night winds blowing
But follow truth's unerring line,
   My bark with holy prudence steering,
Nor even for Helen's love resign
   The hope that waits the persevering.

"Oh! stretch to life's extremest span,
   The brilliant course of earthly pleasure;
How looks the space assigned to man
   Lost in the vast eternal measure.
Rank, fortune, love, earth's highest bliss—
   All life can yield of sweet or splendid—
Are but a thing that scarcely is,
   When, lo! its mortal date is ended.

"So swift is time—so briefly lost,
   The fleeting joys of life's creation:
What seems the present is the past,
   Before the mind can mark its station.
On earth we hold the spirit blest,
   That learns to bear affliction cheerly,
And what we call and fancy rest
   Is brief annihilation merely.

There's demon spite in forms that seem,
　　As fair as angels just descended;
There's demon spite in eyes that gleam,
　　With softness and devotion blended.
That trusted friend, who knew alone
　　The secret of their midnight meeting,
Revealed the whole with serpent tone,
　　To Helen's sire the tale repeating.

One summer eve, returning late
　　From vespers in the convent tower,
With weary feet young Helen sate,
　　Reclining in her garden bower.
Now long forgot that earthly light,
　　Now vanquished long each wild emotion,
As stars in sunshine fading quite,
　　So love was lost in pure devotion.

True, blanched was the rosy cheek,
　　And wasted now the taper finger,
And faintly kind and sweetly weak,
　　The sounds that on those thin lips linger;
But 'mid the wreck a hope prevailed
　　Of bliss that duteous souls inherit;
And still the more the body failed,
　　The stronger grew the heavenly spirit.

Hark! voices at the garden gate!
　　With startled ear young Helen listens,
Where, in the dewy sunshine late,
　　The bowering laurel brightly glistens.
Forgive the act——nor harm, nor blame,
　　Her thoughts perceived, nor wrong intended;
But she has heard Matt Hyland's name
　　With words of menace darkly blended.

"I thank thee for the duteous tale.
 To-night, within his lonely island,
A sailor band shall cross the vale,
 And bind the heels of young Matt Hyland.
A seaman on the heaving deck,
 Then let him plough the cropless water,
In battle stern or hideous wreck
 He'll learn to woo his chieftain's daughter!"

What now shall wretched Helen do?
 By all betrayed—by all forsaken.
What foot to seek his cot, and who,
 With warning voice, his soul to waken?
She clasped her hands, she raised her eyes,
 Then swift through copse and thicket gliding,
To Hyland's cot the lady hies,
 In heaven herself and him confiding.

Alone she sought the evening wood,
 Alone she reached his silent dwelling,
And on his threshold bright she stood,
 Her tale of warning quickly telling.
With wonder wild Matt Hyland heard,
 His grateful eyes delighted raising,
Like sinner to repentance stirred,
 Upon his guardian angel gazing.

"And is it mine to bid thee fly!
 And see thy native valley never—
To tell thee hope must surely die,
 To say farewell!—farewell for ever
To hear thy guiltless doom alone,
 From her whose reason most approved thee:
Thy only fault, that thou hast none!
 Thy only crime, that Helen loved thee?

"Deserve farewell! Since thus we part,
　　And lasting exile darkens o'er thee,
Here let me pour my opening heart,
　　In all its fervent truth before thee.
Yes, here beneath the solemn night,
　　'Mong listening woods and waters lonely,
Receive my troth, and promise plight—
　　I love thee all—I love thee only!

" If it be blameless bliss to know,
　　In danger wild, or pleasure thrilling,
One bosom shares thy joy or woe,
　　One heart divides each varying feeling.
That balm, my parting boon receive,
　　For home, and rank, and state, and splendour
All, all, for thee my heart would leave:
　　All, all, but heaven, for thee surrender.

" And said'st thou poverty would chill
　　The truth that in my heart is burning,
That, pinched with want, and scared with ill,
　　My thoughts would falter—home returning?
Thou little know'st what woman's heart
　　Can dare when love and woe are nearest,
The torture, thus with thee to part,
　　Is keener far than aught thou fearest!"

Pensive his air, and few his words,
　　Like those who secret woe dissemble,
And mournful as the various chords
　　That in the rising breezes tremble.
Humble his state, but high his mind,
　　With unaffected force discerning,
And feelings pure and thoughts refined,
　　The simple bosom's noblest learning.

"Farewell!" he said, with brimming eyes,
    And clasped hands, devoutly kneeling:
Delighted awe and wild surprise,
    And grief within his bosom swelling.
"Farewell! I had no hope—and yet,
    'Twas sweet to hear the soft wind sighing,
And watch the sun arise and set
    Upon the towers where thou wer't lying.

The summer's heat—the winter's snow,
    The wild birds in the woodland singing,
And streams that glide, and flowers that blow,
    Sweet thoughts of love and thee were bringing.
Farewell! my freedom thus preserved,
    At risk of all thy soul can tender,
From Hyland's heart has more deserved,
    Than one like him can ever render."

"Farewell!"—she shrieked—her father's form
    Upon the threshold stood before her,
And, dark as autumn's gathering storm,
    His gloomy brows were lowering o'er her.
"Remove your lady to the hold!
    And bind that slave in heaviest fetters;
How came he by that clasp of gold?
    The hind must mate among his betters.

Thou loitering knave, why waits't thou? Hence!
    Be still, and do thy chieftain's bidding!"
Bereft of hue, and life, and sense,
    They bear her from the cot, unheeding.
Nine moons had slowly rolled away,
    (Long lapse of undiscovered treason,)
Nor, ever from that dreadful day,
    Had Helen known the light of reason.

PART IV.

O war! thou necessary ill!
　　What lingering curse shall he inherit
Who, stirred by fell ambition's zeal,
　　Presumes to rouse thy wasting spirit?
Dark foe to human weal, who draws
　　His sword, the bands of peace to sever,
Without the plea of righteous cause,
　　Woe! woe! shall rend his soul for ever.

The heart, when perilled deep in fight,
　　That warmest glows with warlike spirit,
Is not, in thy all-piercing sight,
　　The highest in the ranks of merit.
For oft it turns with selfish aim,
　　Untouched by nobler thoughts of duty,
In greedy quest of idle fame,
　　Or idler smile of passing beauty.

Such virtue claims the beast of prey,
　　In equinoctial desert lonely,
Who dares the chance of battle fray,
　　For passion or dominion only.
But man, illumed with heavenly light,
　　Should join the din of mortal clangour,
Alone for justice and the right,
　　And then with slow reluctant anger.

We scorn the wretch, with coward hand,
　　When danger toward his home is bending,
Who shuns to aid the patriot band,
　　For helpless age and youth contending.

In reason's eye not less abhorred
    Is he, with hardened soul unsparing,
Who reckless grasps the desperate sword,
    For cause or consequence uncaring.

With steady eye the truly brave
    Behold that fatal term appalling,
Not scared, like passion's conscious slave,
    With outstretched arms the world recalling,
Nor callous to eternal cares,
    In heaven deserted, calm, unshaken;
For charity alike forswears
    The self-devote and self-forsaken.

For, oh! in this our fallen state,
    So frail are even the best and purest,
Their sum of conscious ill is great,
    Who seem in truth to stand securest.
He deepliest feels the yoke of sin
    Who firm in Virtue's mail hath bound him,
And he whose eye is turned within
    Will lightly heed the flattery round him.

Could we, with understanding gaze,
    But calmly view this transient being,
Our souls would shun the sound of praise
    As from the hiss of serpent's fleeing.
By meditation's tranquil beam
    Our minds would read existence clearly,
And see how false—how mere a dream,
    Is all the world esteems so dearly.

There is a pride that outward shows,
    In haughty port and diction swelling,
While lip, and eye, and brow disclose
    The monster in the bosom swelling.

Such pride to open sense revealed,
  Like outward wounds with slight endeavour,
Is often by reflection healed,
  And banished from the heart for ever.

And, oh! there is a stubborn sprite,
  Within the inmost soul abiding,
That shifting flies the gaze of light,
  In bright disguises ever hiding.
Self-diffidence, with downward glance,
  And timid speech it oft resembles,
Even while with secret arrogance
  Each pulse within the bosom trembles.

* * * * *

* * * * *

Wild wonder spread through all the vale,
  And many a friendly eye was clouded,
When Rumour told the mournful tale,
  In cottage lone and hamlet crowded.
How Hyland, from her father's home,
  Had sought to lure his chieftain's daughter,
Now doomed in exile wide to roam,
  A seaman on the western water.

" And who," they said, " will now confide,
  In outside fair, and seeming blameless,
If forms like his at heart can hide
  Deceit and ingrate treason shameless?
For soul in nobler shape enshrined,
  Yet never lived in Erin's island;
And where can truth a shelter find,
  If falsehood dwells with young Matt Hyland.

* * * * *

* * * * *

The boat is launched—the dripping oars
   Glance in the fitful moonbeams holy;
The youth has left Mague's gloomy shores,
   His forest paths and dwelling lowly.
With forehead gloomed with silent grief,
   And dreaming eye and heaving bosom,
His glances catch each passing leaf,
   And drooping bough, and closing blossom.

While pale upon the furrowed wake,
   The moonlit waters brightly bubbled,
Then settling calm as summer lake,
   Slept in the gentle light untroubled.
And frighted in her covert high,
   The curlew rose on whirring pinion,
And startled with her lonely cry
   Hushed silence in her lone dominion.

And far away by ruined wall,
   And shieling low and hold of power,
By lofty Court's embattled hall,
   And Ballycullen's guarded tower.
Where eastward, from the Candle Rock,
   The death-light lung its tiny lustre,
Before uptorn by sulphurous shock,
   Bold warriors round Fitzgerald's cluster.

All purple shone the morning's beam,
 When from Mague's bosom gently gliding
They reached old Shannon's mighty stream,
 O'er swell and breaker gaily riding.
Full many an isle and headland gray,
 And wooded cliff behind them leaving,
E'er moored, in Labasheeda's Bay,
 They reached the ship at anchor heaving

Broad looming 'gainst the surly South,
 From her black hull, robust and swelling,
Full many a grim and muzzled mouth
 Of ordnance fenced the Ocean dwelling.
Above, old England's banner flew,
 From high top-gallant gaily streaming,
The gilded stem, in many a hue,
 With dread Eliza's name was gleaming.

Wild wonder Hyland's heart enthralled;
 His bosom heaved, his accents faltered.
For merry England's wooden walls,
 What eye can see and rest unaltered?
Her hearts of oak and armed array,
 What heart can mark that knows her story
Nor long to join their wild huzza,
 Nor burn to share their patriot glory?

Enrolled amongst that gallant crew,
 Soon Hyland lost his rustic bearing:
Robust in limb and brown in hue,
 A manlier form and gesture wearing.
Well pleased to serve his native land,
 He treads the deck, a seaman steady
And plies his art with dextrous hand,
 And apprehension apt and ready.

Oh, youth! in thy exulting prime,
  Those earthly woes but lightly shake it,
That, known and felt in after time,
  Sink deep into the heart and break it.
With friends or native land to part,
  Then faintly shades life's morning splendour,
Hope holds the world within her heart,
  And time and space like slaves attend her.

To coil the rope—to climb the yard,
  Nor heed the billows' swinging motion,
To watch alone, when driving hard,
  The night wind tore the wintry ocean.
Mildly to bear each varied ill,
  Each labour of his new condition,
And more than all, to bear his will,
  In meek, unquestioning submission.

Such now was Hyland's altered life,
  But well he bore the ills that pained him;
Say, ye who read the bosom's strife,
  What power amid these toils sustained him.
What kept his youthful mind at rest?
  His brow without a cloud to shade it?
What treasure of the blameless breast?
  A heart at peace with him who made it.

His mates, who marked his bearing mild,
  With scorn beheld the pious stranger,
They deemed his mother's precious child
  Unfit to stand the shock of danger.
But ne'er to question or resent
  Did Hyland turn when anger pleaded,
His mind was all on duty bent,
  And left the idle scoff unheeded.

He was not of the fickle school,
　　Who, launched on life in boyhood's season,
Find argument in ridicule,
　　And in a sneer convincing reason.
The star that from the shore of youth
　　His eye beheld with pure devotion,
That cynosure of heavenly truth,
　　Now led him o'er the world's wide ocean.

'Twas morn, and o'er the western main,
　　With favouring gales, the ship was steering.
When, lo! the hostile flag of Spain
　　Far o'er the distant wave appearing.
A sail! a sail! each gladdening face
　　Is bright with mingling joy and wonder,
And soon the level guns of chase
　　Sent o'er the deep their echoing thunder.

But nought, the gallant foe declined
　　The strife, with coward sail retreating,
But hove against the freshening wind,
　　And calmly waits the menaced meeting.
Soon side to side, in stern array,
　　With ready decks they ride the water,
And wait beneath the rosy day
　　The signal of the opening slaughter.

As high o'er cliff or seething main,
　　By lone Kilkee or heathy Callan,
The bustard eyes the soaring crane,
　　With eager beak and ready talon:
So hove the hardy British sloop,
　　Against that ponderous hulk stupendous,
Though towered the Spaniard's armed poop,
　　Above her mizen peak tremendous.

Ye British tars, behold your prey!"
    The Captain's voice was heard no longer,
Lost in the brief and stern hurra,
    From deck and yard arising stronger.
" Those maids of Spain, in times to come,
    This day shall oft recall with sorrow;
Go! send your iron greeting home:
    Up ports! and give the foe good morrow!"

The hulls that on the sunny brine,
    All sullen lay and slowly heaving,
Gave answer to the battle sign,
    With sudden din and stillness cleaving.
Hurra! above the foaming main,
    They join in combat, close and gory,
For Philip and the hills of Spain!
    For England and Eliza's glory!

Hurra! the shot is thickening fast,
    As hail against the roof in winter.
Crash, bolt, and yard, and shrieking mast,
    Each scattering wide the mortal splinter.
Loud rings each hull, as frequent sweeps
    The ponderous ball with sightless motion,
While echo, from her lowest deeps,
    Answers around the listening ocean!

In volumes rolled the sulphurous smoke,
    That did the dreadful scene environ,
While deep at heart the groaning oak,
    Full oft received the rending iron.
Staunch by his gun each seaman stood,
    Unmoved amid the uproar stunning,
Though oft he saw the seamed wood,
    All ruddy with the carnage running.

"Their range of metal trebles ours,"
   The Captain cries, "and fast is telling,
Haste, gallant lads! while darkly lowers
   The favouring cloud between us swelling."
With brief "hurra!" the tars replied,
   And settled ardour, firm and steady,
And hurry down the vessel's side,
   With boarding pike and hanger ready.

Soon bursting from that gloomy shroud,
   Their eager blades are seen advancing,
Bright glittering from the murky cloud,
   Like lightning flash at midnight glancing.
Huzza! behold that hardy band,
   Upon the Spanish deck engaging,
With sword and pistol, hand to hand,
   The fight for death or conquest waging.

Struck lifeless, by a random shot,
   The first lieutenant died unshrinking,
When prompt, at need, Matt Hyland caught,
   The ensign from his grasp in sinking.
And up the shroud he hastens quick,
   With naked hanger nimbly hieing,
Though fatal drove and gathering quick,
   The leaden shower around him flying.

Thrust follows thrust, and blow on blow,
   And many a cheek in death is paler,
Oh! nobly fought the gallant foe,
   But who can check the British sailor?
Ere long the upper deck they gain,
   And rushed beneath with ardour glowing,
Where raged the thickening fight amain,
   And many a hero's blood was flowing.

Oh! who that saw that piteous strife
  But must have felt his bosom rending,
To see so many a gallant life
  In clamour and in carnage ending?
Thus unarraigned of fault or crime,
  To see so many a son of glory,
Cut off in life's exulting prime,
  Oh! young in years! in valour hoary!

Ha! while the strife prolonged in vain,
  Still raved amid the dead and dying,
What daring hand the flag of Spain,
  Sends o'er the wave, dissevered flying?
See! fluttering in the gale, instead,
  The banner of the western island,
And high upon the top-mast head,
  The gallant form of young Matt Hyland.

Now gradual o'er the distant wave,
  The smoky veil aside was flying,
And to the pitying vision gave,
  The scene of strife, all stilly lying.
There locked in death's unyielding grasp,
  Full many a valiant hand was sleeping,
That now no more returned the clasp,
  Of sorrowing messmates o'er it weeping.

Loud shouts of conquest rend the skies,
  "She strikes! Hurra! the Queen for ever!"
"And yield!" the British Captain cries,
  "Since vain is now each wild endeavour.
Ye fought like men, like men give o'er!
  Your sword!—if life be precious, save it!"
"Es Hora bueno—si, Senor,"
  The Spaniard said, and smiling gave it.

"Since I have lost the gallant ship
　　King Philip to my care intrusted,
Why should I vainly wish to keep
　　This bauble in its scabbard rusted?
By cartel freed, some happier day,
　　I yet may dare the wave and weather,
And it may be our lot to play
　　That gallant game again together."

"Now, who was he?" the Captain cries,
　　Who first with fearless heart undaunted,

*　　　*　　　*　　　*

*　　　*　　　*　　　*

Out spoke that tar, with forehead bare,
　　Who erst on Mague's sweet winding border,
Received the youth in far Adare,
　　A seaman pressed by Desmond's order,
"'Tis he! the simple rustic swain,
　　We brought from Erin's lovely island."
They turned and saw, amid the train,
　　The modest form of young Matt Hyland.

"Receive," the Captain said, "thy meed
　　Of praise, since thou hast won it nobly;
Full soon the Queen shall hear thy deed
　　Who seldom thanks a servant coldly.
Right nobly hast thou played thy part,
　　And loudly shall thy zeal be spoken,
For sure thou barest as staunch a heart
　　As ever kept its faith unbroken."

Loud murmurs rose from all the crowd,
   In kind accordance warmly glowing,
While lowly young Matt Hyland bowed,
   His cheek with modest fervour glowing.
For England, ho! They man the prize
   With British hands, alert and ready;
With swelling sails and favouring skies,
   Their homeward course directing steady.

But while each tar with joyous heart
   Indulged at will the burst of pleasure,
Matt Hyland on the deck apart,
   Out-poured his soul's overflowing measure,
When o'er the deep arising dun,
   The eastern shades he saw advancing,
And westward far, the sinking sun,
   From ocean's bosom upward glancing.

"Thee! late, when woe was gathering nigh,
   I called with suppliant aspiration!
Thee! now, in triumph warm and high,
   I hail with grateful invocation!
Thou saw'st me torn by lot severe,
   Far from mine own beloved dwelling,
And kindly heard'st with favouring ear,
   The grief within my bosom swelling.

"That hand in all his varied course,
   That Israel's banished child defended,
It hath not lost its saving force,
   Its task of mercy is not ended.
That eye in many a trying hour,
   That watched for him each coming danger,
It hath not lost its guardian power,
   But still regards the friendless stranger.

"Thy precious boon—this mortal life,
　　Important term of man's probation,
He must not risk in mortal strife,
　　For sake of erring reputation.
They truly hold the righteous mean,
　　Who like a sacred trust receive it.
Not clinging to life's changing scene,
　　Nor rashly prompt, uncalled to leave it.

"Our thanks we owe for life preserved,
　　For victory gained and danger ended,
For many a blessing undeserved,
　　To struggling mortals oft extended.
In triumph or defeat we own
　　Thy power alike with meek devotion,
For battle is the Lord's alone,
　　On gory field or foaming ocean!"

For England ho! the westward sun
　　Is hid beneath his ocean pillow,
Away, away, o'er waters dun,
　　O'er roaring surge and swelling billow.
Soon anchored in the moonlit Downs,
　　They pause till morn's returning glory
Shall spread throughout the island towns,
　　The tidings of their joyous story.

The second morn returning bright,
　　Had roused the crew to life and duty,
And smiling in the grateful light,
　　The world awoke to joy and beauty;
When lo! what dazzling pomp is seen,
　　What pageant gilds the sunny water;
'Tis England's mighty Island Queen,
　　'Tis hapless Boleyn's royal daughter.

Loud thundering from the battered shore,
    Where bright the sunny wave was beating,
The salvos gun's awakening roar,
    Out-bursting gave its mighty greeting.
Wide echoing o'er the glassy wave,
    That in the aerial tumult trembled,
Three cheers the gallant seamen gave
    On deck and yard in files assembled.

Loose o'er the sea, the standards droop,
    Around the Queen in regal splendour,
Majestic on the lofty poop,
    Where England's courtliest dames attend her.
And oft with kindling smile she spoke,
    And lofty brow and bearing royal,
Of England's gallant "hearts of oak,"
    And "wooden walls," and "subjects loyal."

Well pleased the crafty monarch learns,
    That foremost in the fight engaging,
Was one of Desmond's hardy kernes,
    Less grateful war full often waging.
"The Desmond is at last our friend,"
    She said, "and well the name he merits,
Who to his Sovereign's aid can lend,
    Such frames robust and faithful spirits.

But let not coming ages see,
    In history's page the tale recorded,
That e'er such generous deed should be,
    For England wrought and unrewarded.'
She said, and from the scabbard drew,
    A blade in polished splendour shining,
While low before the wondering crew,
    Young Hyland kneels with head declining

"Thus still," resumed the royal maid,
  "By all who rule our prosperous nation,
Be merit with its meed repaid,
  Let worth have place of birth and station.
A servant staunch on sea or shore,
  As e'er drew blade for Albion's Island,
A ship-boy and a hind no more,
  Arise, a knight, Sir Matthew Hyland!"

*　　*　　*　　*

*　　*　　*　　*

With spirit calm and unelate,
  In meek self-knowledge still protected,
Young Hyland bore his altered state,
  In bearing mild and unaffected.
Nor arrogance or vicious shame
  Revealed an inward pride unholy,
But still he was to all the same,
  At heart the lowliest of the lowly.

Three years on stormy waters wide,
  Young Hyland roamed with zeal unceasing,
While each revolving season viewed,
  His merit and his praise increasing·
And still the less his spirit prized
  The fame his faithful service won him,
The more neglected and despised,
  Did honour shower her smiles upon him

Though oft he cheered the gallant crew,
    Against their country's foes in danger,
For private wrong he never drew
    His sword on countryman or stranger
Nor, mindful of the early truth
    That warned him 'gainst each rising passion.
Did vice allure his constant youth,
    Though glittering in the name of fashion.

But, tossed upon the ocean foam,
    Or shining in the ranks of splendour,
His constant heart still turned to home,
    With faithful glance reverting tender.
When, calm at eve, the autumn sun
    Beyond the crimson wave descended,
And o'er the eastern waters dun,
    The solemn moon was rising splendid.

"Though long a sorrowing exile grown,
    With homeward thoughts in vain returning,
And sad at heart, and inly lone,
    With wishes vain my soul is burning
Still round each cherished haunt of youth,
    My ardent mind is fondly clinging,
Still memory turns with changeless truth,
    To scenes of past emotion winging.

'Oh, dear in every change to me,
    Sweet lady of the western ocean,
My longing heart looks back to thee,
    With all an exile's deep devotion!
Fresh bloom each smiling garden there,
    Each fertile vale and sunny highland!
Heaven bless my own beloved Adare—
    Heaven guard my dear, my native island!"

PART V.

Humility! oh, loved of heaven,
　　Triumphant in thy holy terror,
By self-confiding impulse driven,
　　Thou dost not tempt the brink of error;
But, homeward borne and shuddering still,
　　Thou keep'st afar thy faithful station,
Thou shunn'st the coming shade of ill,
　　And fli'st as guilt, remote occasion.

The warrior trusts his mailed might,
　　His practised skill and valour solely,
But he who arms for virtue's fight,
　　Must shield his soul in prudence lowly.
In human wars he wins the plume,
　　Who boldliest writes his name in story,
But here, the souls who least presume
　　Are highest in the ranks of glory.

The wreath in mad ambition's race
　　Is his, whose speed can first obtain it,
But in the quest of heavenly grace,
　　Who lowliest seeks will surest gain it.
Alone in this celestial fight,
　　When countless foes unseen assemble,
There's valour high in timorous flight,
　　'Tis heroic zeal to fear and tremble.

Nor mid the strong and searching strife
　　That ever haunts youth's opening season,
For lasting safety and for life
　　Trust thou thine own unaided reason.
But upward borne on fervent wings,
　　With filial hope divinely burning;
Go seek at mercy's fountain springs
　　For strength renewed and love returning.

Three years had slowly rolled away,
  (Long lapse of undetected treason),
Yet never from that fatal day
  Had Helen known a joyous season.
With merry speech and radiant smile,
  No more she joined the banquet splendid,
But, frequent, towards that solemn aisle
  With secret pace devoutly wended.

Yet though each bud of young delight
  Within her gentle heart had perished,
Though changed by sorrow's early blight
  Each wreath of bliss her youth had cherished,
Though fallen within her altered mind,
  Unpractised fancy's air-built towers,
Hope still around the ruin twined,
  And wove her undecaying flowers.

Still in her gentle eye serene,
  And on her brow angelic, beaming,
A clear seraphic light was seen,
  Like morning twilight sweetly gleaming.
Less oft, perchance, within her breast
  Wild joy arose, tumultuous swelling,
But there, in calm unchanging rest
  Celestial Peace had made her dwelling

Oft when beside their evening fire,
  With cheerful faggot brightly shining,
She sat before her noble sire
  With paly cheek and brow declining.
With secret pang his heart was rent,
  And oft upon his midnight pillow
He grieved that e'er in wrath he sent
  Matt Hyland o'er the western billow.

But most his pitying thought it stirred,
   That while her heart was inly mourning,
Nor moistened eye, nor look, nor word,
   Recalled the woe within it burning;
That still with fond confiding smile
   She met her father's kind affection,
And strove, with many a gentle wile,
   To hide her spirit's deep dejection.

Oh, I would give the fairest hall
   That stands in Desmond's wide dominion,
Could I that fatal doom recal,
   Or he his chieftain's lost opinion!
For what, alas, is lordly power
   If peace withhold her light enchanting?
And what the gain of land or tower
   Where sweet domestic bliss is wanting?

But let him roam in exile lone,
   Forsworn in heart and base in spirit,
For favour to the traitor shown
   Is wrong to virtue and to merit.
For rank may cover low degree,
   And worth may rise as worth has risen,
But, oh! what grace of dignity
   Can veil the hideous brow of treason?"

Not thus with her whose vengeful tongue
   That dark calumnious tale had spoken,
With fell remorse her soul was wrung,
   By fearful dreams her sleep was broken.
To her the toll of convent bell,
   Seemed like a fatal omen falling,
And every stroke a gloomy knell,
   That warned her heart of woe appalling.

She started when the sudden wind
    Along the boughs came swiftly fleeting;
She started when the village hind
    Her pathway crossed with lowly greeting
The warder's blast—the funeral wail
    Of tidings new or unexpected—
To her sick spirit told a tale
    Of coming ill and guilt detected.

When dark across the evening heath
    The shades of night were slowly creeping,
Disastrous thoughts of woe and death
    Came o'er her bosom wildly sweeping.
Life's vanished ease in vain she seeks,
    From scene to scene unquiet flying;
Her haggard eyes and wasted cheeks
    Revealed the inward worm undying.

Even scenes of old, in summer bloom,
    And summer fragrance sweetly springing,
Seemed altered by the boding gloom
    That round her conscious heart was clinging.
When turned her cowering glance on high,
    Her spirit shrunk, her bosom trembled,
For every cloud that crossed the sky
    Fantastic forms of woe resembled.

The morning mists in volumes rolled,
    The shades that wrapped the wooded valley,
The secret haunt, beloved of old,
    In glen apart or moonlight alley;
The measureless abyss that gleamed,
    Reflected in the watery mirror,
To her disordered fancy teemed
    With mystic shapes of gloom and terror.

For conscience, thy unsparing asp
    Keen watch within her soul was keeping.
There firmly clung with fearful grasp,
    And venomed fang and eye unsleeping;
Till in her spirit's altered mood
    Fair Nature lost her wonted graces,
And earth, and air, and fire, and flood,
    Seemed peopled with avenging faces.

Nor rest she finds at midnight deep,
    Nor respite from her fears in slumber,
Dark fancies scare her broken sleep,
    And spectral dreams her soul encumber.
Then buried friends uncalled arise
    In gloomy throngs, her fancy daunting,
With warning hands and dreamy eyes
    Around her silent chamber haunting.

Then on her soul with vivid force,
    In hues distinct and deeply tinted,
Fear's ghastly limner, stern remorse,
    Full many a boding sight imprinted.
Earth's mouldering dust to life restored,
    Uprushing at the trumpet's clangour,
And gleaming high the dreadful sword
    Of justice waking in her anger.

But most she feared the solemn gloom
    Around the church-yard gathering lonely,
While darkling lay each voiceless tomb
    By yew or cypress sheltered only.
Then deep within her shuddering breast
    The fears of childhood found admission,
For souls by secret guilt oppressed
    Are still the prey of superstition.

Thus restless on from day to day
  She dragged along a wretched being,
To every random fear a prey,
  From her own thoughts affrighted fleeing.
Though Desmond's gold her treachery paid,
  Small joy received the conscious maiden.
For heavily her bosom weighed
  With unatoned injustice laden.

She knew not when with artful smile
  And hypocritic zeal affected,
She strove to hide the secret guile
  That all her guilty course directed,
How plainly through that shallow guise
  Her lady saw the lurking danger,
But read in Helen's peaceful eyes
  A mind to all her guilt a stranger.

'Twas dawn—upon the leafless vale
  The winter sky was darkly scowling,
With fitful force the southern gale,
  Along the frozen sward was howling.
Slow swung the lonely convent bell,
  Amid the stormy twilight breaking,
Where, watchful in each narrow cell,
  The penitential train were waking.

Ha! see beneath the misty ray
  Through sleet and snow-drift swiftly hieing,
What footstep marks the devious way
  Toward that high porch affrighted flying?
With backward glance and floating hair,
  Upon the driving gust dishevelled,
As in her bosom blank despair,
  Or haunted frenzy wildly revelled.

"Quick—quick—receive the broken words
  Upon my struggling breath that gather,
A moment hold—ye rending chords!
  A moment hear—oh, holy father!
Oh, death reserve thine angry dart,
  Thus o'er my shuddering soul suspended,
Nor pierce this sick and sinking heart,
  Till all my hideous tale is ended.

"Oh, once to me the morning light
  Arose in sweet and peaceful splendour;
Oh, once to me the falling night
  Brought still repose and visions tender,
For once within my youthful breast,
  Religious peace had made her dwelling,
And lulled in bright and holy rest
  Each pulse of passion wildly swelling

"Ah, happy days, when calm at heart,
  In conscious innocence reposing,
Content, I filled my lowly part,
  From breaking dawn till daylight closing.
When that pure light which shone within,
  Gave all without its tranquil beauty,
And lovely looked each rural scene,
  Lit by the heavenly light of duty.

"Ah, happy scenes for ever changed,
  Ah, hours of sunny peace departed,
When through each woodland haunt I ranged,
  An infant free and careless hearted.
When, hushed beside the whispering Magra,
  'Twas ecstacy to sit and ponder,
Or by its waters winding vague,
  At close of summer eve to wander.

" Then sweet at dawn that convent toll,
   Slow mingling with the choral number,
Upon my tranquil spirit stole,
   And softly broke my morning slumber
But altered now, that solemn choir
   Overwhelms my soul with boding sadness
And in my bosom wakes a fire
   That turns each rising thought to madness.

" Yet not by sudden impulse changed
   In that pure course my spirit faltered,
From fervent love at once estranged,
   Like vales by rushing tempests altered.
No, seldom thus Devotion's flame
   Hath in one gust of passion perished,
Nor bosoms stooped to guilt and shame
   Where piety and peace were cherished.

" One night—my shuddering fancy still
   Recalls that dread prophetic vision,
When unoppressed by conscious ill,
   My heart was lulled in thoughts elysian—
One night I had a fearful dream,
   While yet a child I lived sincerely,
But vainly scanned its mystic theme,
   Till time revealed the sense too clearly.

" Methought I roved on shining walks,
   'Mid odorous groves and wreathed bowers,
Where, trembling on their slender stalks,
   Fresh opening bloomed the early flowers;
Thick hung the fruit on every bough,
   In ripe profusion clustering mellow,
While o'er the peaked horizon's brow
   The evening ray fell slant and yellow.

'Slow pacing through the fragrant shades
   With calm majestic mein advancing,
O'erawed I saw a queenly maid
   With piercing eyes divinely glancing.
Deep wonder chained my reverent tongue,
   My form was bent with greeting lowly,
While silence o'er the garden hung,
   As if the ground she trod was holy.

"'And who art thou?' with eager tone,
   I cried aloud, 'whose presence thrilling,
Though lately seen and yet unknown,
   Can reach the utmost springs of feeling.
And oh! what sweet secluded scene
   Here shines in rural beauty splendid,
Where summer bloom and vernal green,
   With ripe autumnal wealth are blended?'

"With smiles that broke as sunshine bright,
   Their lustre to my soul imparting,
And tones that sent a pure delight
   Delicious through my bosom darting.
'Devotion is my name,' she said,
   'And mine are these delicious bowers,
From purest fountains ever fed,
   And bright with undecaying flowers.

"'In this sweet haunt thy blissful life,
   Shall glide like meadow streamlets flowing,
Unreached by sounds of demon strife,
   Unknown to passion and unknowing.
For thee, these fragrant airs shall rise,
   For thee shall blow these opening roses,
Till far beyond yon twilight skies
   Thy heart in endless peace reposes.

"'Yes, thine shall be this calm retreat
   Of summer bloom and peaceful beauty,
If thou observe with prudence meet,
   And watchful care, one easy duty;
'Tis but to tend one golden lamp,
   With faithful hand and spirit heeding,
From wasting airs and vapours damp,
   His pointed flame attentive feeding.

"'While heavenward thus, ascending bright,
   In holy lustre still increasing,
Thou keep'st thy pure unearthly light,
   With vestal heed and care unceasing.
Sweet peace of heart shall haunt thy bower,
   And safety watch unsleeping near thee,
And happy in thy parting hour,
   Celestial hope shall stoop to cheer thee.

"'But if the faithless thirst of change,
   Or slow consuming sloth should move thee,
Then dread those countless foes that range,
   Terrific in the air above thee.
They cannot pierce thy radiant sphere
   While faithful hands that flame shall cherish,
But woe to thee if slumbering near,
   Thou leav'st its saving light to perish!'

"Upward I looked with shuddering awe,
   And in the growing gloom that bound us,
Full many a dismal shape I saw,
   Slow winging in the air around us.
Grim-visaged death and fierce despair,
   And unbelief with aspect sneering,
And ruin with affrighted stare,
   Disastrous through the mist appearing.

"Heart-stricken at the direful sight
   Awhile I stood appalled in spirit,
But cheered by that celestial light,
   I took my lonely station near it.
Dissolving on the fragrant air
   No more I saw that form before me,
But by the sweetness breathing there
   I felt her influence still was o'er me

"Awhile I kept, with watchful heed,
   My task of duty and of pleasure,
Exact at eve and morn to feed
   That holy flame with ample measure.
Those smiling walks and various flowers
   Each day I hailed with bosom tender,
Nor e'er beyond those happy bowers
   Indulged the idle wish to wander.

'But soon the scene familiar grew,
   Of peace unchanged my heart was weary,
Till in the thirst of pleasures new,
   Even that sweet scene looked blank and dreary.
Oppressive seemed that task unchanged,
   That light had lost its radiant beauty,
For when the will is once estranged,
   Oh! heavy weighs the yoke of duty.

"Why need the fearful end to tell?
   One eve beside the lamp reposing,
Deep slumber on my spirit fell,
   My lids in gradual darkness closing.
Terrific sounds my slumber broke,
   That lamp had quenched in darkness lonely
And shivering in the gloom I woke
   To see the coming ruin only.

"So passed my dream, and it hath proved
    The symbol of my waking story—
My youthful hours thus swiftly moved
    In thoughts of peace and heavenly glory.
So gradual, while with lessening zeal
    Devotion's ardent flame I cherished,
Did sloth upon its fervour steal,
    Till in my darkening soul it perished.

"Oh, if there be a healing force
    In sacred rite or counsel holy,
To quench the fire of dread remorse,
    Relieve its victim bending lowly!
'Twas I who wrought, with lying tale,
    Woe, undeserved, for young Matt Hyland,
Now wandering in the western gale,
    An exile from his native island!

"The Desmond held my words for sooth,
    And paid them with his golden treasure,
But conscience, with avenging tooth,
    To anguish turned the short-lived pleasure.
My waking thoughts are filled with gloom,
    And when the veil of sleep is o'er me,
Dark scenes of woe, beyond the tomb,
    In gloomy force arise before me.

"Last night, when scarce a struggling beam
    Of moonlight on the vale was shining,
Oppressed by many a boding dream,
    I lay upon my couch reclining.
While in the midnight solitude
    Hoarse murmuring broke the wintry billow,
The sheeted ghost of Melcha stood
    Terrific by my lonely pillow!

With voice whose piercing tones conveyed
   Through all my soul a speechless terror.
"Where is my son?" exclaimed the shade,
   "My child unknown to blame or error?
Perhaps 'mid whitening breakers cast
   On some wild coast, relentless scowling:
Even now for him that wintry blast
   His stormy song of death is howling.

"But happier in his ocean tomb,
   In blameless death, he sleeps securely
Than thou, to that appalling doom
   The traitor reaps, devoted surely.
Ah, tremble for that dreadful hour
   When man shall rise to judgment waking,
For pain shall be thy lasting dower
   When light and joy for him are breaking!"

Delirious with prophetic fear,
   At dawn I left the silent dwelling,
When distant on my watchful ear
   The matin hymn came faintly swelling.
And now, even now, within my heart
   Again I feel that boding sadness.
Save! save me from that demon guest!
   Oh, save me from those thoughts of madness!

"Quick! quick! receive the broken words,
   Upon my struggling breath that gather;
A moment hold! ye rending chords!
   A moment hear! O holy father!
Grim conscience free that iron clasp,
   Since now the dreadful tale is spoken:
Pale fear relax thy frozen grasp,
   And leave my wretched heart unbroken!"

"Vainly to me," with drooping head
    And pitying accents whispered slowly—
"Vainly to me," the father said,
  "Thou showest thy hidden deed unholy.
Vainly to heaven for peace and rest,
    Thy prayer shall rise, rejected ever,
While yet the wrong is unredressed,
    Even to the wronger's last endeavour.

"Go seek the Desmond in his hall,
    Where lone he wastes each joyous season,
That foundless tale of guilt recall
    Around that tangled skein of treason!"
Deep shuddering shrank the timid maid,
    Her face within her hands concealing,
And silent long and pondering staid
    With sudden fear and anguish thrilling.

"Oh! how," she said, "can mortal brook,
    In shameless confidence reposing,
The piercing light of Desmond's look,
    Such tale of infamy disclosing?
O father, in the Desmond's ear,
    Breathe thou that fearful revelation:
For howsoe'er the tale he bear
    Alike shall be the reparation!"

"Alike for him, but not for thee,"
    The father answered, calmly speaking:
"More peaceful far thy heart shall be
    Thyself that guilty silence breaking,
The Desmond's glance thou could'st abide
    With that unholy falsehood swelling,
Thou well could'st bow thy bosom's pride
    To do the ill thou shunnest in telling.

"Such difference may'st thou ever heed
    Between remorse and true repentance
One mourns at heart the guilty deed,
    One fears alone the coming sentence.
Cast thou thy happy part with those
    Who share, my child, the purer feeling
And what thou did'st for Virtue's foes,
    Blush not for Virtue's self revealing.

"How many doomed in cureless woe
    To feel the inward worm for ever,
Could they that lingering pain forego,
    Would gladly use such light endeavour!
Then still resist that evil shame
    That limed holds thy struggling reason,
And meekly take that transient blame—
    Light penalty for heaviest treason."

He said and left the holy aisle,
    The arched cloister slowly seeking,
For now, with cold and cheerless smile,
    The winter day was broadly breaking.
Thy strains, Sedulius, bursting free,
    Arose in solemn sweetness blending,
A solis ortus cardine,
    Harmonious with the sun ascending.

Before that lonely altar now,
    Her fervent hands devoutly wreathing,
The maiden bows her reverent brow,
    A prayer for peace and mercy breathing.
Like that fair light, out-bursting clear,
    On scenes in wintry gloom benighted,
Hope stole upon her bosom's fear,
    And peace its morning star beam lighted.

"Yes—frown the chieftain as he may,
　　Howe'er oppressed by shame and terror,
I will retrace that tangled way,
　　Unfolding all the maze of error.
I will unsay that treacherous tale
　　And clear the fame of young Matt Hyland,
And he shall see his native vale,
　　And tread again his native island!"

PART VI.

Nor always in this vale of tears
　　Hath fair desert his meed awarded,
Nor earthly good nor ill appears
　　By measured rule of right accorded.
For justice holds her final doom
　　Still o'er the reckless world suspended,
Till that appointed hour of gloom
　　When man's elective power is ended.

Then if by gathering woes oppressed
　　Thou se'est fair virtue here encumbered,
Or vice upborne with haughty crest
　　Amid the sons of glory numbered.
Oh, never lend impatient lips
　　To question or complaint unholy,
But wait that great Apocalypse
　　With humble hope and reference lowly.

Dread day of vindication! Then
  Ye strong in self-sufficient reason,
Who walk amid the sons of men,
  Triumphant in your transient season.
Ye scoffers of the lowly few,
  Who tread the paths of meek devotion
How idle, in your altered view,
  Will then appear each stunted notion.

Ye who have made your gods of gold,
  Ye dabblers in the slime of pleasure,
Who for a pottage-mess have sold
  Your birthright of celestial treasure,
Oh, dread that long abiding time,
  When, in the general wreck assembling,
Each son of unrepented crime
  Shall drink the menaced cup of trembling.

Yet sometimes heaven in mercy here
  Will lift the yoke from struggling merit,
Lest, bowed beneath the weight severe,
  Despair should crush the feeble spirit.
They best may hope such influence kind
  Oppressed by fortune's frown distressing,
Like Hyland, with discerning mind,
  Who least regard the dangerous blessing.

Slow pacing in the day-beam cold,
  Along the woodland vale returning,
Young Nora seeks the Desmond's hold,
  New hope within her bosom burning
Oh! sweet the earliest glimpse of light,
  To those who track a stormy ocean,
But sweeter far the dawning bright
  Of peace on terror's wild emotion.

That baffled fiend, whose bootless guile
    To dark unmingled hate was changing,
Beheld her leave that holy aisle,
    Along the wintry woodland ranging:
And strove to shake her purpose new
    With startling doubt and inward question,
And 'mid her altering counsels threw
    Full many a deep and dread suggestion.

" Hath reason o'er thy wandering thought
    Her saving empire lost for ever,
Hast thou the Desmond's mood forgot,
    From justice stern departing never?
And wilt thou trust the influence mild
    Of mercy on the soul attending,
Of him who from his only child
    Can turn with iron heart unbending?

" Hast thou so soon the hope resigned
    Of future gain from Desmond's favour,
Hath fortune for thy palled mind
    So quickly lost its witching savour,
That thus a few accustomed words,
    Habitual in thine ear repeated,
Have all untuned hope's ready chords,
    And all her brilliant aim defeated?

" Yet if, on bright ambition's path,
    No fragrant leaf hath power to charm
Let thoughts of Desmond's coming wrath
    Resistless in its might alarm thee.
Perchance ere long thy lot may be
    To hang a corpse on yonder island,
Triumphant sight for all to see
    Who mourn the doom of young Matt Hyland.

Again, again, in Nora's brain,
    Confused, her slumbering fears awaken;
Again by thoughts of coming pain
    And earthly shame her soul is shaken.
All trembling through the postern way
    She passed into that lordly tower,
And long in musing anguish lay
    Concealed within her secret bower.

Hark! at the door, with whispering call,
    Who breaks her mood of anxious feeling
'Tis he who, in the banquet hall,
    To Desmond holds the wine cup kneeling.
"Haste, Nora, haste! since break of dawn,
    I've sought thee at the chieftain's order,
Nor found thee on the misty lawn,
    Nor on the river's darkening border.

"Some matter, sure, of import high,
    The chieftain's noble mind encumbers,
That, ere the morn-beam crossed the sky,
    So early broke his wonted slumbers.
Since midnight, in the eastern hall,
    He wakes by one cold rushlight only;
There slow his thoughtful footsteps fall,
    Like one who keeps some vigil lonely"

With sinking heart and trembling frame
    Young Nora leaves her secret bower,
Oppressed by fear of instant shame,
    And Desmond's swift avenging power
Within his chamber pacing lone
    With paly brow serene she found him,
While, from the deep embrasure thrown,
    The morning light fell cold around him.

Long time, with brow inclined, he stood,
    And arms athwart his bosom folded,
In deep deliberative mood,
    Like form by artful sculptor moulded.
Then, glancing towards the panelled oak,
    Lest listening ears his speech should gather
Thus joy-bereaved and sorrowing spoke,
    In mournful tones, the anxious father.

" When first this wretched tale," he said,
    " Thou breathed'st with faithful tongue revealing
I know thy honest heart was led
    By duteous care and loyal feeling.
Yet not the less its import wild
    For me has wrought unmeasured sorrow,
While thus I see my only child,
    Slow sinking, droop from day to morrow.

" I thought the still-effacing power
    Of time might cure her spirit's sadness,
And gradual, like a bruised flower,
    Her heart might ope to light and gladness;
But vain my hope, from day to day
    She sinks in silent anguish pining,
In health-consuming slow decay,
    With sweet submissive heart declining.

" If right I read my daughter's thought,
    Not inward disappointment only,
Nor passion in her breast has wrought
    This secret grief abiding lonely;
For cheerful seems her voice and eye,
    With watchful heed unmurmuring ever,
And oft she checks the rising sigh
    With spirit-touching sweet endeavour.

"But self-accusing, stern remorse
  For Hyland, still in exile, mourning,
Hath set, with deep and branding force,
  Its stamp within her spirit burning.
That traitorous youth, too lately known,
  In all his dark deception shameless,
His blackening guilt she makes her own,
  And holds the wily ingrate blameless.

"Soon childless in my natal hall,
  By every earthly hope forsaken,
In woe for me each night shall fall,
  In woe each weary morn awaken.
Strange feet, when Desmond sleeps in earth,
  Shall tread his old familiar bowers,
And aliens to his blood and birth
  Shall rule the Desmond's lordly towers.

"But, still, let truth and right prevail;
  Let justice hold her place unmoving,
Nor yield with wavering impulse frail,
  Such base, presumptuous guilt approving
For better live, and die bereaved
  Of every ardent aspiration,
My bosom once with joy received,
  Than gild deceit with rank and station!

"Meanwhile, in penitential deeds,
  I'll seek some potent influence healing,
To staunch the festering wound that bleeds
  Within my bosom keenly thrilling.
I'll seek beyond the eastern sea
  Some saintly shrine, a pilgrim lowly,
Nor vainly linger here to see
  My daughter's life-beam fading slowly

"Perchance some taint of secret pride,
  Or early unatoned error,
Or passion, still unmortified,
  Hath wrought for me this doom of terror.
In meditation's purged sight
  Has heaven the searching power accorded,
To bring such hidden stain to light
  Within the bosom lurking sordid.

"E'en now I hear, in Shannon's mouth,
  Matt Hyland's ship again is heaving,
Victorious from the hostile south,
  With conquering prow the waters cleaving.
Perhaps, in this awakening light,
  He views each creek and well-known island,
And soon, in Desmond's high despite,
  May tread again his native island.

"But let him share that triumph brief,
  By sure, though late, remorse attended,
For me, engulphed in whelming grief,
  Resentment in my breast is ended.
Enough that he shall see no more,
  While lasts for me life's mournful season,
These smiling lawns and winding shore,
  Made lonely by his thankless treason.

"For, oh! throughout this loved vale,
  Each scene the breaking morn discloses,
When sweetest breathes the vernal gale,
  When liveliest spring the summer roses;
The tender bower, the woodland wild,
  Yon stream that flows in murmuring sadness,
But mind me of my pining child,
  And all her vanished hours of gladness.

"O Helen, Helen! thus forlorn,
   While yet thy lamp of life is shining,
It, sick at heart, I sigh and mourn
   To see thy gentle frame declining,
How lone will seem this echoing hall,
   How deep shall be my daily sighing,
When, dark beneath her funeral pall,
   My child in Death's cold arms is lying.

"Ah me, ah me! I dread the day—
   Ah me, I dread that hour of mourning,
When, barefoot through yon arched way,
   From distant pilgrimage returning,
The warder at my voice shall bend,
   And hail his lord with mournful greeting,
And tell of Helen's saintly end,
   Sweet Helen's dying words repeating.

"For, oh! to me the merriest song
   By Zephyr sung at hush of even,
On odorous pinions borne along,
   Melodious in the vaulted Heaven,
Could never fill my charmed ear
   With such delicious joy abounding,
As Helen's well-known accents dear,
   Like falling silver sweetly sounding

"But blessed be the counsels high
   Of him who rules this wide creation:
For how can man's presumptuous eye
   Fore-know the eternal dispensation?
Perhaps e'en while with hope grown cold
   And hearts in careless anguish bending,
We mourn throughout the altered hold,
   Bright joy is at the gate attending.

"For thee, to whom our thanks we owe
    For Desmond's ancient fame defended,
What can thy grateful Lord bestow
    Co-equal with thy service splendid?
In distant regions wandering far,
    'Mid barren wilds or breakers hoary,
Be still a bright propitious star,
    To old Fitz-Gerald's name and story."

While thus the sorrowing chieftain spoke,
    Around her frame convulsive bending,
Young Nora drew her hooded cloak,
    With stifled sobs her bosom rending.
But when she heard his kind "farewell!"
    Resistless grew the struggling feeling,
And shrieking at his feet she fell,
    For mercy to the Earl appealing.

"Oh, best of masters and of friends,
    Forgive—forgive, a wretch unholy,
Who envious wove for basest ends
    This web of crime and melancholy.
Not Hyland's are the guilt and blame,
    Not Hyland's is that blackening treason,
On me should fall the weight of shame
    With juster cause and fairer reason.

"Oh, hide awhile that glance severe,
    Till all my hideous tale is ended,
Lest lost I sink with conscious fear,
    Ere yet the wrong be half amended.
Like him who man's Redeemer sold,
    By horrors of the night afrighted,
I bring again that guilty gold
    For which my bosom's peace was blighted.

"'Twas I who framed that soundless tale,
    Whose influence wrought for young Matt Hyland
Long exile from his native vale,
    His natal cot and lonely island."
She said, and all her guilt confessed;
    She told him how he wronged his daughter;
And blameless poor Matt Hyland pressed,
    And sent him o'er the western water.

Long time the Earl, with look amazed,
    Like one from mid-day sleep awaking,
Upon the prostrate maiden gazed
    With troubled bosom inly aching.
Till all the dark conviction broke
    Resistless on his breast descending,
And, trembling through his frame, he spoke;
    With grief and wonder mildly blending.

"A falsehood!—ha!—and thine the word!
    What murderess!—thine the guilty story,
Whose import keen as traitor's sword
    Lies rangling in my breast and gory.
And thou for Desmond's hand hast filled
    That chalice of exceeding anguish,
Beneath whose withering influence chilled
    I've given my daughter's life to languish!

"And blameless was my saintly child!
    And guiltless, too, my faithful Hyland!
By Desmond's causeless rage exiled,
    An outcast from his native island!
Oh, web of mischief darkly wrought!
    Oh, rashness, rashness, past the telling,
What cloud obscured my darkling thought,
    What frenzy in my heart was swelling!

"Not thine, not thine this hideous blame,
　　With me should rest the guilt, the terror,
Who, jealous of our ancient name,
　　Too soon received that slanderous error.
For Hyland's wrong, for Helen's peace,
　　Too late, alas, too late discovered,
And many a vanished hope of bliss,
　　That round my doting fancy hovered!

"But go! the task were idle now
　　Thy motive or design to question,
Had any told this tale but thou
　　My mind had scorned the wild suggestion.
The morn that now in tumult breaks
　　Should end for thee life's guilty season,
But that thy free confession takes
　　Some shadow from the hue of treason."

He said, and from the hall withdrew,
　　While trembling rose the wretched maiden,
And shuns each menial's envious view
　　With heart confused and sorrow laden.
Alone, in speechless shame, she lay
　　Concealed within her secret bower,
Till cheerless closed the wintry day
　　And darkness sunk on vale and tower.

Not sudden in his daughter's ear
　　The Earl revealed these words of gladness,
Lest, bowed beneath the shock severe,
　　Even joy might aid the work of sadness.
But gradual, as with altered mind,
　　He mildly spoke of young Matt Hyland,
And owned the hasty doom unkind
　　That sent him from his native island.

Thus slowly as the summer dawn
　　With ray on ray successive breaking,
Each shade of lingering gloom withdrawn,
　　Delight in Helen's heart was waking—
Delight, at Hyland's fame redeemed,
　　At Desmond's old regard returning,
Once more in Helen's glances beamed,
　　Within her ardent spirit burning.

Again the ruddy freshening blood
　　In Helen's joyous veins was rushing,
Again with early health renewed
　　Young Helen's brightening cheek was blushing.
For now the only earthly care,
　　Despite her bosom's pure endeavour,
That held its rankling influence there
　　Was banished from her heart for ever.

*　　*　　*　　*

*　　*　　*　　*

In sweet Adare, the jocund spring
　　His notes of odorous joy is breathing,
The wild birds in the woodland sing,
　　The wild flowers in the vale are breathing.
There winds the Mague, as silver clear,
　　Among the elms so sweetly flowing—
There fragrant in the early year,
　　While roses on the banks are blowing.

The wild duck seeks the sedgy bank,
   Or dives beneath the glistening billow,
Where graceful droop and clustering dank
   The osier bright and rustling willow;
The hawthorn scents the leafy dale,
   In thicket lone the stag is belling,
And sweet along the echoing vale
   The sound of vernal joy is swelling.

All hush and still the breezes slept
   On flowery lawn and murmuring water,
When Desmond to the chamber crept
   Where slumbering lay his beauteous daughter.
He softly kissed her brow of pearl,
   And gently pressed her golden tresses,
And said, "Arise, my darling girl!"
   And woke her with his fond caresses.

"Arise," he said, "my daughter dear,
   I did not know you loved so truly,
There's lasting bliss for duteous fear,
   And thanks for service rendered duly.
I've sent my knights to Shannon's side
   To bring thy exile to our bowers;
And thou shalt be Matt Hyland's bride,
   And he shall rule thy father's towers.

Arise! arise! in sweet Adare
   The village maids and youths assemble;
Already in the sunny air
   The sounds of sylvan music tremble.
Throughout the town the tale is told
   That Desmond longs again to greet him,
Expectant in the festal hold,
   With open arms and heart, to meet him.

"Nor fear I for our ancient name,
　　In such unwonted union blending,
Lest Desmond reap his country's blame,
　　From dignity of place descending;
For he hath come of high degree,
　　From regal blood of old O'Connor,
And won upon the stormy sea
　　His gallant way to rank and honour.

"Oh, once again from Helen's smile
　　Shall Desmond's heart contentment gather,
Once more shall Helen's mirth beguile
　　The sadness of her aged father.
When by our hearth at evening close,
　　Thou heard'st in sweet, domestic leisure,
How first this wondrous change arose
　　That turned our household gloom to pleasure!"

First low to Heaven, with grateful heart,
　　The maiden bent in speechless feeling,
That Heaven had ta'en the injured part,
　　Young Hyland's stainless truth revealing
Nor ceased her infelt thanks to pay
　　For joy restored and vanished mourning,
'Till boisterous menials ran to say
　　That Hyland was in sight returning.

Ah, sweet Adare; ah, lovely vale!
　　Ah, pleasant haunt of sylvan splendour;
Nor summer sun, nor moonlight pale
　　E'er saw a scene more softly tender.
There through the wild woods echoing arms
　　Triumphant notes of joy were swelling,
When, safe returned from war's alarms,
　　Young Hyland reached his native dwelling.

With joy she wept to hear the tale,
   Around her father's bosom clinging,
While shouts arose in all the vale,
   And bells in gay Adare were ringing.
With kerchiefs gay and wreathed flowers,
   Bright shone the festal scene surrounding,
And blithe from all the woodland bowers
   The harp and rustic pipe were sounding.

Prepare, prepare the festal board
   With rushen torches brightly burning,
Make welcome meet for joy restored,
   And peace renewed and Hope returning.
For now along the crowded way
   They hail him to his native island,
And there they held a wedding day,
   And made a Lord of poor Matt Hyland!

Oh, ever thus, let worth be found,
   Triumphant in each varying danger
Be merit still with conquest crowned
   To suffering as to guilt a stranger;
Here oft, as in the promised land,
   Where joy shall reign unchanged for ever,
May mercy aid with succouring hand
   Unfriended Virtue's high endeavour!

Ye wanderers in the narrow path
   To bright perfection's portal leading,
Though chilled by storms of worldly wrath,
   Forlorn ye toil and inly bleeding.
Still firmly hold with faithful zeal—
   Far, far beyond all earthly pleasure—
Integrity through woe or weal,
   And Hope, who builds in Heaven her treasure.

So may your well-tried patience find
　　The cup of anguish meekly tasting,
In this bleak world a peaceful mind,
　　And *there*, a welcome bright and lasting
So may, even here, your bosoms share
　　The transient good that life can render,
And in affliction learn to bear
　　The sharper test of worldly splendour.

THE END.

GISIPPUS;

OR

THE FORGOTTEN FRIEND.

"Freeze, freeze, thou bitter sky,
Thou dost not bite so nigh
      As benefits forgot!
Though thou the waters warp,
Thy sting is not so sharp
      As friend remembered not."
"As you like it."

GISIPPUS:

A PLAY IN FIVE ACTS;

AS PERFORMED AT DRURY LANE.

BY

GERALD GRIFFIN.

Dublin:
JAMES DUFFY & CO., LTD.,
15 WELLINGTON QUAY.

PREFACE.

The following play has been brought before the public under rather peculiar circumstances. The author of "The Collegians," to whom it owed its origin, had, in the early part of his literary career, a strong turn for dramatic writing, and so long ago as the year 1823, had produced no less than four tragedies. The first of these was begun while he was yet in his eighteenth year, and Gisippus, the last of them, before he had completed his twentieth. He went to London in the summer of that year, filled with the high aspirings after literary fame which are characteristic of that passion in early youth, and which were strengthened, in his case, by a temperament peculiarly ardent and sanguine, and by his want of experience of the difficulties with which its attainment is usually beset. His intention was to get one of them performed at one of the great theatres, if possible; but at that time the public taste was vitiated by managers who yielded to the depraved appetites of the multitude, instead of endeavouring to correct them. Mechanical wonders, cataracts of real water, brilliant scenic representations, and sights of an amphitheatrical and popular character, usurped the place of the legitimate drama, and after many distressing difficulties, and much valuable time sacrificed in the attempt, he gave it up as hopeless. Gisippus is the only one of those plays that has been preserved among his papers; the rest there is no trace of, and it is presumed they have been destroyed. It may perhaps be interesting to notice what the author himself says of it in a letter to his friends in Ireland, a short time before this determination was come to. "But what gives me the greatest satisfaction respecting it is, the consciousness that I have written *an original play*. That passion of revenge, you know, was threadbare" (he alludes to the subject of one of his former pieces). "Banim has made some suggestions, which I have adopted; I will finish it immediately, place it in his hands, and abide the result in following other pursuits." Some time after the author's death, his friends having become acquainted with Mr. Charles Kean when he was in the south of Ireland, were induced to submit it to his judgment. In a letter received from him soon after, he says: "I have read Gisippus with the greatest attention, and though fully impressed with the beauty of the language and the high talent displayed throughout, yet I should fear its success as an acting play, and, indeed, should be sorry to produce it on the stage." They have been given to understand that subsequently it was submitted to the manager of one of the most respectable of the lesser theatres, who seems to have been much less touched by the beauties of the piece than Mr. Kean, for when taxed subsequently by one who more fully appreciated its merits, with the want of judgment shown in letting such a play "slip through his fingers," he stated that, "he had only read it on the outside of an omnibus." These circumstances, however, are only mentioned for the purpose of showing that the legitimate drama has had difficulties to contend with that could not readily be anticipated, and that the merits of a piece have not hitherto been sufficient to prevent its rejection. As the author's friends, notwithstanding these repeated discouragements, felt very confident of the excellence of the play, and as the latter part of Mr. Kean's expressed opinion seemed so decided and strong, they could hardly bring themselves to believe he had given the subject all the consideration it deserved. They therefore determined to make one attempt more, and placed it in the hands of Mr. Macready, who, after having perused it, pronounced a decided opinion in its favour. They cannot help expressing a high degree of satisfaction, at having their previous feelings on the subject thus strengthened by the decision of a person of Mr. Macready's good taste and judgment, and they look forward with confidence to the public for a confirmation of his opinion, and for the encouragement of that desire which he has manifested to give the English drama the position its merits entitle it to.

THE MANAGERS OF COUNTRY THEATRES are requested to observe, that the play of "GISIPPUS" must not be represented.

GISIPPUS.

ACT I.
SCENE I.—A STREET IN ATHENS.

Enter CHREMES, PHEAX, *and* MEDON.

MEDON.
The sweetest, fairest, loveliest maid in Athens,
Although I be her brother that do say it.

CHREMES.
Sum all perfection in one little word,
And say—the wealthiest maid in Athens.

MEDON.
Nay,
Gisippus does not care for that! He loves
Too deeply,—and too fervently for that.
And yet, I think, not the *less* truly for it!
The shafts of the boy God ne'er wound less surely,
For being tipt with gold!

PHEAX.
But, prithee, Medon,
When goes the wedding forward?

MEDON.
Why, he hath waited
The changing of her humour these three years,

In patient fondness; and it seems not like,
Now he hath bent at last her stubborn will,
Unto the fashion of his own—and weaned
Her memory from that phantom-love that haunted it,
He'll stay the consummation of his joy
O'erlong.   But look you yonder!

PHEAX.

Ha!   'Tis Fulvius!

CHREMES.

Returned so soon from Corinth?

MEDON.

How!—what Fulvius?

CHREMES.

You should have heard Gisippus speak of him.
He is his other self; his Pylades—
The young Roman Student!

MEDON.

As I know him not,
And have some matters that command me hence,
I'll leave you to accost him!—Fare you well.
(Exit MEDON *and* PHEAX.)

Enter FULVIUS.

CHREMES.

So early from your studies, Fulvius?

FULVIUS.

A smile!   I've searched half Athens for a smile,
And never found it.   What a heavy time
I spend here with you Greeks!   I soon shall quit
Your Academic groves, and I am glad on't.

CHREMES.

Of all men you should not complain of dulness,
Yourself a very Cynic.   You have not

The capability of pleasantry;
Our maids of Athens find you cold and harsh,
And given to thinking.

FULVIUS.

I'll be so no longer!
'Tis true I had a cause!   (*Muses.*)

CHREMES.

And do ye still
Dream of this fair Corinthian vision? Oh!
How passionate a sigh was there!

FULVIUS.

Peace! Peace!

CHREMES.

To pine for years upon a boyish fancy,
And let the thousand bright and real beauties,
That court your praise, flit by you all unheeded?
Shame! Shame! You ne'er again will meet your old love,
(And though you should, you've found her most unworthy,)
Then cast that memory to the winds.   Look round ye!
There are bright eyes and fairer forms in Greece,
And hearts less false, believe me.   I have seen ye
Before this fair Corinthian fancy seized you
Flatter a graceful robe, with such a spirit;
And make such furious protestations!   Oh!
But now your manhood is forgotten.

FULVIUS.

No!
Give me your hand—You have well counselled me,
And thou shalt see me changed to what I was,
From this time forth—No! My lost love shall find
I can be free and generous as she was.—
The first fair form I meet, I bend the knee to;
I'll be no pining fool to die forsaken,
And have my name and fortune chronicled

Among the tales of true-love victims—Hark thee,
I'll think of her no more.

CHREMES.

Bravely resolved!

FULVIUS.

I say, I'll think of her no more!

CHREMES.

And wisely!
And gallantly 'tis said.

FULVIUS.

No, by the Gods
I never will!

CHREMES.

Well, you have said enough on't—
Here comes Gisippus with his wedding face on!

FULVIUS.

Gisippus?

CHREMES.

There's a smile!—you longed to see one;
The smile successful love wears—Are ye bid
Unto the bridal?

FULVIUS.

Ay—but know not yet
The lady of the feast—nor sought to learn
Ere this.   What!   Gisippus?

Enter GISIPPUS, *and a Slave.*

GISIPPUS.

You are well met—
I'm glad to see you wear so gay a brow
To honour our espousal—(*To Slave*) To your mistress—
Bid her expect me earlier than she looked for!
I've sought you, Fulvius.   (*Exit* SLAVE.)

FULVIUS.

I shall now, at length,

Behold this paragon, your bride, and know her.
Do you find her still a paragon?

GISIPPUS.

And think you
Love can be led by circumstance so easily?

CHREMES.

Ay—passion hath its change of seasons, sir;
And 'twere as vain to hope eternal summer
As an eternal faith. This is with you
The spring of courtship—which calls up the flowers,
The fairest flowers of Love—your blooming fancies—
Your fragrant love thoughts, murmuring vows and
    prayers,
But even as nature's spring—love's too must roll
Away—and then comes your adored honeymoon,
Love's summer of enjoyment—next, his autumn
Of lukewarm liking, verging to indifference,
The time of shrugs and yawns and absent thoughts;
And then his winter comes—frosty and dry,
Sharp, biting, bitter—cunning in cold taunts—
Making the evening hearth, so late a paradise,
A place of harsh uncomfort. Then, O Love!
How suddenly thy changeful votaries
Find thy Elysium void!—from the pale poet,
Who wooed the groves in song-lorn melancholy,
To him, the blustering terror of the field,
Who sighed like Boreas, and made love like war—
All, weary grown of the ignoble bondage,
Look back with scorn upon the yoke they've spurned,
And wonder how the silly toy had power
To make them sin so palpably 'gainst wisdom.—

GISIPPUS.

Peace, scoffer!—

CHREMES.

True—that speech was for a married man,
Not for a mateless turtle like myself.—

I'll leave you with a proselyte I've made
Within this hour;—(no very worthless votary;)
You will confirm the change I have begun.
                              (*Exit* CHREMES.)

GISIPPUS.

Come to my bridal, Fulvius. You shall see
Some beauties worth the wooing, though they lack
The eagle spirit of your Roman maids.

FULVIUS.

And I shall deem them lovely in that want—
Those eagle spirits are too grand for me.
Such forms may grace a painter's canvass well,
Grouped in a legend of the Commonwealth,
But by an evening fire are cold companions.
Woman was made for love, and not for wonder.
Give me the pliant—soft—and human fair—
But heaven defend me from your soaring beauties!
Your love is none of these?

GISIPPUS.

Come with me, sir—
Let your own judgment answer you.

FULVIUS.

And tell me,
You are indeed the happy one you seem?

GISIPPUS.

Happy!—Ah, thou cold Western—thou dull scholar,
Made up of crabbed systems, I'll not talk
With thee of that thou canst not comprehend.
And yet if thou hadst seen her, Fulvius—
Although thy breast were frigid as the stream
That curdles through the usurer's withered veins,
Thou still wouldst own my happiness. But yet—

FULVIUS.
Nay, if your fortune may admit that clause,
I shall not envy you.
GISIPPUS.
One thing troubles me—
FULVIUS.
Ay—I should wonder else. Did you then look
To rest your happiness on a woman's will
And find it unalloyed? What is this seasoner
Of yours?
GISIPPUS.
Why, nothing. It hath taken birth
In thought alone—a doubt of love too sensitive
To give even rapture's self free entertainment.
Some old affection combated my love—
That still is made a mystery. Faith stands
On unsure grounds where confidence is wanting—
And hers I lack—But let doubt find out me,
I'll not seek it, nor do—She's mine—and I
Could trace no lingering of the hesitation,
That chilled my earlier wooing, in the deed
That made her mine at length. But fare ye well,
I'll meet you straight and bring you to her house;
My joy must not be lonely as my grief was.
FULVIUS.
There's something more than beauty to content ye?
GISIPPUS.
There are, as you will see, some fair possessions;
Yet, Fulvius, by the honour of my love
I had no thought of these when I became
Her suitor.
FULVIUS.
I believe you.
GISIPPUS.
And it was not

x

My fortunes placed my need beyond them neither;
Had this not chanced, I were a ruin every way.
Two thousand sesterces were all I owned,
And those I was a debtor for; I staked
My villa to command them.   Do you wonder
That I should thus send my last venture forth
On the frail prospect of a woman's kindness?

FULVIUS.

I rather wonder that hath not deceived you.
But frankly, I am glad to see you happy,
And like yourself again.

GISIPPUS.

Oh, I have but now
Begun to live—Until this morn my soul
Ran its career in darkness—and the world,
Fair unto those who live in fortune's smiles,
Was unto me a weariness—but this
Hath poured a flood of light into my soul
That no succeeding night can chill or darken.
(*Exeunt severally.*)

SCENE II.—THE GARDENS OF SOPHRONIA, WITH GROTTOES, &c.—MUSIC.

Enter SOPHRONIA *and* HERO.

HERO.

SOPHRONIA!   Not a word!   Is it to hide
A blush or tear, that veil's so closely drawn?
Dear friend, speak to me; on my heart your silence
Falls like an augury of ill, least fitting
Of any to a day like this.

SOPHRONIA.

Oh, Hero!
Do not question me. I have not known (too late
I find it) all my spirit's weakness.—Oh!
What an inconstant thing is woman's will—
On what a trifle may the happiness
Of a whole existence hang! A summer wind
That is but air—nothing—may turn an argosy,
And the poor word in weary weakness uttered,
Hath power to bind beyond release or hope
A life's whole destiny.

HERO.

The Gods have made
Thee their especial care.

SOPHRONIA.

Ay—yes.

HERO.

Sophronia, some grief is at your heart; may I not share
  it?

(SOPHRONIA *avoids her.*)
This is not like yourself, Sophronia—friend—
(*Retiring conversing.*)

Enter FULVIUS *and* CHREMES.

CHREMES.

Why fortune must have ta'en her bandage off
To shower such graces on you. You must dedicate
A temple to the goddess. From the Emperor?
Sent for to Rome already?

FULVIUS.

I have here
The letters which command my presence there;
I am promised honours. If you be not bound
Too closely to your native city, Chremes,
Let not this change divide us—Share my fortunes,

And be to me a memory of what
Gisippus was till love made friendship light.

     CHREMES.
We'll speak of this again ere you leave Athens.
Did you not say he should have met you here?

     FULVIUS.
A little further on—
   (FULVIUS *fixes his eye on* SOPHRONIA, *who
    is talking with* HERO.)

     CHREMES.
'Twill be no grateful tidings for his ear,
Those news of your return to Rome.

     FULVIUS.
That form!——

     CHREMES.
You do not think of leaving till the festival
Be past?

     FULVIUS.
How dim and wavering is the recollection
That stirs within me? There's some faint similitude
To an old memory I cannot now
Distinctly summon up.

     CHREMES.
What's this? Why gaze you so?

     FULVIUS.
It is the loveliest form I've looked upon
Since I have entered Athens!

     CHREMES.
It is indeed,
A bust for Dian's self.

     FULVIUS.
If she had left
Her wild wood for the portal of her temple,

To give her votaries a visible *audit*,
She could not move my admiration more—
I'll speak to her!

CHREMES.

You cannot think it, sure?
This is some lady of high estimation!
You are changed indeed!   What plea have you to offer?

FULVIUS.

I care not.   Let chance, which gives the occasion,
Be kinder yet and furnish me with matter.

CHREMES.

You are a madman!   (*Stopping him.*)

FULVIUS.

You are a coward!   Off!
A pitiful, dull trembler.   Hark you, sir;
Go you and marvel yonder, at her state,
And see it bend to me—'Twill do so!   Hush!
Be dumb—she speaks!—

CHREMES.

You will not be advised?

FULVIUS.

Psha!   No—away!—   (*Exit* CHREMES.)
Now, by Cytherea,
Here is no common beauty.   Would she but lift
That veil!   There is a sadness in her air
And motion.   Oh! if that veil hide beneath it
A sorrowing brow, when shall a smile be worshipped?

SOPHRONIA (*to* HERO, *coming a little forward.*)

But, trust me, since that "yes" was wrung from me
I have not rested.   You must come more frequently,
Else I grow serious as the fate that waits me.
Farewell!   I wait Gisippus here.

FULVIUS (*aside*).

Gisippus!

Some fair friend of the bride— (*Exit* HERO.)
(SOPHRONIA, *coming forward, suddenly
meets* FULVIUS *and starts back.*)

SOPHRONIA.

Ah, heaven!—

FULVIUS.

Your pardon, lady!
Do ye start from me as it were a spectre
That crossed your daylight path.—You shake and
    tremble!
These groves are silent, but not desolate,
And many ears are waking near you—Say
What is there in an honest face to terrify you?
As, sure, mine seems no other.

SOPHRONIA (*aside*).

It is Fulvius!
'Tis the same gallant air—the noble form
That caught my first affection—Years have made
But little change upon him.

FULVIUS.

How she regards me! (*Aside.*)

SOPHRONIA.

He knows me not! (*Seeming to go.*)

FULVIUS.

You would not go, lady,
Leaving me thus unsatisfied?

SOPHRONIA.

I know ye not, sir!

FULVIUS.

I am a Roman, and a friend of Gisippus!
A scholar too, just weaned from the harsh studies
Of your Athenian schools, and turning now
To find a gentler lesson in the fair
And varied volume nature lays before me!
A diligent and most untiring learner,

Could I but hope
That most excellent pattern of her skill
This morning shows me, might continue ever
My study and my inspiration.

SOPHRONIA.

You
Are pleasant, sir!

FULVIUS.

I have a failing that way—
Oh!
Could you but feel the wrong you do that brow
When you would make it minister to scorn,
No heart would mourn the absence of its light.

SOPHRONIA.

Vain men! And do ye seek to cozen us
With flattery so palpable as this?
You know it fair, and yet have never seen it!

FULVIUS.

But shall?—(*approaching her.*)

SOPHRONIA.

No. Named you not Gisippus, Roman?—

FULVIUS.

He is known to you?

SOPHRONIA.

He is.

FULVIUS.

His promised bride, too?

SOPHRONIA.

Should be my near friend.

FULVIUS.

And we thus stand at distance!—Now, by Nemesis,
I thought we should be friends. I know not why,
But though we sure have never met before,
That form already grows upon my soul

Familiar as a memory of its childhood.
Our sages teach (and now I find them reasonable),
There is between the destinies of mortals
A secret and mysterious coincidence
Drawn from one mighty principle of Nature;
A fixed necessity—a potent " must,"
That sways mortality through all its harmonies!
That souls are mingled and hearts wedded, ere
Those souls have felt the dawning of a thought:
Before those hearts have formed a pulse, or yet
Begun to beat with consciousness of being!
My heart is governed by a fate like this,
And drawn to thee, unknown—unseen.

SOPHRONIA.

Beware!
I am your friend and warn you. Trust me not,
Earth never formed a being half so false.
To him who shuns me, I can be more just;
To him who wooes like thee with heart on lip,
A very icicle.

FULVIUS.

I will believe you!—
'Tis beautiful, and so art thou—'tis fragile
And false—so ye would have me think ye—Bright,
So is thy beauty—sparkling as thy wit!
'Tis radiant as thy form; and it is cold,
And so art thou!

SOPHRONIA.

I am a dull diviner
If that speech were not meant for one, a foolish friend
Of mine, at Corinth once, who threw her heart
Away, thinking it given to a Roman youth.

FULVIUS.

At Corinth, lady!
Spoke you of Sophronia?

SOPHRONIA.

Why,
I named her not!—you've known her, then?

FULVIUS.

I have;
I pray you hear. There is a friend of mine—
A poor weak youth—Oh! hear me—for my life
Is wrapt in his, and that is failing fast.
He loved her—and she wronged him. Knew ye this?

SOPHRONIA.

No, truly. And yet I might say I knew her
(Her very heart) even as mine own.

FULVIUS.

She was
The fairest, yet the falsest thing that e'er
Made light of confidence. Her eyes looked brightest
When they were silent perjurers—Her voice
Sweetest when turned to deep deceit—Her smile
Pleasant as health, yet death's worst messenger!
This is my memory of her. Years, alas!
Have passed since I beheld her! Lives she?

SOPHRONIA.

Yes,
And for a new love. She has lived to learn
The wisdom of forgetfulness. 'Twill be
Some comfort to your false friend to hear this!

FULVIUS.

Oh! I was never false—Proud I might be,
I am—but though in very stubbornness,
I steeled my heart against the scorn that pained it;
And like the slave whose struggling in his chains
Makes them hang heavier and corrode more deeply,
The influence that I sought to smile away
But clung more sensibly about my heart,

Binding it down unto its first affections
More firmly while my laughing lip denied
The dear allegiance—Would Sophronia knew this!

SOPHRONIA.

Ay, if she had but known this!

FULVIUS.

Ay, idle sorrow now;
For had I sought her and bowed down my heart
Yet lower than its boyish pride could stoop,
It were in vain, for she esteemed the fancied wrong
Her own, and would have spurned the suit and me.

SOPHRONIA.

Oh, women have forgiving tempers, Fulvius;
You should have made the trial—

FULVIUS.

Ha!—that tone!—
I stand as one in mist—Am I deceived?

SOPHRONIA.

But now, indeed, 'tis late. Sophronia is
In Athens—and forgiveness past her power.

FULVIUS (*approaching her*).

The veil! In mercy! Oh, my anxious heart
And throbbing brain! The veil! Nay, raise it, lady,—
And snatch me from the agonising dream—
Say, do I err?
Or does my heart deceive me when it claims
That voice, for one familiar with its oldest
And best remembrances? It grows upon me
More rapidly and surely—My Sophronia,
Oh love! life! happiness! (*She throws back the veil.*)

SOPHRONIA.

Hold there!

FULVIUS.

No, no!

By thine own unchanged beauty, I do swear,
I am as innocent of wrong to *ye*
As aught in virtue or in truth!

SOPHRONIA.

It matters not;
I am no more mine own to meet thy faith,
Although I should believe it.

FULVIUS.

Say thou dost!
And where is he who dares dispute the consequence?
I do remember somewhat, lightly spoken
And hastily, (which thou wilt sure recall, love,)
That chills my breast to think on. Nay, put off
That distant air—Wave not your hand thus coldly,
As you would scatter sorrow with the action
Upon the heart that loves you. Register
My pardon, even by a look, and say
Unkindness sleeps between us and love wakes again.

SOPHRONIA.

It is too late, now.

FULVIUS.

Wherefore? Are you not
The same free Grecian maiden? I can see
No mark of bondage on you.

SOPHRONIA.

But there is
A heavy bondage. I am bound.

FULVIUS.

To me! (*Eagerly.*)
Think you I could forget that vow, Sophronia?
Truth, love, and justice are my witnesses,
(And surely you will honour them,) the heart
That stilled its beating to record the pledge,

Tenders it yet among its living pulses,
The dearest memory there!

SOPHRONIA.

This must be ended.
Fulvius—I am indeed—

FULVIUS (*interrupting her*).

Although thy lips,
Which are the beauteous ministers of Truth,
Of virgin Truth herself, had sworn that, lady,
I must not credit ye.

SOPHRONIA.

Then fare ye well,
The time must undeceive you.

FULVIUS.

Hold, Sophronia!
If any fearful, creeping, heartless slave
Have made a base advantage—O my blindness!
That I should leave to such a venomed slanderer
The opportunity he dared not vindicate—
But name him—and I will redeem thy pledge
Though I should tear it from his heart and give thee
A reeking witness with it.

SOPHRONIA.

'Tis a name
Will lay a quieter and heavier influence
Upon your spirit, Fulvius. You are sensitive
In friendship as in love?—

FULVIUS.

Ha! (*Starts back.*)

SOPHRONIA.

I am here
The mistress of the revel—Hark! Oh heaven!
My lord approaches—O forgive and leave me!

FULVIUS.

Your lord?

SOPHRONIA.

My husband—Gisippus! Your friend!
Oh! fly!

FULVIUS.

My friend? (*Abstractedly.*)

SOPHRONIA.

I fear your meeting.

FULVIUS.

Oh!
Avenging Nemesis!—O traitor, Hope!
What was there in the little store of peace
That I till now had laid unto my heart,
Thine eye should covet thus?

SOPHRONIA.

He comes! (*Anxiously.*)

FULVIUS.

I am glad of it! (*Starting round.*)

SOPHRONIA.

Mercy! you would not——

FULVIUS.

In his very teeth
I'll fling my charge—there let it stick, and blacken!
Ye bards, whose tales of Grecian faith are cherished,
In strains that credulous fancy dotes upon,
Your ashes shall no more be hallowed now.
It was a lying spirit moved ye!—Hence!
Thou art become a plague unto my sight,
A blot and stain upon the virgin air.

(*Music is heard within,* SOPHRONIA *sinks on her knee.*)

O arise, my love!
How swift a shame runs burning through my veins!

You should not kneel—What, though you are heartless,
    love,
You still are queen in this—Beautiful falsehood!
Ye have spells about ye—and I would curse,
Yet can but gaze into thine eyes, and bless thee.
What would ye I should do?

SOPHRONIA.

I've been to blame,
But now repentance is in vain. I fear
The anger of my lord, for I am now
Bound to obedience. Seem not to know me, Fulvius!
The fate that's on us passion cannot alter,
But may confirm.

FULVIUS.

Fear not. I will be governed.—

Enter GISIPPUS, MEDON, CHREMES, *ladies, guests, &c.*
Music plays, while seats, &c., are arranged
*—*GISIPPUS *leads* SOPHRONIA *to a seat—*
FULVIUS *remains unobserved, leaning against
a side scene up the stage.*

GISIPPUS.

Here in these silent groves we will attend
The lighting of the Hymeneal torch.
How pure, how holy is the sacrifice
That waits on virtuous love! How sacred is
The very levity we wake to honour it!
The fiery zeal that passion knows, is there
Tempered by mild esteem and holiest reverence
Into a still, unwasting vestal flame
That wanders nor decays. All soft affections,
Calm hopes, and quiet blessings hover round,
And soft Peace sheds her virtuous dews upon it.
No conscious memories haunt the path of pleasure,
But happiness is made a virtue.

FULVIUS.

Ay!
An universal one—for truth and justice,
Honour and faith, may be cast off to gain it,
Without one conscious shame.

GISIPPUS.

How's this?

SOPHRONIA.

Gisippus. (*Lays her hand on his arm.*)

GISIPPUS.

My love! What would you?

FULVIUS.

Oh! must I endure this?
The action hath struck fire from out mine eyes—
I cannot hold. (*Coming forward.*)

GISIPPUS.

Ha! Fulvius! O dear friend!
My happiness fell short of its completion
Till you had given me joy.

FULVIUS.

Why should it need?
The joy that conscious truth gives will wait on ye,
For surely you deserve it.

GISIPPUS.

Friend and brother,
I thank you.

FULVIUS.

Does the bride?

GISIPPUS.

Nay! ye should spare her.

FULVIUS.

Prudent friend! Wise lover! Now

I see the spring of your half confidences.

GISIPPUS.

What doubt is this?

FULVIUS.

Doubt! Oh! I know thee just;
I know thy tongue was honest—but I know too,
The silent tales a glance may tell—the lies
That may be acted. (*They all rise.*)

GISIPPUS.

Ha! (*Sophronia throws herself between.*)

SOPHRONIA.

Oh! heed him not,
There is some error—

FULVIUS.

All the nods—the looks
By which the absent fool is safely damned—
Ye would not slander me in words, I know it,
But there are ways.

GISIPPUS.

What sudden, horrible fear
Creeps o'er my frame?
There is no likelihood in that. (*Aside.*)

FULVIUS.

Farewell!
Honest Gisippus, fare ye well! Sophronia,
I will not, for the last time, take your hand
With an ill word! (*Kisses her hand.*)
Gisippus, this is all
Your friend claims from your bride—O she was worth
A double perjury! O virtuous pair,
The happiness ye merit dwell about ye
Till ye have learned to laugh at conscience. How!
Am I a wonder, that ye throng and gaze
Upon me? Have I marred the bridal? Oh!

Let it proceed, and pardon me. Hearts worthier,
Marriage ne'er blest; take a friend's word for that—
An undone friend it may be, but that's little.
My last advice is—ye may ne'er remember
The name or fortunes of your ancient friend,
For there's a cause why that should breed ill thinking.
Farewell, Sophronia! O true friend, Gisippus—
Farewell! farewell! (*Exit* FULVIUS.)

MEDON.

What is the cause of this? (*Apart.*)

CHREMES.

Whate'er it be, Gisippus hath it now,
His looks betray it. Mark him!

GISIPPUS.

Hold, my heart!
Rush not too quickly on a divination
So full of fear for thee. Sophronia?

SOPHRONIA.

I am here, Gisippus!

GISIPPUS.

Medon will attend you
To your chamber. I would speak with you alone—
I'll follow you.

SOPHRONIA.

My lord shall be obeyed. (*Exit with* MEDON.)

GISIPPUS.

Kind friends, your pardon for this interruption,
Which should not mar the festival—One hour,
While you attend a measure in the house,
I would bespeak your patience. Then I come to ye!

(*Music plays, while* CHREMES *and the rest go
out, leaving* GISIPPUS *alone upon the stage.*)

GISIPPUS.

Corinth? The mystery of Fulvius—and

Y

Sophronia's old affection? You great Gods,
I see my fate.—The sacrifice you ask
Is great and bitter.—You, who lay upon me
This heavy test—lift up my soul to meet
And wrestle with its potency;—the hour
Is come at length when the young votary, Virtue,
Must prove his worship real—when the spirit
Shall soar above all natural affections,
A wonder and a tale for days unborn,
Or sink, degraded, into self. My love?
My friend? How suddenly the word unmans me!
My heart is weak,—and I but pant and struggle
At the greatness I would master. Yet it shall be so.
Sophronia shall be tried—and should she falter,
It must be done, although my strings of life
Crack in the doing. O! for one brief moment,
Lie still and cold, ye whispering ministers
That stir my blood with selfish doubts and wishes;
Dig memory, sense, and feeling from my brain
And heart, and make it steel to all but that
Which makes yielding painful!

END OF THE FIRST ACT.

ACT II.
SCENE I.—A STREET IN ATHENS.

Enter FULVIUS *and* CHREMES, *followed by* LYCIAS *and* SERVANTS.

FULVIUS.

Friends, let our train expect me on the hill,
Beside the villa of Gisippus. (*Exeunt* LYCIAS, &c.)

CHREMES.

Nay!
Why should you droop thus, Fulvius?

FULVIUS.

I would
We had left Athens yesterday. I grieve
To think upon the wrong I did Gisippus,
And would return and see him once again,
To take a friendlier leave.

CHREMES.

You should say rather
To see Sophronia once again, and make
Your parting yet more painful.

FULVIUS.

No, I have wronged
My friend! The friend that would have died, ere injured
Me, or cast one moment's shadow o'er my heart,
He must think better of me.

CHREMES.

Well, I seek not
To cross your wishes. But I pray you, tell me—
That gloomy looking knave ye sent before
Just now: is he your slave?

FULVIUS.

My freedman, Lycias.

CHREMES.

It is impossible that there can be
An uglier man.

FULVIUS.

Or a truer.

CHREMES.

Pish for his truth!
I would not keep such a face about my household
For all the truth in Greece. I have conceived
A strange antipathy against him. What

A dark and scowling glance the sulky slave
Shoots from beneath his shaggy brows!

FULVIUS.

Beware!
Keep such thoughts in your breast and live in peace.
He's a Phœnician; faithful—but revengeful.

CHREMES.

Psha! He shall know my mind a dozen times
In the hour. I'll whip him from his cut-throat looks.
He talks too little to be an honest man.
I'll teach him a more civilised obedience
Than that he showed you now when you spoke to him:
"Lycias, go bid our trains expect me."—"Ugh!"
    (*Exit sulkily, frowning back on* FULVIUS.)

FULVIUS.

I'll see him; once again will see Sophronia.
Why should I doubt my resolution?—Yet
If she should smile—and heaven is in that smile—
May she not win me back
To the delusions of my wooing hours,
And blind my vision to the onward path
That honour points to? No, no, it must not
Grieve Gisippus to think upon our friendship.
He shall yet deem nobly of me. (*Exit* FULVIUS.)

SCENE II.—THE HOUSE OF SOPHRONIA.

Enter MEDON *and* SOPHRONIA.

MEDON.

Away—tell me no more!

SOPHRONIA.

I have heavy reasons.

MEDON.

They should be such indeed to o'erweigh that

You now have urged. Delay the bridal! Bid
Our friends disperse, and keep their mirth untasted
For another morn? Fie! fie! Have you a name
To care for? What a scandal will it bring
Upon our fame! A man, brave, learned, honoured,
Worthy the noble lineage he sprung from,
Worthy as fair a fate as thou couldst give him,
Were it made doubly prosperous. What, think you,
Made you thus absolute? I'll know the cause
From which this fancy springs, or hear no more.

SOPHRONIA.

Then you shall hear no more, for while I live
The cause shall sleep within my lips, though none
But the ear of solitude should hear it spoken.

MEDON.

Sophronia, I know well 'tis some device
To break this contract.

SOPHRONIA.

No, my brother.

MEDON.

But
My heart is set upon it. His noble birth,
His eloquence, his influence in the city,
Are wanting to support our growing name.
My plans, hopes, all are based on this alliance.

SOPHRONIA.

But to defer—

MEDON.

Defer! What did you promise?
Why did you mock us then with your consent?
What shall be your next humour? We'll attend it.

SOPHRONIA.

Why should you be so quick to speak unkindness?
It was to please you, Medon, I consented.
I did not then look for a life of happiness,

But now I feel content shall scarce be mine.
Yet as I hope for that, I swear to thee
I do but seek to meet the pledge I've given,
And with a firmer fortitude redeem it;
I have no other hope. Oh! brother, if
Indeed you would be deemed such, grant me this,
And—ha! he is here—

Enter GISIPPUS.

GISIPPUS.
I am sorry that I startle you,
Medon; what is there in your gift, Sophronia
Should sue thus humbly for, and find you cold?

MEDON.
I would not have it known—and if she holds
My love at aught, she will be silent on it.   (*Exit.*)

GISIPPUS.
Forget this peevish bickering of your brother,
And hear me speak.

SOPHRONIA.
At least, Gisippus, you
Can have no cause to chide!

GISIPPUS.
Why, there, Sophronia!
How like a conscious one you spring to anticipate
The shadow of an accusation. I
Said not I came to chide you; but indeed
You've judged aright, and you shall hear my charge!
The promise you have pledged me, you redeem
In words; your looks are cold; they freeze my heart,
And tell me it is cheated with a mask
Of constrained seeming.

SOPHRONIA.
Whither does this lead?

GISIPPUS.
Your converse, friendship,

You say are mine. But I would yet be lord
Of more than these! without it they are valueless;
'Tis an ideal good, excelling substance—
'Tis trust, 'tis confidence, Sophronia.

SOPHRONIA.

Nay, there, at least, I'm free.

GISIPPUS.

Indeed, you are?
And therefore 'tis I value it and seek it.
Give me your hand. You've had proof of my love,
Now try me further. Lay your heart before me,
Naked as it appears to your own thoughts,
With all its aspirations. You may find
That I can act as worthy and as free
A part, as if I ne'er had stooped so low,
To win the love that hath at last deceived me.
For though, my heart can witness, I do prize
My love, beyond the life-blood that flows through it,
I would not weigh it 'gainst your happiness,
The throbbing of one pulse. Believe, and trust me.

SOPHRONIA.

You are too noble!

GISIPPUS.

Do not think that, Sophronia,
Nor let your generous fear to wound a spirit,
Too sensitive, affect your confidence.
The rigid schools in which my youth was formed,
Have taught my soul the virtue that consists
In mastering all its selfish impulses!
And could I bring content into your bosom,
And bid that care, that pines your delicate cheek,
And pales its hue of bloom, (fit paradise
For the revelry of smiles!) resign his throne there,
My heart, without a pang, could lose ye!   (*Aside.*)
It burns, while I belie it!

SOPHRONIA.

I have heard you
With wonder, that forbids my gratitude.
How you have humbled me! O Gisippus!
I will deceive you yet—for you shall find,
Although I cannot practise, yet I know
What greatness is, and can respect it truly;
I would requite your generosity,
And what I can, I will. Do not distrust me
From my seeming! I have plight my promise,
And it shall be fulfilled.

GISIPPUS.

My fears were just, then?

SOPHRONIA.

Let them be banished now! My noble monitor,
When I shall make advantage of your goodness,
Virtue forswear me! You have waked my heart
To duty and to honour; they shall find
An earnest votary in it.

GISIPPUS.

Duty and honour,
Ye have spoken it worthily, Sophronia.
Yet these are cold words—Oh! how beautifully
That fiery carriage shows upon ye! How
Ye shine and sparkle in your hourly changes!
O woman, what an empty boaster man is,
When he would strive against your empire! How,
When he would soar at lonely excellence,
Ye cling upon him with your potent weakness;
And when he is content to creep beside ye
In the dull circle of material happiness
Ye fire him to a longing after greatness.
He hath the strength of the huge ocean-wave,
But you—you are the planet by whose influence
It mounts or falls. Have you spoke this too hastily,

Or do you feel that firmness in your nature,
Which you have quelled in mine?

SOPHRONIA.

The guests attend us,
If you will longer hesitate, I'll doubt
The welcome my assent meets.

GISIPPUS.

Beautiful miracle!
Oh! you shall find how dearly I esteem it.
Farewell! I will but see all placed in readiness
Without, and then attend you. O you have sent
Joy, like a strong light, through my darkened spirit!
Farewell! the rite shall be prepared. (*Exit.*)

SOPHRONIA.

The sacrifice—
The double sacrifice! We have been made
The victims of our own caprice.

Enter NORBAN.

NORBAN.

Sophronia,
Fulvius would speak with you.

SOPHRONIA.

Ha! Peace! Where is he?
Not for the world. Away!

Enter FULVIUS.

FULVIUS.

The wings of peace
Shelter your heart, Sophronia, though they leave
Those that have loved you comfortless!

SOPHRONIA.

Your coming
Is most ill-timed. I would not for thy life
Gisippus saw ye here.—Norban!

NORBAN.

I am here, Sophronia.

SOPHRONIA.

Remain on this side, and be sure you warn me
When Gisippus returns!

NORBAN.

I will obey you.

SOPHRONIA.

Why have you come?

FULVIUS.

You are so dear to me,
So coiled and wound about my heart, that I
Am glad to find my presence is unwelcome to you.
I come to take my leave, for ever!

SOPHRONIA.

How?
Do you leave us then, indeed?

FULVIUS.

I am for Rome.
The path of worldly fame and honour lies
Smiling before me. All the dignities
That young Ambition covets may be mine,
And fair Success invites me, like a bride.
How joyously my spirit once had leaped
To meet her smile and merit it. But now,
Its earliest impulse hath been chilled and wasted—
Its earliest hope o'erthrown.

(GISIPPUS *enters quickly behind*
NORBAN, *unseen by him.*)

GISIPPUS.

Fulvius! (*Starts backs.*)

SOPHRONIA.

Do not speak thus, Fulvius.
This is not manly in you.

FULVIUS.

O, my love!
(For I must call you such, though I have lost you)
You have bereft me of all nobleness,
And made me what you should contemn.

    (NORBAN *turning accidentally discovers* GISIPPUS *and starts.* GISIPPUS *grasps his arm, points to his dagger, and motions him off.* NORBAN *departs.*)

GISIPPUS.

A watch set, too! (*Apart.*)
This is the bride now,—this—O prudent woman—
Angel and devil in one hour! My friend, too!
Peace! peace!

SOPHRONIA.

Nay, look not thus dejected, Fulvius.
Think it is our fate which masters us,
And strive against it firmly.

FULVIUS.

Alas! sweetest,
You counsel me in vain. Do not despise me
That I am wanting in that stern command
Of natural feeling, and that scorn of circumstances
That shields the breast of Gisippus.

GISIPPUS.

Well put,
My friend!—This is the friend—the bridegroom's friend!—
Ha! torture.

FULVIUS.

Do not envy me the luxury
Of yielding to the pressure of my fortune,
The heart is not mechanical—nor owns
The empire of the will.
It is the universal law of nature,
That where the hand of suffering presses hard

Complaint should follow. There is a relief
In the abandonment of utter sorrow
That only sufferers know!

SOPHRONIA.

Weak sufferers, Fulvius;
The unreasoning slaves of impulse and excitement,
Would you depress your nature to the level
Of mindless—nay, even of inanimate things?
The victim at the stake will howl and whine;
The plant, unwatered, droops; but man should meet
The malice of his fate with firmer carriage.
Alas! look on the life of the happiest hero;
What is it but a war of human pride,
With human suffering? the mind, the soul
In arms against the heart! their ally, reason,
Forcing the aching wretch to suffer greatly,
And own no influence of fate! What, still
Unmanned at parting? Pray you, Fulvius,
Resolve me this.

FULVIUS.

What is't you ask?

SOPHRONIA.

Suppose—
(I do but dream now while I speak of this)—
But say that it were possible our loves
Might yet be favoured!

FULVIUS.

Ha!

SOPHRONIA.

Beware, young Roman!
I speak this as a dreamer. But suppose
Cisippus, who you know is very worthy,
And loves you as a friend—

FULVIUS.

Alas! I've proved that—
But ill requited him—

SOPHRONIA.

I pray you, hear me.
Suppose your friend should give me back the promise
That I have plight—(O most unwillingly!)
And leave me free to make my own election,
Wrong or dishonour set apart—

FULVIUS.

I hear ye.

SOPHRONIA.

How would my freedom move ye?

FULVIUS (*rapturously*).

As my life
Restored beneath the lifted axe.

SOPHRONIA.

We should rejoice then!

FULVIUS.

We should pale the front,
The Afric front of night, with revel lights,
And tire her echoes with our laughter!

SOPHRONIA.

Ay,
And Gisippus would laugh, too.

FULVIUS.

Ha!—(*Fulvius droops.*)

SOPHRONIA.

He'd be
The loudest reveller amongst us. Ay,
We should be famed in story, too. The best,
The truest friends—self-sacrificers!—Oh!
Our monuments should be the memories
Of every virtuous breast,—while Gisippus
Might find his own dark tomb, and die forgotten.

FULVIUS.

What mean you?

SOPHRONIA.

Cast aside that dull respect
Of fair opinion and the world's esteem,
Which is the death of many a happiness.
You are for Rome?—Our fate is in our hands—
The world may call it perjury in me,
In you, foul treachery—but we can live
Without the world's approval, (can we not?)
And laugh at self-reproach, too?

FULVIUS.

Sweetest warner,
Mine honour is not dead, though it hath slept—
What would you do?

SOPHRONIA.

I'd wake that worthiness
Within you, which I know you own. Oh! Fulvius,
You now may see how dearly I have loved you,
Since I had rather lose you—(ay, my first,
Old idolised affection!)—than behold you
Second to any in your own esteem.

FULVIUS.

In yours, and virtue's never!—Do not fear it—
I came to take my last farewell, Sophronia—
Come; I can throw my helm upon my brow,
And shake my crest upon the battle field,
And bare my bright steel with a grasp as firm
As his whose arm is nerved by glory's zeal,
Not by the madness of a broken heart.
An honourable cause—a fiery onset—
A peal of war—a hush!—one thought on thee!—
And there's an end of Fulvius and his love!

GISIPPUS (*coming forward a little*).
That speech was like ye, Roman!

SOPHRONIA.

Oh, now you are

The gallant soul you have been; and shall be
The cherished memory of my heart. Oh! Fulvius,
It is a sullen fortune that subdues us.
But we have trifled with her early smiles,
And now must strive against her hate. Farewell!
Forget me and be happy.

                FULVIUS.

It must be
My solace to remember you, Sophronia,
But only as a rightful sacrifice
To honour, and to friendship. Dear Sophronia,
Let me be careful of his peace to whom
The Gods have given you now. He knows not yet
Of our affection. Let him never know it.
Time, absence, and the change of circumstance,
May wear me from your memory—(never droop
Your head to hear it,) and you may yet be
To Gisippus—all—but away with that—
Farewell, at once, for ever!

        (*They are separating, when* GISIPPUS
            advances quickly.)

                GISIPPUS.

Stay, Sophronia!

                SOPHRONIA.

Ha! we are lost!

                GISIPPUS.

Lost? How? Why? wherefore, lady?
You, Fulvius, too!—Look on me calmly, Roman,
You've known me long—beheld me in all changes,
And read my spirit in its nakedness.
In what part of my life have I betrayed
A mean or selfish nature?—Ay! that gesture
Would tell me—never.—Wherefore am I then
So worthless of your confidence? I must
Turn eaves-dropper to gain it. Not a word!—

You were eloquent but now. Ha! ha! You'll say
You had an inspiration then—

FULVIUS.

Gisippus—

GISIPPUS.

Now, can it anger you, that I have played
A mirthful humour on ye both? I've known
Long since of this, and did but seek to punish ye
For your distrust.——Oh, I have laughed at ye—
To see your fears, and must again—(*Aside.*) O Gods,
My brain is scorched!—(*Puts his hand to his forehead, and pauses.*)

FULVIUS.

What mean you, Gisippus?

GISIPPUS.

You say right, I was wrong to trifle with you,
But now the jest is ended—I shall laugh
No more—O never—never!
I pray you, pause one moment——

FULVIUS.

My kind friend!

GISIPPUS.

(*Rising slowly, and assuming a gradual firmness.*)
Come this way, Fulvius! Sweet Sophronia!
(I must no longer call thee *my* Sophronia,)
Give me your hand too. As you gave this hand
To me, even while your heart opposed the deed,
I give it now to one who loves you dearly,
And will not find that heart against him. There,
You are one. And may the Gods, who look upon
Those plighted hands, shower down upon your heads
Their dearest blessings. May you live and grow
In happiness; and I will ask no other,
Than to look on and see it; and to thank

My fate that I was made the instrument,
To bring it to your bosoms.

FULVIUS.

Oh, my heart's physician!
Was this indeed designed, or do you mock us?

GISIPPUS.

This way a secret passage will conduct you
To the temple porch. Medon I know has set
His soul upon my marriage; but let me meet
That consequence—the lightest. Your bride waits;
Nay, fly! Stay not to question nor to speak;
The interruption may give space for thought,
And thought may bring—madness! Away! the rite
Attend you. Medon is not there—nor any
Who may prevent you. With my sword and life
I will defend this passage.

(FULVIUS *uses an action of remonstrance, but yields to the impetuosity of* GISIPPUS, *and leads* SOPHRONIA *out at an upper entrance.*)

Gone! Alone!
How my head whirls, and my limbs shake and totter
As if I had done a crime. I have. I've lied
Against my heart. What think ye now, wise world?
How shows this action in your eyes? My sight
Is thick and misty—and my ears
Seem dinned with sounds of hooting and of scorn—
Why should I fear? I will meet scorn with scorn;
It is a glorious deed that I have done.
I will maintain it 'gainst the wide world's slight,
And the upbraiding of my own rack'd heart.
Oh! there I'm conquered!

(*Sinks into a seat, in a desponding attitude.*)

(Hymn without.)

When thy rite, as now,
  By youthful tongues is spoken—
And youthful hearts record the vow,
  That never may be broken—
Loves like these, 'tis thine to bless;
  Theirs is perfect happiness!

CHORUS.
                    Loves like these, &c.

(The curtain slowly falls during the chorus.)

END OF THE SECOND ACT.

ACT III.

SCENE I.—A PUBLIC PLACE, NEAR THE HOUSE OF SOPHRONIA.

Enter MEDON *and* FRIENDS.

MEDON.

Married to Fulvius! A free maid of Athens
Bartered unto a stranger—All my schemes,
Each plan for our advancement, crushed and scattered—
But we can reach him. There is none amongst you
But is a Medon, friends!

ALL.

Not one!

MEDON.

Then all
Bear on their brows a portion of this slight
Gisippus throws upon our house. An age
Will not restore us the ascendant. What
May he deserve who sunk us thus in Athens?

FIRST FRIEND.
A worse shame than he gave.

SECOND FRIEND.
We'll send our slaves
To scoff him in the streets.

MEDON.
I have a deeper penance for him—
Meet me an hour hence by the Areopagus,
You shall know more.

FIRST FRIEND.
We will not fail. *(Exeunt all but* MEDON.*)*

MEDON.
Away, then!
He's ruined, and I am not sorry for it,
Ho! Pheax!

Enter PHEAX.

PHEAX.
Do not stay me—I must find
Gisippus, and prevent his ruin—

MEDON.
How—

PHEAX.
I fear to wait the telling—

MEDON.
You may safely,
He will come this way shortly.

PHEAX.
There's a clamour
Among his creditors, with whom, indeed,
(For a philosopher,) he is well provided,
And pledged, I know, beyond his means. They say
He gave away, with your Sophronia's contract,
The only hope of compensation left them;

But now I met old Davus, the rich usurer,
Taxing his withered limbs, to seek his pleader;
One shrivelled arm close pinioned to his side,
The hand fast clenched upon a musty parchment,
Which, next his skin, looked fair; the other wandering,
With bony fingers stretched, in the act to grasp,
(Fit emblems of the miser's double craft,
Getting and keeping)—his small weasel eyes
Glanced every way at once—his countenance
Looked like a mask made out of an old drum head,
In which the bones at every motion rattled
From mere starvation. Flesh is a garment, sir,
Far too expensive for his use. Oh! how,
As he went hobbling by me, I did curse
The law that has forbid the art of beating;
I never had so much ado to make
My right foot keep the peace.

MEDON.

I am glad to hear this. (*Apart.*)
Go you to Rome with Fulvius?

PHEAX.

Ay, to-morrow—(*Enter* GISIPPUS.)
O Gisippus, I've sought you. You are like
To speed ill if you tarry here.

GISIPPUS.

Trouble me not—I know it.

PHEAX.

There are three of them
Have ta'en possession of your villa. Nay,
'Tis said the sale of that will not half quit
The charges you have drawn upon your 'state,
And they assail your person—Davus has
Already sued for that.

MEDON.

So, Gisippus—

GISIPPUS.

So, Medon—

MEDON.

This is all you merit now
From me, I am sure. You soon shall find that I
Esteem the wrong you've done me, at its value;
Your jeering shall not serve. How will you excuse
Your thankless slight?

GISIPPUS.

Good Medon—I have nothing,
Nothing to offer in excuse; my foul
And heinous crime must e'en lie on my head;
And so—good day.

MEDON.

I've something for your ear first.

GISIPPUS.

You look like one who would not be at peace
With the world, nor with himself. If it be so,
You could not find a wretch in Greece more apt
To meet you at midway, than he who stands
Before you now.

MEDON.

I am very sure of that,
But you mistake my resolution quite;
You should have deeper cause, sooner, for this bravery.
There's Davus, in whose danger you are placed,
He will be crying for his sesterces!
Look not to me for aid.

GISIPPUS.

To thee? Away,
Vain and presumptuous man! I hold thee

So high in my esteem to be thy debtor,
If thou should'st sue for it.

MEDON.

You shall hear from me.

PHEAX.

This is his nature.

GISIPPUS.

Oh! I blame him not.
We that do study things in their first cause
Are not so quickly moved by the effect.
'Twas his fate that denied him so much heart
To comprehend
An act of free, disinterested friendship;
Of friendship and of love, deep love, Sophronia!
Gods!—there are men upon this earth who seem
So mixed and moulded with that earth—so like
Mere dull, material engines—that for all
The purposes for which man looks to man,
It were as well a piece of curious mechanism
Walked in humanity's name and wore its semblance.

Enter THOON.

Oh! you are come?—

PHEAX.

I much fear Medon's malice
May work some evil 'gainst you; I will follow him
And bring you news should any danger threaten. (*Exit.*)

GISIPPUS.

Well, what says Davus?

THOON.

He says you have deceived him villanously,
And he will give no time.

GISIPPUS.

Did you not tell him
That which I bade you, as touching Fulvius?

THOON.

I did, and so much mercy found I in him,
He gave you one whole hour to try that chance.

GISIPPUS.

Chance? Pish!—Ah, heaven! they are here!—

Enter DAVUS *and* OFFICERS.

DAVUS.

Yonder's your prisoner.

GISIPPUS.

Where's the time you promised?

DAVUS.

I am changed,
And will not trust you—Fulvius is for Rome.

GISIPPUS.

I tell you now again, as I have said,
You shall not be defeated of your own.
Before night close, I will satisfy you,
But leave the means to me.

DAVUS.

I will not take
The promise of a sibyl, if the certainty
Rest in my hands. Advance!

GISIPPUS.

Then, by the Gods—(*drawing*)
My freedom shall be dearer than my life,
Or his who dares assail it.

DAVUS.

Heed him not—
You've numbers, and authority to aid you.

GISIPPUS.

They shall be needed.

Enter FULVIUS *and* NORBAN.

FULVIUS.

Hold! hold! Gisippus—
       (GISIPPUS *sheathes his sword and crosses*
         quickly to DAVUS)

GISIPPUS (*apart to* DAVUS *earnestly*).
By the honour of my name—by all I've lost,
And all I hope to gain—I swear to you,
You shall be satisfied before to-night;
But leave me now—and free till then.—Hush! speak
    not;
My hope—life—hangs upon it.—Let me pray you,—
I will deserve this kindness. At my villa—
Thou knowest the spot—You'll find me grateful, Davus.
     (DAVUS, &c., *go out.* GISIPPUS *remains looking*
       after them.)

FULVIUS.

What men are these? What meant this brawl, Gisippus?

GISIPPUS.

Insolent knaves!—I was about to amerce them for it,
Had you not crossed me. Words, bred from a trifle,
And now forgot. Fulvius, I give you joy.

FULVIUS.

Thanks for the cause.

GISIPPUS.

I have something, Fulvius,
If you are not o'erpressed in time, to give
Your private ear.

FULVIUS.

Go to your lady, boy—
I will attend her quickly.   (*Exit* NORBAN.)

GISIPPUS.

How shall I tell? Will it not appear
As I took ground upon my claim, and sought
The very time it could be least resisted? (*Aside.*)

FULVIUS.

What, musing, Gisippus?
What would you stay me for?

GISIPPUS.

And yet—to think—(*aside*)—
For such a—nothing—which, without regard
To that which cannot be repaid, he owes me,
And far above,
My very life should now be put in question,
Or more—my freedom here—

FULVIUS.

What syllogism—(*advancing to him*)—
Do you hunt down now, Gisippus? Pray you, jump
To your conclusion, and dismiss me quickly.

GISIPPUS.

I'm glad to see your ancient spirit live again.
I do him wrong to hesitate—to be silent.—(*Aside.*)

FULVIUS.

Gisippus—
Thus do we stand. My time is limited
By her, to whom, as yet, I owe it all;
You can allow for this?

GISIPPUS.

Indeed! so absolute?
Well, I will not obstruct your pleasures, Fulvius—
You had better leave at once.

FULVIUS.

Psha!—now you are angry.

GISIPPUS.

Come—I will tell thee that which troubles me,
And in few words. When your Sophronia—
So soon cut short?

Re-enter NORBAN.

NORBAN.

A message from the Questor.

Enter a CENTURION, *who gives a packet to* FULVIUS.

FULVIUS.

Come to prevent my wishes?—(*Reads.*)
                    Ha! my friend—
Now give me joy, indeed. I'm greeted here
With an appointment, from the Emperor,
In the Eastern wars—If fortune hold her humour
I shall be rich in every happiness
That friendship, love, and honour can bestow—
As the mad promise of the wildest hope
That ever killed Content.

GISIPPUS.

Your joy is mine—

FULVIUS.

I have a faith in that.

GISIPPUS.

Now, Fulvius, hear me—

FULVIUS (*to Centurion*).

If memory err not widely, 'tis four years
Since, in those very regions, Anthony
Unwove the web Ventidius had spun
With Roman toil, and dyed with Roman blood—
You served him in those wars—   (*Centurion bows.*)
                  Come to my house,
You are my guest until we leave together;
We will retrieve the shame of that discomfiture,
And call young glories from Armenian fields
To grace the statues of our children's children.

(*Exit with* NORBAN *and* CENTURION.)

GISIPPUS.

Why welcome then imprisonment and ruin?

Light hearted youth; and yet it is but lightness;
'Tis true, a gift not freely given, is none,
And gratitude itself is compensation;
Then what care I, if his remain unpaid?

Re-enter FULVIUS.

Ay, memory, have ye woke?

FULVIUS.

I had forgot—
Friend? Gisippus!—

GISIPPUS.

I thank thee, Fulvius—
I thought you should not leave me. Didst thou know
How deep a fear thy coming hath dispersed,
You'd say I had a cause——

FULVIUS.

What fear?

GISIPPUS.

No matter—
'Tis gone—you are returned—and I am satisfied—
I will suspect no more.

FULVIUS.

Did you then doubt me?
I had forgot you told me 'twas a matter
Of serious import that you wished to speak on.

GISIPPUS.

And so it is. But at some other time
I can detail it more at ease—you're now
Too happy to attend me. Will you promise
To come this even to my villa, near
The suburbs, and I'll give you all?

FULVIUS.

Most willingly.

GISIPPUS.

You, bridegrooms, have short memories. Will you strive
To keep it on yours, Fulvius?

FULVIUS.

Good Gisippus,
I will not swear, but I will say, indeed,
The friendship I profess lies not wholly
Upon my lip as that request would say;
'Twill be no toil to keep it on my memory.

GISIPPUS.

Enough. Let ruin shake her wintry wings
Over my sunny fortunes—blight and darken them!
Let blistering tongues be busy with my name,
And that—and all the comforts I have known
Pass from me, to return no more—thou, Fulvius,
Shalt have no part in the dread consummation,
And I can bear it calmly.

FULVIUS.

Yet I hope
You ne'er may *need* that consciousness.

GISIPPUS.

I thank thee,
And it is my hope too. Farewell, my friend,
But fail not of your word, if you would have
That hope made true. Hope is not kin to fate,
And there's a discord when they meet and jar,
The heart's ease dies to witness. Fare ye well!
(*Exit* FULVIUS.)

I am a truster—and I fear a fond one,
And yet could doubt—What, Pheax!

Enter PHEAX *rapidly.*

PHEAX.

Oh, Gisippus!

GISIPPUS.

What is the matter? Give your wonder words.

PHEAX.

You are my friend. Oh, I have a tale for you!

Gisippus, if you take my counsel,
You'll not remain in Athens.

GISIPPUS.

Not remain
In Athens!

PHEAX.

No—'tis known—

GISIPPUS.

What's known?

PHEAX.

That you
Have given Sophronia to the Roman.

GISIPPUS.

Oh!
They know it? I am glad of it. They know
That I have given her to her ancient love,
And my first friend. What do their wisdoms say
Upon this novel guilt? If it be crime
To give my love, life, soul away,
For thou to me wert all, Sophronia—
To tear up my own comfort by the roots
To make a garland for another's head,
Then I have sinned most deeply, and my reason
Shall venerate their censure.

PHEAX.

Oh, Gisippus!
You jest upon a——You are in peril!
All Athens is incensed against you and
Your Roman friend. They practise on your safety,
Even this moment they are met
Before the Areopagus.

GISIPPUS.

I pray you, Pheax,

What statute in our code makes give
Cold, miserable slaves!

PHEAX.

Nay, 'tis not so;
The charge is deep and foul.

GISIPPUS.

What is it? Ha!

PHEAX.

I dare not say it.

GISIPPUS.

Come, come, out with it? Quick!
There is more daring in your silence.

PHEAX.

Thus then
They have spoken loudly of your wants, my friend,
And Fulvius' wealth. You start? Ay, that's the
  charge!
They trump it to the state that you have had
Mean views in this. But it has struck you deep,
You do not speak? You do not answer me?

GISIPPUS.

I cannot speak my thought! I'm wonder! rage
And wonder all!——(*Pauses.*)
The furies tear their hearts—lash them with worse
Than the fell stings they've cast on mine! Gods! what?
Make venal that I gave my peace to purchase;
And to my friend!—Give me the slanderer's name,
That I may tear the lying tongue from out
His jaws, and trample on the——I am choked,
I cannot find a voice to curse them.

PHEAX.

Friend!

GISIPPUS.

Gold! trash!
What? truck and barter name and happiness!

Who could have dreamed this? Oh! this stabs home.
Though that the devil of gain had mastered so
Men's hearts, they felt and owned no warmer impulse,
None but a devil could have foreseen a slander
So tainting, and so foul. Pah! it is vile!

PHEAX.

Let it not move you thus.

GISIPPUS.

Let it not move me!
I tell thee, were this calumny but breathed
In the silent of the night to a deaf ear—
Could I but know that it was born in thought,
Though never uttered—'twould move me more than
    ruin,
Than loss of wealth and every temporal good.
But, told through Athens! registered in her courts!
O Jove, destroy my consciousness at once,
And, that way, give me rest!

PHEAX.

But Fulvius—

GISIPPUS.

Ay, well thought on. Fulvius!
You'll meet him ere this even. Whatever falls,
Bid him remember his appointment with me.
These troubles rush in floods upon me now,
And I must ask another hand to stem them.

PHEAX.

Where do you meet, then?

GISIPPUS.

At my villa.

PHEAX.

There!
You are deceived, my friend.

GISIPPUS.

He has promised.

PHEAX.

Trust me,
He cannot do it.

GISIPPUS.

I tell thee, he hath promised.

PHEAX.

He has deceived you then.

GISIPPUS.

How? On my need?
Deceive me?—Fare you well! Believe me,
You are deep in error, sir. (*Exeunt severally.*)

SCENE II.—BEFORE THE VILLA OF GISIPPUS —EVENING.

Enter FULVIUS *and* ATTENDANTS.

FIRST ATTENDANT.

Your lady is before;
She waits your coming.

FULVIUS.

Stay! is not here the villa of Gisippus?
Come—follow—I will send a packet to him,
To tell him of this sudden chance. The train
Is gone before?

SECOND ATTENDANT.

It is, my lord.

FULVIUS.

Away, then! (*Exeunt.*)

Enter GISIPPUS.

GISIPPUS.

I'll have thee only,—let them take all else,
My natal bower, home of my infancy,

My hope's first nurse thou wert, and thou shalt be
The tomb of its decline.   Hark ! hush ! a stir ?
(Goes towards the villa.)
All's still as death !   Davus has not been here
With his minions.   Fulvius too not yet arrived;
He's not impatient in it—and yet, weighing
His feelings now by those which once were mine,
His stay should not make me so   Soft, you ! Chremes!
Appointed too, for travel !   *(Enters the house.)*

Enter PHEAX, CHREMES, LYCIAS, *and* FESTUS.

CHREMES.
Go overtake thy comrades.   *(Exit Festus.)*
Here, did he say ?   *(To* PHEAX.*)*

PHEAX.
Who, my friend ?   Medon ?   Yes !
He bade me tarry here, but for one hour
He would attend you.

CHREMES.
I cannot stay his snail-paced movements; Fulvius
I see is hurrying on—we must overtake him !
Haste, fellows !   You wait Gisippus here.

PHEAX.
Ay, and could wish it were with more of comfort.

CHREMES.
Medon and I escort the bride to Rome.
Lycias !

LYCIAS.
Well !

CHREMES.
Now,
What think you of this honeymoon travelling ?
How will it meet the approval of your lady ?

LYCIAS.
I busy not myself about my betters
But to obey them.

CHREMES.

You are right.

LYCIAS.

I wanted not
Your word for that.

CHREMES.

I have a strange foreboding
That you and I will quarrel one day.

LYCIAS.

Like enough.

CHREMES.

Thou art the most ill-favoured knave!

LYCIAS.

I am glad
You think so.

CHREMES.

Why?

LYCIAS.

I shall think better of
My looks from this day forward.

CHREMES.

Do I lie, then?

LYCIAS.

Few Greeks make much of that.

CHREMES.

Go, join the train;
But that thou art an useful slave, and I
Have weightier matters now upon my hands,
I'd beat respect into thee!

LYCIAS.

Hate and hypocrisy
May come that way—Respect's a sturdier fellow.
But that *you* are my master's friend, you should not
Repeat that threat, Greek!— (*Exit* LYCIAS.)

CHREMES.

Did you ever see such an ill-conditioned slave?
But fare ye well. Dull life for you in Athens,
Whilst we are revelling in Rome. Tell Medon
I could not tarry. I must needs see Fulvius,
He's yet in sight—Farewell. (*Exit* CHREMES.)

PHEAX.

Farewell, good Chremes,
Too light of heart e'en for a passing thought,
That bears gloom with it. Gisippus not arrived—
Oh, my friend! (*Enter* GISIPPUS *from the house.*)
You are true to your appointment.

GISIPPUS (*advancing*).

Is it a fault?

PHEAX.

Now, I'll be sworn you have not yet forgiven me
For doubting Fulvius.

GISIPPUS.

And did you doubt him?

PHEAX.

No. You say truly. Him I do not doubt.
His will, I am sure, is true—It is the circumstance
Prevents him from fulfilling his engagement.

GISIPPUS.

Prevents him?

PHEAX.

Why, you surely do not now
Expect him?

GISIPPUS.

Pheax, I beseech you, leave me;
Your jesting is ill-timed.

PHEAX.

You are too petulant

My friend. Have you not heard that Fulvius
Has been commanded for Armenia?

GISIPPUS.

All hath been told me. Now, I pray you, go!
I know he has had letters of such import,
And that he will obey them and depart
To-morrow even.

PHEAX.

This even, my friend.

GISIPPUS.

To-morrow even—

PHEAX.

This even—
This night—this very hour—He hath arranged
All—There has been a second messenger,
To bid him to the camp this very hour.
Chremes goes to Rome, with Medon and Sophronia;
Nor is it like they will again behold
Your friend, 'till the campaign be ended.

GISIPPUS.

Pheax! my friend!

PHEAX.

Nay—
I seek but to prepare you for the truth!
I will not answer thee
In words; but look you yonder!   *(Pointing off.)*
'Tis his train—
You know he bade them wait on yonder hill.

GISIPPUS.

I see it!—but—but—O ye mighty Gods,
Can there be truth in this? He is not with them.
He has sent his train before, and tarries yet,
T——Ho! they disappear along the hills,
And if he lied in speaking of the time,
Why may not all be false that he has uttered?

The Gods do know I fear the consequence
No tithe so much as finding my heart fooled
In its free confidence.   You still look doubtingly;
Do you think he will deceive me?   Do you think
He will not come?   Have I given up my love, my all,
To worthless hands?   Do you think?—O peace!   I will
As soon cower on my knee, and dread the toppling
Of far Hymettus on my villa here,
As a fall in Fulvius' friendship, or the word
He once hath plight.   I stand upon his honour,
And 'tis proud ground.   Oh, I can laugh at doubting!
(A distant shout is heard.)
What are those sounds?

PHEAX.

Do you not know your cause
Is now in question?   I came to tell the news,
Which I am grieved to utter—but 'tis true,
That it goes hardly forward.

GISIPPUS.

Let it go
Even as it will.   I care not now—I'm heedless
Of all the external proprieties of life.
I have braced up my heart to meet the worst
That fate can cast upon my fortunes.   All
That men call evil, I can meet and suffer:
While one—one only fear is spared me.
Enter CHREMES (with a letter).

CHREMES.

Fulvius sends—

GISIPPUS (*eagerly*).

Ha! sayest thou?   Well!   O unbeliever, look,
And let thy spirit blush for grace! (*To* PHEAX.) What
    says he?
Where didst thou leave him? How? When will he come?
Speak! speak!—

CHREMES.

He cannot come, Gisippus. (GISIPPUS *starts*.)

PHEAX.

He is with his train ?—

CHREMES.

He is far before it, Pheax. He has taken horse
With the Centurion.

PHEAX (*to* GISIPPUS).

Look not on't thus ghastly !
What is the consequence that makes you dread
His absence thus ?

CHREMES.

He bade me say, this letter
Would give you his reason. (*Exit* CHREMES.)

GISIPPUS (*after a pause, taking the letter*).

Merciful Jove ! Is't so ?
I was mistaken in thee, Fulvius. Honesty
Hath oft before been made the dupe of seeming
Look ! as I tear this scroll——(*Pauses.*)
      By the just Gods,
I thought there was but one true heart on earth,
And was deceived—It is as black and false
As hell could make it——As I tear this scroll,
Piece after piece, and crush it in the dust,
So I abjure the wretch who mocked me with it,
For ever !—What ?—O, I'm rightly dealt with,
Most justly—oh, most meetly—Mighty heaven !
I cannot see well yet—Forgot !—forsaken !

PHEAX.

I'll write to him—

GISIPPUS.

I'll cleave thee to the earth,
If thou wilt say that word again !—No, no,
The gratitude that must be roused from slumber,

Is never worth the waking—Let it sleep! (*Shouts.*)
Again! hark!—

PHEAX.

Be at peace; I see the citizens
Are coming forth.   Remain! I'll soon return,
And tell thee of the issue. (*Exit* PHEAX.)

GISIPPUS.

Now I would
That there were fierce wars in Greece!   O Gods!
The comfort of a lawful suicide!
The joy of hunting after death, when life,
Grown hopeless, goads us to the chase! the rapture
Of meeting him bare-breasted on the field,
Amid the roar of fight that shuts out thought,
And rushing to his blood-red arms, without
The fear of the high heaven's displeasure.

Re-enter PHEAX.

Friend!
The judgment? hath it passed?   Stay! Stay!
I read it in thine eyes.   It is a doom
Too terrible.   But—Well! the sentence?

PHEAX.

You've been decreed the slave of your chief creditor,
Davus.

GISIPPUS.

Not that!   A sword and buckler, Gods!
And an unfettered hand!   Then, Fate, I dare thee
To prove my heart is softer than a man's
Should be.   Cast me free upon the world,
With all my injuries upon my head,
I still will move your wonder—and mine own;
But slavery!

PHEAX.

There is
A way to shun it.

GISIPPUS.

Ha!

PHEAX.

Fly!

GISIPPUS.

O cold ingrate!
That he should leave me thus! 'Tis well—

PHEAX.

They come!

GISIPPUS.

You do not—cannot feel how much he owes me;
But you are right, I am free yet!   (*Rushing out.*)

    Enter MEDON, *with two or three friends meeting him.*

MEDON.

Not so.

GISIPPUS.

Ha! hence! thou causeless hater! Art thou come
To look upon the proud man's ruin? Hence!
I have no part with thee.
Thou art to me a thing material,
Mindless, and heartless—a mere physical hindrance;
As such I put thee from my path, unmoved,
And so forget thee.

    (*He passes* MEDON, *and is going out rapidly, when he is met by* DAVUS, *who enters accompanied by a* SICILIAN MERCHANT *and* SOLDIERS. GISIPPUS *is seized.*)

MEDON.

Ha! ha! How this scorn,
Becomes the slave of Davus!

DAVUS.

Not *my* slave!
O not my slave indeed. I have sold ye, Gisippus,
To this worthy man. He sails for Sicily
To-night, and you must with him.

GISIPPUS.

Sicily?—(*Pausing.*)
Ha!—Rome—I am content.

DAVUS

You would be proud
To know how dearly I have sold ye, Gisippus.

   (*Shows a parchment to him, which* GISIPPUS
    hands to PHEAX.)

GISIPPUS.

Give this to—ha! ha! my young friend!—and bid him
Bind it up with his laurels—Fare ye well!

   (*Giving his hand listlessly to* PHEAX.)

PHEAX.

All will be well yet, Gisippus.

GISIPPUS.

Ay, like enough;
Fare ye well. Rome? (*Aside.*) It may be done.
 Come on;
I am ready to attend you, sirs—the dust
Is on my head, I'll be a patient bondsman.

   (*Exeunt* MEDON *and* PHEAX *at one side,*
    GISIPPUS *and the rest at the other.*)

END OF THE THIRD ACT.

ACT IV.

SCENE I.—A MAGNIFICENT ANTE-ROOM IN THE PALACE OF FULVIUS, AT ROME.

(Chorus and shouting heard without.)

HYMN.

Welcome home! welcome home!
Guardians of the weal of Rome.
Over land and over sea,
The eagle's wings spread gallantly.
Guardians of the weal of Rome.
Welcome home! welcome home!

(During the chorus, which is heard nearer and more distinctly, SERVANTS *and* MESSENGERS *with letters pass over the stage.)*

FIRST SERVANT.

It is our lord.
They're now before the palace.

SECOND SERVANT.

Haste, man, the show'll be past.
Are we too late?   *(To* MACRO, *entering.)*

MACRO.

No questions now.   I've letters for Sophronia—
Lead me to her—   *(To* SERVANT.)
You'll be in time for Fulvius;
He's now passing—Lead on, sir.'

SERVANTS.

Hark!—come—come.

(Exeunt MACRO *and* SERVANTS.)
Enter MEDON *and* CHREMES *with* NORBAN.

MEDON.

Go, boy—wake up your lady.

NORBAN.

She is ill, sir.

MEDON.

She must not be ill, sir;
Ill on the morn of her lord's triumph!—Go—
He will be terribly angry if he come
And finds her ill. Bid her get well again,
And speedily, if she would keep his favour.

NORBAN.

I'll tell her so, sir. (*Exit* NORBAN.)

MEDON.

Do so, sir. I know
The cause of this; some new neglect from Fulvius.

CHREMES.

Why do you let him treat your sister so?

MEDON.

Why do I let him treat myself still worse?
These swift successes have completely changed him;
He's prouder than the Emperor, and looks
On his old friends as they were born his bondsmen;
All but you, Chremes. You are still his friend,
His bosom counsellor; for poor Sophronia,
She is the first wife that was ever jealous
Of her husband's reputation.

CHREMES.

We must let him
Tire of his high-flown wishes quietly.
Some check of fate may humble him, and turn
His heart unto its old affections yet.

Enter SOPHRONIA, *attended.*

MEDON.

Good day, Sophronia—

CHREMES.

Madam, I have news for you

You will be glad to hear. Your lord comes hither;
The Senate have decreed him an ovation
For his late conquests in Armenia.

SOPHRONIA.

How does he, sir?

CHREMES.

Much discontented still.
He says, had th' Emperor been half so prosperous
He had had a triumph, and fifteen days' thanksgiving,
But *he* must rest content with an ovation—
A poor ovation.

SOPHRONIA.

Nothing would content him—
The honours he aspires to, when he gains them,
Look mean and worthless in his eyes, but this
Becomes not me to say.

MEDON.

What, do you mourn
At this?

CHREMES.

He is made Prætor too.

SOPHRONIA.

I would
I were once more in Athens—never knew
What love—nor what neglect was.

MEDON.

Ay—I know
Who would have made a kinder husband. Now
You are sorry for your scorn of Gisippus.

CHREMES.

Hush!

SOPHRONIA.

Have you heard of *him* since, Chremes?

CHREMES.

No, madam.

SOPHRONIA.
Poor Gisippus!—Nor told my lord his fate?

CHREMES.
Madam, I thought that would have been a vain cruelty
Till I had found Gisippus, and given Fulvius
The power of yet redeeming past neglects.

SOPHRONIA.
Perhaps you were right.

CHREMES.
O! I am sure I was.

SOPHRONIA.
When may I look for Fulvius? If he thinks
My welcome worth the having, he is sure of it.
I shall be glad to see him.

CHREMES.
I pray you, seem so, madam,
He will be disappointed else.
He was impatient, so he bade me say,
Until the Senate's will dismissed him home,
To hear his sweetest welcome from your lips.
(Shouts without.)
They come!

MEDON.
'Tis he, Sophronia! *(Shouts.)*

OFFICERS *(entering).*
The Prætor!
Enter FULVIUS, *attended as from a triumph.*

FULVIUS.
Oh! young Athenian,
I am glad to see thee!—From the General this—
This greeting from the Prætor—and a long kiss
From the Roman boy, who wound himself into
The heart of a proud lady some while since
By a temple porch at Corinth.

SOPHRONIA.
My dear lord!

FULVIUS.

These weighty honours which my country throws
Upon my hands, wean me from quiet fast.
I would they let me stay in humbleness,
With thee, and found some more ambitious mark
For favour. Ay, you smile, but it is true.

SOPHRONIA.

I would it were, Fulvius.

FULVIUS.

It is, believe me. Come, where are your sports?
I must have nought but smiles and happy faces
For these few days at least, the Senate gives me;
But ever holiday looks from thee, Sophronia.
Come, let us see your revels.

(Exeunt all but CHREMES *and* LYCIAS.*)*

CHREMES.

I saw thee grinning at the porch but now
As I passed in, what meant ye?

LYCIAS.

Do not ask me;
I am at your command, give me your orders,
And let me go at once.

CHREMES.

Then make all ready;
Bid the dancers shake their legs and put their toes in
    order,
And the musicians puff themselves into wind-gods,
Men of immortal lungs. Let the cook look to it.
If he so far forget his office as
The matter of a snipe's wing burnt, he dies;
We'll have him served up in one of his own dishes,
And save a goose by it—Lastly, for thyself;
When you have done this, get into some corner,
And be not seen until the feasting's ended—
That face would mar all merriment—

LYCIAS.
I hear you.

CHREMES.
And no more silent jeers or sneering, if
You love unbroken bones.

LYCIAS.
Pish! pish!

CHREMES.
Speak out, dog,
What say you?

LYCIAS.
I hate talking.

CHREMES.
You hate every thing,
I do believe.

LYCIAS.
A great many.

CHREMES.
Empty fool!
Where learned ye this affected sullenness?
You are ever growling. Do you never bite?

LYCIAS.
I have no cause.

CHREMES.
Fool, knave! Are these no cause?

LYCIAS.
None. Do your words pinch, maim, or wound me? Say,
I call you idiot—brainless boy—puffed beggar.
Do these words leave their marks upon ye? Ha!
(Chremes strikes him.)
You have done it now!—
(Seizes Chremes and draws.)

Enter FULVIUS *and* MEDON.

FULVIUS.

Ho! Lycias! how is this?
A dagger drawn in your lord's house?—Vile slave,
Do you dare indulge your ruffian humours here?
What, Chremes, too!—

LYCIAS.

He struck me without cause.

CHREMES.

Why, faith—I did so.

FULVIUS.

I am weary of
Your causeless jarrings, and must end them quickly.
For you, sir, here's a quittance for your services—
I have done with you—(*Gives money.*)

CHREMES.

Nay, Fulvius—'tis too much.

FULVIUS.

It shall be as I say—Away!

LYCIAS (*to* CHREMES).

Remember
You struck me without cause.

FULVIUS.

What does he mutter?—

CHREMES.

I care not.

LYCIAS.

You may care ere long.   (*Exit* LYCIAS.)

FULVIUS.

This letter
Despatch to Baix, to the Emperor.
I have a herd of clients yet to see;
Chremes, attend me, we will soon dismiss them,
And then I have a charge of grave import
For thee, ere I proceed unto the capitol.   (*Exeunt.*)

SCENE II.—NEAR THE CAPITOL, BEFORE A POOR INN.

(Distant Music heard, at intervals.)
Enter MUTIUS *from the inn.*

MUTIUS.
This way, sir, this way. I have now at last
Told you my mind; I pray you, understand
The course that I would have you take.

(GISIPPUS *enters from the house in a mean garb; his countenance pale and wasted, his hair hanging neglected on his shoulders, and his whole appearance completely changed. He leans against the doorway.*)

GISIPPUS.
I pray you, do not send me forth to-night.
I am a stranger in Rome, and even falls already.
I will but draw my toga o'er my head,
And lie against your fire.

MUTIUS.
It must not be.

GISIPPUS.
Are you so hard? Well, Roman, I'll not press it,
But pray you, say what festal sounds are these
That ring through the wide city? Whose is yon mansion?
It is a splendid one.

MUTIUS.
Splendid indeed?
What else should be the abode of Titus Fulvius?

GISIPPUS (*coming forward quickly*).
Of Titus Fulvius?

MUTIUS.
Titus Fulvius. Are you
So long in Rome, and know not Titus Fulvius?

If you would feast your eyes with the sight of a great
    man,
Stand close; he will come this way presently;
You'll not mind fasting for three days after.
(Exit into house.)

GISIPPUS.

Know Fulvius?
I had known less of man, and more of peace,
Had I ne'er known him. O weak, failing pride!
Do ye desert me now I need ye most?
Will you, who have upborne my soul against
The tyranny of passion, leave me now
To humble in my fall? O for a spot
Of green Greek turf! a little——to hide
My woes, my memory, and my doubts together.
Where must I wander now? The dews of night
Fall on me, and I have no home of shelter
To shroud me till the morn break.
I will seek one——
But—what do I behold? The gate is opened,
And—hush! my sense, be steady for one moment—
That's Chremes—and—By all my miseries,
'Tis he! himself! Where shall I hide me? Heavens!
                    (Knocks at the door.)
What, ho! within! They come upon me this way.
Well! wherefore should I shun him? Let him blush;
The shame's not mine——I grew to this for him.
Ha! should I stay?——I'll try
If he will know me yet. But I'll not speak;
No, no, I'll merely look into his eyes,
And——

(Flourish of trumpets without. Enter FULVIUS *and* CHREMES, *with lictors,* CITIZENS *pressing on him;* GISIPPUS *stands on the opposite side of the stage, gazing intently on* FULVIUS, *his toga drawn close around his neck, so as to conceal part of his features.)*

FIRST CITIZEN.
My noble lord—
SECOND CITIZEN.
My lord, I pray you, hear me—
FULVIUS.
Good citizens, I cannot now attend.
If you will meet betimes at the capitol,
I will to-morrow hear your grievances,
And if their remedy lie in my power,
Rest assured you shall not feel them long.

(*He looks at* GISIPPUS.)

FIRST CITIZEN.
Then we will meet there, Fulvius.

FULVIUS.
As you please,
It shall be as I say; believe me, friends.

CITIZENS.
Do you hear that? " Friends!" Long live our noble Prætors.

(*Shout. Exeunt* CITIZENS.)

(FULVIUS *again looks at* GISIPPUS, *who lowers his toga a little, as he meets his eye.*—FULVIUS *turns carelessly away.*)

GISIPPUS.
The eye can be as vocal as the tongue,
And his hath told me, I am known.

FULVIUS.
You, to your mistress go. Bid her expect me
Yet earlier than she looked for. (*Exit* SERVANT.)

CHREMES.
Fulvius,

I spoke with Varro on that matter now,
He could do nothing.

FULVIUS.

Nothing! Did he give you
His reasons?

CHREMES.

They were of such a kind, he said,
As could be only trusted to yourself;
This letter will disclose them.

GISIPPUS.

Silent, yet?
I would I were beneath the deepest wave
Of dark Tyrrhene, to hope or doubt no more.
There is a fate that chains me to this ground,
A spell about my feet and on my strength,
And I must wait the sentence of his eye.

(FULVIUS *talks apart with* CHREMES.)

CHREMES.

Then as you bid me, Fulvius, I will act;
Though still, I fear, in vain.

FULVIUS.

Have I not said?
Away! if you should fail, I will myself
Attempt him. Will you take a guard along?
You pass the burying ground of Afer, and
The night is falling.

CHREMES.

Not I. I wear my guard upon me. (*Exit.*)

(FULVIUS *motions the lictors forward.
They approach* GISIPPUS, *who stands
full in the way of* FULVIUS.)

FULVIUS (*reading a letter.*)

Varro refuse my first request!

FIRST LICTOR.

Stand back!
Way for the Prætor!

GISIPPUS.

I would speak with the Prætor.

FIRST LICTOR.

Thou speak with him? Ha! ha!

SECOND LICTOR.

A Greek dog bar the Prætor's way in Rome!

FULVIUS.

What words are these? Who's he disputes our way?
Ho! smite him to earth—if he will not
Give room—Back, slave! and know your place.
On, Lictors!

(A LICTOR *strikes* GISIPPUS *aside—they all pass off.)*

GISIPPUS.

Bright Jove,
Art thou the stranger's keeper? Let me press
My head—and crush the thought to rest for ever.

(He presses his forehead with his hands, and remains motionless.)

CHREMES *re-enters.*

CHREMES.

One thing I had forgot. What! gone already.
Ho! Fulvius!

GISIPPUS (*starting*).

Curse him, heavens! whoe'er thou art,
Let dumbness seize thee ever for that word!
I had just then begun to tell my soul
That it was false, that I had never heard
The name, and I was dropping quietly
Into a dull, a thick, oblivious madness.
That busy, meddling tongue has waked my heart
To memory, sense, and agony again.

CHREMES.

What means this?

GISIPPUS.

O! I see and know thee now.
You are Chremes, the Athenian? Worthy mates!
He is gone that way—Titus Fulvius,
Did you not call him? You are fitted friends—
Two heartless, thankless, mean self-seekers—villains!

CHREMES.

Madman!

GISIPPUS (*clasping his hands*).
Oh, would to heaven it were so with me!

CHREMES.

Who art thou? what—

GISIPPUS.

I am Gisippus.

CHREMES.

Heavens!

GISIPPUS.

You know me well.

CHREMES (*after a pause*).
Though you had been my brother, Gisippus,
The wondrous, fearful change that has come o'er thee
Had been enough to baffle memory,
Even when instinctive nature helped its efforts.
My friend! my countryman! Could you suppose me
That traitor to old Greece, and pleasant Athens,
To meet her exiled son, and the companion
Of my school days, and pass him knowingly
In a strange land? I pray you, be convinced,
That you have wronged me. I have sought you long
And now rejoice to find ye. By this hand,
This hand that I am glad to grasp—I do.

GISIPPUS.

I must believe you, sir—

And yet though I should grieve to think you scorned me,
I should not wonder. In this dark, false world,
Nothing shall ever now surprise me more.
Pray, come not near me, sir; you are a soldier,
And wear the arms of honour. I have, too,
A sword, but long forgot the use of it;
I am an abject thing—a beaten wretch.
Furies and hell! O peace! peace! Sleep and death!

CHREMES.

What is it moves you thus?

GISIPPUS.

O cursed memory!
You see me where I stand before you, Chremes.
It was not so when you have known me better;
You can remember what I was. You know
How sweet, how fair a light of promise, fortune
Shed on my days of youth. You know how warmly
My confident soul opened itself to Fulvius.
You know, too, somewhat more than at this time
My tongue can freely utter. Would you think
How all that has been answered?

CHREMES.

With a truer
And deeper gratitude than you believe.

GISIPPUS.

This is that gratitude—indeed a deep one,
Too deep for me to find its virtue. Hear!
When I left Athens,
Despised and hated by my fellow citizens,
Yet nought repenting that which I had done,
I toiled for freedom, gained it, and set forth
To Rome. You start? Was that a meanness? No!
True, he had wronged me; and my pride was stung by it.
Alas! you know not, friend, how very quietly

And silently that same tall fabric, pride,
Is sapped and scattered by adversity
Even while we deem it still unmoved, unshaken;
He was my friend once—and my life now, having
No aim nor object. I said with myself
That I would look once more upon the happiness
I had raised from the wreck of mine own hopes,
And so to death or solitude. Look hither, sir;
Here—here, I met him, here he bade his slave
Strike me from out his path!—his own high hand
Scorned the low office——here his ruffian smote me,
And here I stand to tell it!

CHREMES.

Yet!—

GISIPPUS.

No hasty judgment!
Believe me, I'm not sunk so low to bear that—
But a strange numbness crept upon my senses,
And left me cold and powerless.

CHREMES.

You
Are over apt—(and 'tis most natural in you)—
To fancy what you feared was real—Trust me,
You are deceived to think that Fulvius knew you;
His fortunes have indeed altered him strangely,
But yet he is not what you deem him.

GISIPPUS.

This
Is kindly meant in you. I thank you for it,
But I have eyes and ears, and a heart, Chremes,
To see and hear and feel what passes round me,
Even as it doth pass. Fulvius knew me well!
I thank you, though, that you should seek to give me
The bliss of thinking otherwise.

CHREMES.

Gisippus,
You do not go yet?

GISIPPUS.

Wherefore should I stay?

CHREMES.

Come with me to his palace.

GISIPPUS.

To his palace!
What? Be indeed a beggar?

CHREMES.

Here me, Gisippus.

GISIPPUS.

You are the only man that knows of this;
How if you should betray me now, and publish
My shame unto the world? You are like to do it.
I have known liars with as clear a brow
As that. And if you should, by the just Gods,
I would not rest, sleep, wink, till I had torn
Your heart out and destroyed——But you'll not do it;
You know me better. If you'd have me honour you,
You will not speak of this to your general.
Farewell! I'll meet ye soon again!

CHREMES.

My friend!

GISIPPUS

No friend! I charge ye; call me brother Greek,
But friend! No, no, friendship and I have found
Each other out, shook hands, and parted quietly.

(*Exit* GISIPPUS.)

CHREMES.

He's gone! poor Gisippus! how worn, how changed!
Here is an humbler for the pride of Fulvius.
But may not some device be yet invented
To reconcile the friends once more?
As I proceed, 'tis worth the plotting.

SCENE III.—A BURYING GROUND—NIGHT.

GISIPPUS (*discovered*).

GISIPPUS.

This is his court;
Here does he hold his reign of stirless fear,
Silence his throne—his robe of majesty,
The hue of gathering darkness. Here, his minister,
The night-bird, screams, and the hoarse raven iterates
His warning from the left. Diseases flit
Like spectres through the gloom, clothed in damp mist
And tainted night-air—yet the grim slayer
Will send no kindly shaft to me.

(*He leans on a tomb.*)

Will the dead
Afford me what the living have denied—
Rest for my weary limbs, and shelter? Here
At least I shall find quiet, if not ease,
And host who do not grudge their entertaining,
Even though the guest be misery. Colder hearts
Than those which rest within this sepulchre
I've left in all the health of lusty life
Informing bosoms harder than its marble.
Then I will be your guest, ye silent dead;
Would I could say, your fellow slumberer!

(*He enters the tomb.* CHREMES *wrapped in his mantle passes over the stage dogged by* LYCIAS. *A clashing of swords is heard without.*)

CHREMES.

What ho! help! murder! villain! (*Within.*)

LYCIAS (*within*).

Do you feel me now?

CHREMES *(within).*
Too deeply.
LYCIAS *(within).*
There's a quittance for ye.
(GISIPPUS *re-enters from the tomb, draws, and rushes off*—CHREMES *staggers in, wounded. He falls near the tomb.*)

CHREMES.
Ah! villain! He has cut me to the veins,
Revengeful villain! Oh!

Re-enter GISIPPUS, *his sword drawn.*

GISIPPUS.
The ruffian has escaped. What luckless wretch,
Has thus been made his victim? You great Gods!
Chremes!

CHREMES.
Whoe'er thou art, I pray you give
These scrolls to—to—— *(Dies.)*

GISIPPUS.
This is thy justice, Death!·
I who would greet thee with a lover's welcome,
And kiss thy shaft, have wooed its point in vain;
This wretch, whose hope was green, thou seekest un
 called.
Relentless destinies! Am I become
Such an abomination in your sight
To love me is perdition? Where—oh, where
Is my offence? But there may yet be hope,
Breathless and cold! My last friend, fare ye well!
(Voices within—" This way! this way!")
They come. Is it not now within my reach?
I have it! It shall be so! *(He stains his hands and sword with the blood of* CHREMES, *leans forward, kneeling over the body.)*

Enter CITIZENS, *with torches, &c.*

FIRST CITIZEN.
This way the sounds proceeded. Did you send
To warn the Prætor's guard?

SECOND CITIZEN.
Yonder they are!

Enter MEDON *and guard.*

MEDON.
'Tis as I feared. Chremes! unhappy countryman!
Who has done this?

FIRST CITIZEN.
Do you not mark that man
With bloody hands who kneels beside the body?
He is the murderer.

MEDON.
Speak! if thou art he—
Confess, it will be useless to deny it—
Confess——

GISIPPUS.
Why, what confession do you need?
I am here before you, in my hand a sword
Unsheathed, his blood upon that sword—yet warm
From the divided breast. What would ye more?
Can words declare more?

MEDON.
Guards, away with him!
Away with him to the Prætor! Yet one word—
What moved ye to this act?

GISIPPUS.
I had my reasons.

MEDON.
Take him away.

GISIPPUS.
Now I have made it sure.

MEDON.

What dost thou say?

GISIPPUS.

I say, that I rejoice
In that which I have done. Do as you list!

MEDON.

Away with him!   (*Exeunt.*)

END OF THE FOURTH ACT.

ACT V.

SCENE I.—THE PALACE OF FULVIUS.

Enter FULVIUS *and* SOPHRONIA.

FULVIUS.

Ay, I have heard enough. Why should I tax
Your brother with this base and coward act,
That am myself more base in my neglect
Than he in his revenge? Poor Gisippus!
Banished from Athens, sold to slavery!
And now a wanderer without home or name,
Perhaps the tool of some low taskmaster,
Or the cold inmate of a nameless grave.

SOPHRONIA.

Yet, Fulvius.

FULVIUS.

Ha! how say you?

SOPHRONIA.

Do not turn
Thus sullenly away, nor yet look on me

With that regard of cold reproach. I know
No more than thou of this unhappy chance,
And mourn it full as deeply.

FULVIUS.

They were all
Your friends who did thus.

SOPHRONIA.

And is that my crime?

FULVIUS.

I would give all again that I have gained—
My present joy—the memory of my past,
And all my hope of future happiness,
To stand beneath the roof that shelters him,
And know my gratitude not wholly fruitless.
Oh! I am torn with vain regrets!

SOPHRONIA.

For my sake,
Speak not of this to Medon. What is past
His ruin could not better. If you love me
You will not——

FULVIUS.

If I love ye! Do you make
A doubt of that, now?—If I loved you not
I had been now at peace with my own heart,
I had not brought a stain upon my soul
That no repentant sorrowing can whiten.
Had I not loved thee better than fair virtue
I might be now an honourable friend,
And those quick rushing memories that crowd
Upon my heart in thick and painful throbbings
Might shadow it with that calm, peaceful influence
Of gratitude discharged, and friendship cherished,
Which makes remembrance sweeter than enjoyment.
I've loved ye but too well!

Enter NORBAN.

NORBAN.

My lord—the murderer
Of Chremes bade me give these scrolls unto you,
The dying man had placed them in his hands.

FULVIUS.

Have you spoke with him then?

NORBAN.

By your command,
I went into his dungeon at the sunrise.
I found him waking then. His wasted form
Lengthened out in the dust—one shrivelled hand
Beneath his head, the other with lank fingers
Parting the matted hair upon his brow,
To take the greeting of the early light
Upon its sickly swarth—his eyes were fixed
On nothing visible, a dead, dull light
Was in them, the cold louring of despair;
His whitened lips were parted, and his teeth
Set fast in fear or agony. I spoke—
My words dropped harmless on his ear. I sought
By kindness to attract his note, and placed
Before him food and wine—he pushed them from him,
Then looked into my face, shrunk back—and hid
His own within the foldings of his garment.

FULVIUS (*turning over the scrolls*).

Ay, here is Varro's answer. Had it come
But one hour sooner, I had saved a friend by it,
And here——ha!

NORBAN.

Madam, mark my lord!

SOPHRONIA.

What, Fulvius!

FULVIUS.

Joy! triumph! rapture! He's in Rome—Away!
Fly! seek him—all! The man who finds him first
Shall be a God to Fulvius.

SOPHRONIA.

Whom?

FULVIUS.

Gisippus!
My old friend is in Rome. O ye kind Gods,
My heart is gushing towards ye!

MEDON (*without*).

Fulvius!
What, Fulvius!

Enter MEDON *rapidly, a sword drawn and bloody, in his hand.*

MEDON.

He is innocent!

FULVIUS.

Who?

MEDON.

The Greek.

FULVIUS.

How say ye? Are your waking senses liars?
What weapon's that?

MEDON.

The sword of the innocent man,
Whom even now they lead to execution.
It came thus stained in his defence of Chremes,
Not in his murder—Lycias, your freedman,
He has confessed the deed.

FULVIUS (*taking the sword*).

Ha! Gods!

MEDON.

Away!

Will you see a second murder? They are slaying him!
It is an hour since he was taken forth.

FULVIUS.

Fly, Medon, with my warrant, and release him.
Haste! haste! *(Exit* MEDON.*)*
   'Tis strange! Some poor life-weary wretch
Who hoped unwisely in his youth—and droops
To find his dreams *but* dreams.

NORBAN.

I fear, my lord,
They are too late.

FULVIUS.

I would not have it so,
For more——(*Looks on the sword, examines it closely and rapidly—recognises it, and remains fixed in horror.*)

SOPHRONIA.

My lord! You terrify me, Fulvius!
Speak—speak!
   Enter MACRO.
The murderer of Chremes—

FULVIUS.

Liar!
Ho! smite him dumb, some one! My hand is powerless,
My limbs are cold and numb!

SOPHRONIA.

My lord! my love!

MACRO.

His last request.

FULVIUS.

'Tis in thine eye and lip,
Thou comest to tell me I'm a murderer,
The murderer of my friend—and if thou dost,
The word shall choke thy life. (*Seizes him.*)

2 c

> Croak out thy news!
Raven! if they must tell of death—or, peace!
Giv't not in words.—Look me a hope!   He lives?
He does! he does! You've looked me into strength
  again!
  (FULVIUS *rushes out*—SOPHRONIA, *&c. follow.*)

SCENE II.—THE PLACE OF EXECUTION, GISIPPUS STANDING IN CHAINS—DECIUS, GUARDS, &c.

DECIUS.

Remove his chains.

GISIPPUS.
>   Let it be ever thus—
The generous still be poor—the niggard thrive—
Fortune still pave the ingrate's path with gold,
Death dog the innocent still—and surely those
Who now uplift their streaming eyes and murmur
Against oppressive fate, will own its justice.
Invisible Ruler! should man meet thy trials
With silent and lethargic sufferance,
Or lift his hands and ask heaven for a reason?
Our hearts must speak—the sting, the whip is on them;
We rush in madness forth to tear away
The veil that blinds us to the cause.   In vain!
The hand of that Eternal Providence
Still holds it there, unmoved, impenetrable;
We can but pause, and turn away again
To mourn—to wonder and endure.

DECIUS.

My duty
Compels me to disturb ye, prisoner.

GISIPPUS.

I am glad you do so, for my thoughts were growing

Somewhat unfriendly to me.—World, farewell;
And thou, whose image never left this heart,
Sweet vision of my memory, fare thee well.
Pray, walk this way.
This Fulvius, your young Prætor, by whose sentence
My life stands forfeit, has the reputation
Of a good man amongst ye?

DECIUS.

Better breathes not.

GISIPPUS

A just man, and a grateful. One who thinks
Upon his friends sometimes; a liberal man,
Whose wealth is not for his own use; a kind man
To his clients and his household?

DECIUS.

He is all this.

GISIPPUS.

A gallant soldier too?

DECIUS.

I've witnessed that
In many a desperate fight.

GISIPPUS.

In short, there lives not
A man of fairer fame in Rome?

DECIUS.

Nor out of it.

GISIPPUS.

Good. Look on *me* now, look upon my face;
I am a villain, am I not?—nay, speak!

DECIUS.

You are found a murderer.

GISIPPUS.

A coward murderer;
A secret, sudden stabber. 'Tis not possible

That you can find a blacker, fouler character,
Than this of mine?

DECIUS.

The Gods must judge your guilt.
But it is such as man should shudder at.

GISIPPUS.

This is a wise world, too, friend, is it not?
Men have eyes, ears, and (sometimes) judgment.
Have they not?

DECIUS.

They are not all fools.

GISIPPUS.

Ha! ha!

DECIUS.

You laugh!

GISIPPUS.

A thought
Not worth your notice, sir. You have those scrolls
I bade you give the Prætor? Was't not you?

DECIUS.

I think they are now within the Prætor's hands;
His page it was to whom you gave them.

GISIPPUS.

Ha!
Lead me on quickly, then. Did I not say
He should not see them till my death was past?
Not while a quivering pulse beat in my frame,
That could awake one hope of restoration?
What! shall he say I quailed and sought his mercy?
A wavering suicide?—and drag me back
To life and shame! Fool! Idiot! But haste on,
I will not be prevented.

FULVIUS (within).

Give me way!
Way! way!—hold! hold!

GISIPPUS.
Shall I be cheated thus?
Your duty, officers!

DECIUS.
Peace! 'tis the Prætor.

GISIPPUS.
Let me not be disturbed in my last moments,
The law of Rome is merciful in that.

> (FULVIUS *rushes in, and remains on one side of the stage, greatly agitated, his toga elevated in one hand, so as to shut out all the other characters from his view.*)

FULVIUS.
I dare not look! All silent! This is terrible.
I dare not ask! The hue of death is round me.
In mercy, speak! Is't over? Am I late?

GISIPPUS.
I would ye were.

FULVIUS (*clasping his hands*).
I thank ye, Gods, my soul
Is bloodless yet. I am no murderer.
Friend! Gisippus!

GISIPPUS.
O no, you are in error, sir.

FULVIUS.
By all the Gods—— (*approaching him.*)

GISIPPUS.
Hold back! or I will spurn ye,
By all the Gods, proud Roman, it is false—
I'll not be mocked again.

FULVIUS.
Is this a mockery?
Look, Romans, on this man——O Gisippus!

Look on him—Oh, that pale, that wasted face!
To him I owe all that you know me master of!
Life, public honour, and domestic happiness!
Here in this thronged area Fulvius kneels
Before his benefactor—in that attitude
Prouder than when he took his place among
The judges of your capitol.

GISIPPUS.

A Prætor
Kneels at my feet.—Look upon him, Romans!
Hear this, ye purpled ones, and hide your heads!
Behold, how mean the gilded ingrate shows
Beside the honest poverty he scorned—
Start from the earth, man, and be more yourself;
Arch the sharp brow, curl the hard lip, and look
The heartless thing ye are! Court not opinion
By this mean mockery.

DECIUS (*to* FULVIUS).

Rise, my lord!

(FULVIUS *rises dejectedly, and motions with his hand. The stage is cleared of all but* GISIPPUS *and* FULVIUS.)

FULVIUS.

Gisippus,
Are you content yet? I have knelt to you,
Not in the meanness of a crouching spirit,
But dragged down by the deadening self-reproach
That wintered in within my soul. But now
I've borne an insult in the streets of Rome,
Which is unto the honourable mind
What death is to the coward. Now I stand
Erect, and challenge ye to name the sin
Which this endurance may not satisfy.

GISIPPUS (*pausing in surprise*).

You speak this well—sir,—faith, 'tis very well;

Certain, I am wrong. You have done nought you
    have done;
Nor is this air I breathe, sir—nor this soil
Firm earth on which we stand. Nor is my heart
A throbbing fire within me, now—no—no,
Nor this hot head an Ætna. Ha! Farewell!
Nothing of this is so. I am very wrong. (*Going out.*)

FULVIUS.

Yet hold—

GISIPPUS (*bursting into fury*).

What, haughty ingrate! Feel I not
The fasces of your satellites yet on me?
Hold back! cross—touch me, stay me, speak again,
And by the eternal light that saw my shame
I'll gripe that lying throat until I choke
The blackening perjury within! O sin!
O shame! O world! I'm now a weak, poor wretch—
Smote down to very manhood. Judgment lost,
I've flung the reins loose to my human spirit,
And that's a wild one! Rouse it, and ye pluck
The beard of the lion. Gisippus, that was
The lord of his most fiery impulses,
Is now a child to trial. High philosophy,
With its fine influences, has fled his nature;
And all the mastery of mind is lost.

FULVIUS.

Yet would you hear?

GISIPPUS.

Could I chain up my heart,
That bounds unbridled now—and force my sense
To drink your words, it were in vain.
That heart has grown incapable of all gentleness,
And hard to every natural affection:
Ye may as well go talk the warm red blood

Out of that column. Pray, begone—ye vex me!
(*Going out.*)

FULVIUS.

You shall not go. Curse me,—but speak not thus!
Will nothing
Move ye to hear me?

GISIPPUS.

Nothing. Could you conjure
The memory of my wrongs away, and leave me
No other cause for being what I am,
Than that I am so, nothing yet could change me.
Psha! Death! Why do I dally thus?—Away,
See me no more! No more!
Away! Farewell!

(*Turning, and bursting away, he looks off the stage, starts and remains motionless.*)

FULVIUS.

Ha! Sophronia comes! It stirs him.

GISIPPUS.

My dreams have been of this! My sleep has been
Fear haunted, till this vision came to quiet it,
And then my soul knew peace! O ye have been
My memory's nightly visitant.

FULVIUS (*elevating his hand to* SOPHRONIA *within*).
Hush! softly!

GISIPPUS.

Beautiful phantom of my faded hope!
How many thousand, thousand scenes of joy,
Not rudely dragged from rest,
But quietly awakened into light,
By the soft magic of that *wizard* glance
Rise on my soul, as from the dead!

FULVIUS.

Sophronia!

Enter SOPHRONIA.

SOPHRONIA.

I am here to seek ye. They have told me, Fulvius——
Ha! Gisippus! (*Reaching him her hand.*)

GISIPPUS.

Hush! peace, sweet woman! All
Is softening o'er my wounded heart again.
Sophronia, I am glad you do not scorn me;
There is a reconciling influence
About ye, in your eyes, air, speech—a stilling spell,
The wronged heart cannot strive against.

FULVIUS.

Gisippus,
Would you prove that?

(GISIPPUS, *with his eyes still fixed on* SOPHRONIA, *reaches his hand back to* FULVIUS, *who wrings it fervently between his.*)

GISIPPUS.

'Tis not impossible, Fulvius.

SOPHRONIA (*drawing him to* FULVIUS).

Then, for my sake, Gisippus.

GISIPPUS.

All for thee! (*Embracing Fulvius.*)

THE END.

DRAMATIS PERSONÆ.

Sophronia	Miss H. Faucit.
Hero	Miss Turpin.
Gisippus	Mr. Macready.
Titus Quintus Fulvius	Mr. Anderson.
Medon	Mr. Graham.
Pheax	Mr. Elton.
Chremes	Mr. Hudson.
Lycias	Mr. G. Bennett.
Norban	Miss E. Phillips.
Davus	Mr. W. Bennett.
Thoon	Mr. Marton.
Decius	Mr. Lynne.
Mutius	Mr. Waldron.
Festus	Mr. Mellon.
Macro	Mr. Selby.
Roman Centurion	Mr. Bender.
Sicilian Merchant	Mr. Harcourt.

Athenian Citizens, Mr. Montgomery, Mr. Gilbeigh, Mr. J. Smith, Mr. Paulo, Mr. Burdett, &c.

Roman Citizens, Mr. Hughes, Mr. Yarnold, Mr. Grammer, Mr. Priorson, &c.

www.ingramcontent.com/pod-product-compliance
Lightning Source LLC
Chambersburg PA
CBHW030425300426
44112CB00009B/858